A Philosophy of War

A PHILOSOPHY OF WAR

Alexander Moseley

Algora Publishing
New York

ISBN: 1-892941-94-5 (softcover)
ISBN: 1-892941-95-3 (hardcover)

Library of Congress Card Number: 2002-005747

Moseley, Alexander, 1943-
  A philosophy of war / by Alexander Moseley.
    p. cm.
Includes bibliographical references and index.
  ISBN 1-892941-94-5
  1. War (Philosophy) I. Title.
  B105.W3 M67 2002
  355.02'01—dc21

                                      2002005747

Front Cover: Antonio Del Pollaiuolo — *Hercules and Antaeus* (1475)
Back Cover: Albrecht Dürer — *The Four Horsemen of the Apocalypse* (1497)

Printed in the United States

TABLE OF CONTENTS

PREFACE

The philosophical examination of war begins with very general questions: What is war? What is the relationship between human nature and war? To what extent can humans be said to be responsible for war?

A host of philosophers from Plato to Bertrand Russell have turned their attention to war and its various aspects — what causes it, how it should be fought, and whether it should be fought at all. But, in the history of thought, we often see that philosophers ponder war through the lenses of their own particular eras, sometimes making war or man's bellicosity the driving premise of their entire philosophies.[1] Others who have made a life-long study of war have approached it from the specialty of their own discipline, from, say, biology, history, or anthropology, and have thereby attempted to construct consistent theories. While they may provide useful insights, their theories often echo the grand philosophical visions of war or of man's nature produced by philosophers such as Plato, Aristotle, Augustine, Hobbes, Rousseau, or Machiavelli. Broader and more flexible insights may be provided, especially these days, by freelance writers who have the liberty to draw on a variety of disciplines and hence transcend particular philosophical systems: their liberty of mind motivates this work and hopefully sustains its remit. No discipline should be considered "out of bounds" for philosophy and no philosophical vision should be deemed sacrosanct. The works of academic philosophers possess no monopoly on wisdom, but neither are the works of "experts" intellectually inviolable. Philosophy provokes questions in the individual subjects just as much as it proffers general answers — the conjectures and hypotheses by which people seek to understand life — but it should also respond to the findings from all areas of study.

In this work, philosophy is used to provide an integrated understanding of war, drawing on knowledge from a variety of academic disciplines. The book tackles the definition, nature, and causation of war; except incidentally, it leaves issues of political and ethical philosophy to a planned second volume.

The endeavor entered into here is a philosophy of war that will be broad and wide-sweeping, generalizing where necessary, as philosophy should, yet also bringing the underlying currents to form a general philosophical theory that can be of use to philosophers and to historians, anthropologists, economists, and students of international relations, politics, and the general humanities.[2]

The argument, succinctly put, is that war is the product of beliefs and ideas. War is not inevitable, but many factors make it appealing. Biologically, we are not inevitably predisposed to wage war except perhaps in self-defense, but neither, and more importantly, are we predisposed *not* to wage war. Our biological evolution has afforded us traits and dispositions that complement and interact with the belief systems our cultures and reason create, but they do not in themselves prompt us to fight. Beliefs do.

Beliefs, however, are not necessarily "purely rational" in the sense of being fully articulated, for our ideological systems are largely the products of our actions, our emulations, and our tacit agreements in cooperation, and it is here that war finds its origins: submerged in cultural aspects that generate beliefs in individual agents. But those beliefs, as with the more readily explicated notions our minds produce, are only acted upon by agents who choose to act upon them. Man is not anchored to a belief system, as determinists may argue, for he is free to choose among his beliefs. But what maintains war is that those choices, committed in a context of social cooperation and inherited traditions and expectations, are part of a complex matrix or web of tacit and explicit notions and norms that guide our thinking. A vast host of ineffable, subliminal and liminal "reasons" accompany the choices we make, and those "reasons" (explanations or conclusions that lie below the surface of our thought, or that are generated by social interaction as things that are "just done") are the product of more than one mind thinking consciously, to the best of its ability and mental vocabulary at any given moment. War's origins are hence complex: they are found in the nebulous systems of thoughts generated in cultures over time. But while reason and explication can unravel those origins — and hence explain, to a great extent, why man wages war — the task of abolishing war can never be accomplished by reason alone.

Man cannot abolish war by reason alone for the same reason that man cannot invent a language (for it is a social product that *evolves* beyond the remit and expectations of its inventors). To do that, cultures would have to change and produce countervailing forces that undermine the liminal glory or value of war. Only market economies have ever succeeded in expanding the mutual benefits of cooperation and peaceful intercourse. Only in areas that have developed or evolved cultural networks that swamp latent beliefs in war with other, more compelling beliefs, has war been reduced or abolished. And that, arguably, only takes place where the mutually benefiting arrangements of the market economy spread *and are embedded in* customs and morals, that is, where exchange extends past parochial borders, systematically undermining cultural prejudices by the liberty to trade and socialize with others. But even the market economies' success in reducing conflict is shallow when compared to the deep culture of war, which can be readily — and facilely — drawn upon when the need arises.

The complexity of man and his beliefs means that war is complex too, and hence its abolition is not wholly within the present generation's grasp. So much of man's actions, it will be argued, are prompted (but not determined) by his culture and his historical background, by ideas accepted often *without much thought*, which leaves a concluding theme that some ideas die hard — and war is one of those. [3]

Notes

1. Heraclitus and Hobbes are sometimes characterized as doing so.
2. Generalizations dominate thinking and deserve critical analysis in turn. But the Socratic passion for dissembling opinions and generalizations should not annihilate our concepts beyond recognition so as to produce a conceptual or ethical nihilism or barren landscape devoid of any intellectual or practical pleasure.
3. For those who are aware of the general history of thought, Immanuel Kant's vision of perpetual peace acts as a useful guide to the philosophy developed here. Kant's vision of commercial pacifism — of the expansion of markets and international cooperation, which was so popular among free market economists in the nineteenth century and so attractive to the post-bellum world of 1945, is in principle correct. But Kant relied on the ineluctable progress of mankind to pursue what is naturally in his interests. Unfortunately, humanity is not so easily or always led by natural interests, for beliefs can always get in the way of progress or resolution, and it is precisely those beliefs that sustain war that this book investigates.

CHAPTER ONE: Why a Philosophy of War?

War is a philosophical problem.

For many, this will seem a superfluous description — surely philosophy deals with every subject, and why should war be an exception? To others it will seem a non-starter for, they argue, philosophy deals with ideas, with logic and abstract concepts, whereas war, in its cruel, concrete barbarity, is as far from the philosophical mind as one can get. Leave war, they would argue, to be studied in the sub-disciplines of the arts and sciences. Moralists often appraise or condemn war, and accordingly war may be consigned to the sub-discipline of applied ethics or political philosophy; but by its very nature of questioning, examining, and postulating answers, philosophy deals with life and death, and so with peace and war. But philosophers should not rest there; they should aim to study war in all of its aspects — not just the moral or political issues it raises — and consider what war's connections are to systems of thought presented by philosophers: for politicians are often influenced by philosophical thought, although they may not realize it. Philosophers should also consider the implications of various theoretical positions on, say, human nature or knowledge, and how they relate to warfare.

If we are living, thinking, imaginative creatures, how could philosophy evade the most disruptive of human affairs? Only by drawing a veil on what we think and how we act. Sadly, this is often the case with the journey into abstract thought, which, for some people, entails the separation of their heads from their bodily functions (which they begin to either ignore or despise). But thinking and action are mutually dependent: what I think about affects my behavior, and my behavior (or that of others) may in turn affect my thinking; but ultimately how we behave is a product of our ideas, of beliefs we learn or create ourselves, beliefs whose origins we often forget. The causal relationship runs from our mind to our behavior, but the nature of beliefs and of ideas is complex. The power of reason to challenge war, or any other form of human conduct, has to be understood within the context of the various origins of the ideas that inhabit our mind, the ability for us to access and to explicate those ideas, and our will to act on our choices.

Non-philosophers soak up philosophical ideas from theories produced in the plethora of disciplines that they study at school or university. Unwittingly, they are hearing echoes of philosophical discourse from previous generations, and these notions, partly-formed conclusions, conceptions, and methodologies (or the lack thereof) affect how they view themselves in the world, how they view others, and how they view the world itself. Philosophers too are not immune from influences; they are as much a product of the time and of previous generations' thinking as anyone else, although they should be more aware of the connections, for that is, in part, their business. As our minds mature, the philosophies (consistent or not) that we produce, or consume, do not lie idle in our thoughts; they provide the framework within which we think, and an intellectual framework can be dynamic and adaptive or fixed and restraining.

Nonetheless, the supposed loftiness of philosophy often turns the mind from recognizing the commonplace and sordid violence of man's history, except to denounce the immorality of man's bodily nature or the nature of other men, i.e., any aspect of his nature other than thinking! Philosophy itself is rarely blamed. But when it is, the mistake is reversed, assuming that war and violence are promoted by wrong-thinking — heresy (and they are, to some extent or other, but it is wrongly concluded that the effects of ideas are universally imposed on plastic, malleable bodies that can only be freed by a mental brainwashing or physical inquisition). The error is that it requires an act of volition to properly learn and to challenge previous ways of thinking, and volition can never be forced.

What I hope to establish in this work is that the principles of war's origins involve all aspects of our nature, culture, and thinking. Although, ultimately, we fight because we *believe* in fighting and our beliefs have to change if we wish to abandon war, the nature of beliefs — of ideas tacit and explicit, liminal and subliminal — means that the task is not simple or readily achievable. The precepts of reason are not sufficient to extinguish man's *passion* for war.

But neither is it the case that reason is the slave of passion, for what we are passionate *about* is determined by the ideational structures we possess: i.e., the values that we believe are of worth, and the expectations, applause, and affirmation of others. Yet most people *believe* that their actions and beliefs are dictated by sources other than their own minds, and so they abandon their thinking and repeat what they already know or what they see in others (and in effect become fodder for propaganda and war). Imitation and repetition form a great part of any individual's behavioral patterns (and to some extent necessarily so), which, when writ large for society, we recognize as cultural patterns — of group ways of doing things.

War is predominantly a cultural phenomenon, but to acquiesce in the belief that it is the product of something other than man's ideas is to acquiesce in determinism, which should be rejected. War is not something that just happens: we actively bring it about and maintain it as a cultural and political institution. But, more often than not, we engage in war because we are (consciously or not) imitating our culture's perceived successes with wars in the past: we volitionally sustain the cultural inertia that maintains war. This is particularly the case when the state usurps control over education and the direction and wealth of the economy: its possession of a monopoly on the use of force in the domestic arena provides the state with the means to retain and rechannel atavistic cultural prejudices that tend to linger in centrally-controlled states. Constraints on freedom of expression and commerce act to diminish the speed at which outdated forms of behavior can evaporate naturally.

To present a sweeping conclusion of the philosophy of war garnered from the chapters of this work, my theory is that although the propensity to war resides within us biologically (for pacifism plainly does not), war is predominantly the product of our choices and beliefs.

However, what is meant by "beliefs" includes all particular aspects of human action that are learned, copied, or imitated, as well as considered explicitly by thought and language, argued over, and critiqued. Beliefs are resoluble into implicitly and explicitly held ideas, and imputed values as well as rationally-considered interests. Beliefs determine the values and interests we seek: they motivate as well as describe. In turn, ideas invoke a host of thoughts, conjectures, and fantasies that may or may not be consistently ordered into a governing philosophy in the mind and may or may not be reflective of reality. What is crucial to understand is that beliefs do not exist as ethereal (epiphenomenal) entities — they reside within thinking, acting, breathing, living beings, who deign to exercise their minds, or not, and whose brains have evolved to participate in conceptual thinking to some degree or other.

The philosophical vision of war presented is hierarchical to the extent that what is learned is deemed to be of greater significance in explaining war than what is inherited. But, more importantly, no artificial borders or barriers should be drawn between man's various elements — even the employment of the term "hierarchy" is not something I am completely happy with. Man's elements are constantly interacting — reason is often glorified as the highest faculty we possess, and so it is, but our explicit *present* thinking is not omniscient or unlimited; it is necessarily the product of prior reasoning, of antecedents that have been incorporated in individual psychological structures and in the cultural structures from which we learn so much without having to acknowledge it. In the words of Scottish Enlightenment philosopher, Adam Ferguson, much is the product of human action but not design.

Hence ideas are not just the product of reason construed as an a-temporal exegesis of the truth. Many ideas are inherited from pre-rational tacitly held beliefs that may still motivate us, some even overlapping with biologically-inherited instincts or dispositions; only when ideas are fleshed out by articulated language may they become belief systems proper: that is, theologies and philosophies.

Above the murky area of our evolved biological instincts to defend or to aggress, war is an ideologically created institution. The problem is that many of its ideas may lie rooted in ancient *but learned and chosen* pre-rational structures. Succinctly, we believe that war is the way of the world, it is the way things are done, it resolves disputes, it affirms our existence, it deters aggression, and so on.

The grand vision that war is predominantly an ideological enter-prise is not revolutionary, but what is meant by ideological is in this regard different from the mainstream conception of "ideological". It stems from the work of intellectuals (especially Friedrich Hayek) who are critical of the purely rationalist vision of man — the notion that man is wholly a rational animal, whose explicated reasons necessarily offer objective, impartial, universal accounts of reality and truth. Real-ity and truth exist, *but our understanding of them* — and hence how we act — *is a product of our broad ideological base of explicit and implicit ideas* that incorporate metaphysical and epistemological assumptions, political views, thoughts on the self and the other, manners and mores, etiquette and cultural mannerisms.

The pure rationalist dream negates the tacit and implied, to make all our thoughts explicit and amenable to logic — but that dream be-holds a naïve vision of man, so readily critiqued, e.g., as against the *homo oeconimicus* — the archetypal, coldly calculating utilitarian that suppos-edly represented the economic vision of man or *Star Trek*'s Spock. But reason is not to be downplayed or rejected — irrationality and irration-alism are often the source of much human misery and war, and the les-sons that can be drawn from reason are impressive indictments of war. Similarly, the expansion of our explicit knowledge — concepts that we can agree on as being reality based and which we can use to compre-hend better the nature of our world — offers a path to understand the origins and purposes of our tacitly held (cultural) beliefs. But I do not think that man's reason is sufficient to ascend to omniscience, as Shakespeare's Hamlet notes: "There are more things in heaven and earth, Horatio,/Than are dreamt of in your philosophy."

Inasmuch as reason offers a path to universal ideas, even to a com-mon morality and political idea — and it is the very vehicle by which we examine the world — it presents a thoroughly humanist vision: a vision that seeks to encompass all the world's peoples into a world of peace and cooperation. But, as this work will argue, to be human is to be much more than a pure rationalist (if that were possible or plausible anyway). War is embedded in our articulated ideas and in our tacit as-sumptions and expectations about each other and the world. Reason should attempt to draw much that is hidden to the fore of articulated discussion, *but its task can never be complete.* The philosopher is always a human, always a biological, cultural, and thinking being; and against the positivist ambition which seeks to nullify all aspects of our nature except our mathematical and logical — metaphors are necessary!

War behooves examination, yet usually the theories produced rankle with the simplicity of reductionism, of fitting war neatly into a grand scheme conjured by a single mind with little reference to war itself or to competing theories that may have something to contribute. Reducing war to a single explanatory variable, no matter how encompassing that theory is (nature, nurture, class systems, culture, history, balance of power, genetics, etc.), should be avoided. War performs a multitude of tasks and possesses a multitude of meanings that cannot easily be cast aside or reduced into a single explanation — and this is true of most social phenomena that have evolved through social interaction, such as money, hunting, art, or romance.

The contention — if not the passion — here is that a philosophy of war should draw on knowledge gained from economics, sociology, biology, anthropology, and so on, to produce a working vision of what war is and what it entails. Similarly, it should draw on a variety of philosophical systems that seek all-encompassing explanations of life and hence of war in pursuit of complex truths. In doing so, a philosophy of war should avoid the Aristotelian tendency to assume that the pursuit of explanation — the life of philosophy — should be made *de haut en bas*, looking down upon human nature and action with either the judgment of an Olympian god or pure intellect's condemnation, despising war and the other trappings of the material world (wealth, sex, food, beauty, intelligence, power, etc.). Warfare is a vile business to the intellectually inclined, sometimes even more vulgar than trade, man's other persistent secular occupation. For some philosophers, war is traditionally a problem for the lesser mortal of the statesman, but philosophy should not shirk from investigating its nature and origins; indeed it is just as much a philosophical duty to consider why we attempt to destroy ourselves as to examine the nature of beauty or logic, or whether we should be ethically deontological, utilitarian or virtuous in ethics.

To proceed with the contents, the first chapter grapples with defining war, which is not an easy task. A broad definition of war is presented before moving on to different types of war. Then various philosophical positions are examined for their cogency in explaining war, beginning with theories of determinism, of human nature and of human biology, of culture, and of reason. Reductionist theories are rejected, but as we proceed, the better elements of each theory are taken up to be incorporated into the philosophy of war.

Notes

1.   Just as an aching back is not something that just happens but something we bring about through conscious and subconscious decisions that we have internalised through learning. A back will continue to ache unless we address the thinking processes that cause us to work our backs improperly.

2.   The power of atavism — effectively of tapping into historically deep cultural roots — was evinced in the politics of Milosevic before his fall in 2001. Milosevic, in securing and expanding his own power base, drew upon latent myths and expectations of the Serbian culture to stir up ancient animosities that had been superficially plastered over by the Yugoslavian state. Peace, cooperation, and prosperity between the various ethnic groupings could have been possible had the liberal free trade doctrine been the guide rather than sectarian tribalism.

3.   This is also true of state education that explicitly attempts to bring about a more peaceful and less prejudiced society. The imposition of a model and mode of education on millions of children is not likely to be successful in teaching them to be *critical thinkers*, and the quality of education, as with the quality of any state product or service, will diminish with time. Experiments in multiculturalism consistently fail, for they emphasise differences and end up retaining the tribalism they were designed to abolish.

4.   Methodologically, much of the critique in the work attacks reductionist explanations of war. The motive is taken from David Hume, who warns that the love of simplicity has been the source of much false reasoning in philosophy. What causes war cannot be reduced to a single factor — as with all human actions, there can be many motivating elements. *Enquiry Concerning the Principles of Morals*, Appendix II. p. 90.

> Wars don't change except in name;
> The next one must go just the same.
> — Robert Graves, "The Next War."

DEFINING WAR

If anything is to be studied, it is useful to employ definitions of what one is studying. That way, other people can work out what we are referring to and can offer adjustments or criticisms of our method or the breadth or narrowness of our study, hence allowing knowledge to expand. However, definitions are philosophically awkward beasts, and we encounter the immediate problem that schools of thought approach the method of defining any entity by a variety of paths.[1]

Cicero, for instance, defines war broadly as "a contention by force"; Hugo Grotius adds that "war is the state of contending parties, considered as such"; Thomas Hobbes notes that war is also an attitude: "By war is meant a state of affairs, which may exist even while its operations are not continued"; Denis Diderot comments that war is "a convulsive and violent disease of the body politic;" for Karl von Clausewitz, "war is the continuation of politics by other means." Modern writers such as Parsons tend to expand the violence in war's definition to include propaganda: "In its most general sense, war is the use of physical weapons and forces in a conflict that may be expressed without the use of such weapons and forces." The attempt to formulate a common definition of war has been criticised by Frondizi, who asserts that: "[W]ar does not exist; what exists are wars, in the plural, ranging from tribal skirmishes to World War II," but Liddell Hart, echoing Graves's sentiments above, rightly counters that, "the idea that every war has been different from the last is the delusion of those who know no history."[2]

Defining what war is becomes the first philosophical obstacle. We could ignore it, leaving the definition to be assumed (and often books do ignore defining the very entity they are examining), but that would leave the definition — indeed the examination — floating vacuously and therefore subject to fashionable or political reinterpretations. Ideas matter, and ideas are based on our definitions, or implied understandings, of what we are considering — hence we must not shy away from attempting to define what war generally involves.

To avoid epistemological or linguistic vagueness, it is pertinent to provide a definition, but since any definition of a social enterprise can never be complete, war's definition can only be a *working definition*, subject, if necessary, to change, particularly at its conceptual borders which, as with any sociological concept, are inherently blurred.[3]

The definition offered is that war is *a state of organised open-ended collective conflict*. This is a robust and working definition of war that aptly fits the commonalties evident in wars. It also provides a means, albeit necessarily incomplete and empirically vague, to distinguish wars from fights, riots, and brawls. War is organised, unlike, for example, a street brawl; it is open-ended, unlike a boxing match; it is collective, unlike a personal feud; and it involves conflict that implies non-violent as well as violent hostilities. This definition does not claim war to be a series of battles or clashes, for wars may exist without battles occurring; nor does it claim that the concept includes declarations, states, or the lack of morality and rules.[4] If we establish war as a collective endeavour, other sociological disruptions may compete for inclusion and we must admit that, at the periphery, commotions such as riots may overlap into a low level form of warfare.

Riots are a particularly problematic example. For the most part they are ostensibly not organised and appear to erupt spontaneously, implying a randomness to people's behaviour, as well as to their targets or acts of destruction. However, although they appear not to be organised in any meaningful sense (i.e., politically and strategically), riots are pre-meditated and coordinated at some level, and thus they betoken a sociological shift into warfare. Rioters volitionally converge on encouraging and agitating each other and others, and their targets are those previously singled out on some level of discussion: sometimes strategically and explicitly ("let's hit MacDonalds"), other times liminally ("don't you just hate the ethnic stores?").[5] The occurrence and nature of riots are not as random or unprovoked as a superficial examination would imply: human acts do not come from nothing, nor do they come from the nature of the environment, they come from the beliefs people possess (and choose to possess) concerning their environment, their complaints, fears, expectations, and so on.

Rebellions, insurgencies, uprisings, insurrections, and revolts share collective conflict and hostility with war, but commonly they denote a political goal to alter or to overthrow an incumbent regime. War's definition should avoid specific political conceptions of the world (e.g., the world is only made up of states), as far as that is possible, for the objective of a war may not be the overthrow of a regime — it may be war for glory's sake, war for God's sake, war for ritual's sake or other ends. Often, definitions of war imply that the incumbent target is morally or politically legitimate, which implies a particular political conception of the world, namely that it involves states, and that such states either hold power legitimately or not. In other words, the terms rebellion, uprising, insurrection, etc., are more usefully employed as political-legal terms requiring a political and ethical examination of the claims for legitimacy.[6] Definitions of war (notably the political-rationalist and realist definitions) are prone to such faults; hence, to be philosophically useful, the concept should not initiate normative implications but attempt to describe what war is.

A definition should rest on (at least some) objective criteria to avoid the hollowness and mutability of any subjective definition.[7] Subjective definitions depend on an agent's own particular description of war ("War is what I think it is"). Conceptual nihilism is rendered redundant when we both agree that some series of events do establish that a war is taking place, that is, events deemed *objectively* accessible. For example, if I were to exclaim: "Look at the violence in Jerusalem, there exists war," and you agreed, it follows that whatever concept or acknowledgement catches that agreement, in turn captures an objective "something" that pertains to violent behaviour, which would enable us to distinguish (or at least provides the means to distinguish) violent from non-violent events. Wars are not in the eye of the beholder, but must be objectively defined, as far as that is possible. The term "war" signifies, points to, refers to, and indicates a series of sociological events that we may describe as *a state of organised open-ended collective conflict.*

The terrorist attacks on America on September 11, 2001, were certainly acts of war: they were the culmination of a state of organised and open-ended conflict that a particular organisation, Al-Qaeda, pursued with the West. The definition of war does not require that the combatants be readily identifiable by their dress, nor that there be declarations of war or that armies march to predetermined areas to fight pitched battles: such criteria are the province of ethical discussions, not of war's definition.

This is, as I mentioned, a working definition: a definition that may expand or adjust as new information comes to light with different forms of warfare produced by new technologies, or with insights from anthropological or historical research. The definition should seek to encompass what we commonly agree war involves, as well as to provide a useful objective benchmark with which to recognise war as compared to, say, territorial disputes, riots, domestic violence, or the broader category of conflict.[8] A sociological definition should primarily be *a priori*, yet it should not be removed from empirical matters;[9] it should therefore be robust yet permit flexibility in the face of new evidence — for the word is, after all, a tool in the employment of our minds.

The concept "war" should capture all possible and all historic wars and permit change in our particular knowledge of war and warfare should our information change, for certainly as our knowledge of any phenomenon such as war expands, we are capable of gleaning a better understanding of it.[10] However, such progress is never inevitable, for it requires a concerted, focused effort to learn — to think, to conjecture, to compare and contrast the particularities of one event with another.[11]

War, defined as a state of organised open-ended collective conflict, is distinguishable from other forms of human violence such as battery and murder, riots, and brawls, although at the edges wars involve similar patterns of behaviour and similar levels of violence. It involves groups but is discernibly more organised than riots in which crowds loot and pillage. Organisation can be produced by automatic instincts (e.g., the herd instinct) or by culturally accepted notions that prompt a tacit organisation, as well as by explicitly constructed agreements, constitutions, rules, and goals.

CONTEXTUAL UNDERSTANDING

Language use presumes some flexibility in meaning and understanding that must not be forgotten in analytical investigations of human phenomena. Contextual comprehension is paramount in any literary, poetical, or philosophical analysis of the meaning of sociological terms. Invoking a contextually dependent definition is not new — an entire discipline of the philosophy of language and parallel methods in the social sciences and anthropology emphasise the importance of relativist or contextual analysis, and rightly so, for what is meant by any concept is highly dependent on the context. But commonalities exist by which to distinguish an action or phenomenon from other events; in Ayer's useful example of drinking wine,[12] what is contextual is the *motive* and hence the *meaning* that can be ascribed to the action, but the action itself is distinguishable from the act of pouring the wine away or not drinking the wine, etc. So the motives of going to war may be open to interpretation and revision but the actual act of war is not.

What we know of a concept depends on the particular information that we possess of it and the context of its use; and as our information of a particular event expands, the definition and hence our understanding may become more precise. We may see such epistemic development through human maturation: for example, as children we possess simplistic notions of war involving soldiers fighting — a chaotic confusion, perhaps, just as the Germanic-Franks may have seen it (see next chapter), but as adolescents our understanding of war begins to incorporate the destruction, death and misery caused by physical violence, and as we learn more history we become aware of different types of war — "cold" wars, bloodless wars, ritualistic wars, terrorism, and today even "cyber wars". The Romans defined war to capture the politics and even the legality of war, and stated that it involves two sides at least in a duel of mastery — thereby producing a highly influential rationalist definition that still influences mainstream definitions today; but war is not necessarily confined to politics: it can reside deep in a culture's institutions that lie far removed from law and politics.

What is needed is a definition that acknowledges not only the political side of war, for reasons that will be outlined, but also the cultural and biological aspects. Not all wars involve states or polities: some are primitive reactions to social or environmental factors, while others are perceived as forms of inter-societal rituals.[13] Common elements exist between all wars, although some would deny that possibility: for such thinkers, concepts can only refer to particulars (this war, that war) and a comparison between particulars to form a common conceptual denominator ("War") is a fruitless task.

This philosophical issue must be dealt with, for if no definition is provided, we may not know what we are discussing. Gallie, for example, comments:

> War is, logically as well as physically, a rough-and-ready as well as a brutal and bloody affair. And philosophers and military men have been, for once, at one and right in refusing to waste their time in worrying about its essential nature.[14]

Yet, as Gallie himself notes, "it is of the first importance that we learn how to think about it."[15] The attempt to formulate a concept of war has also been criticised by Frondizi, who asserts that: "[W]ar does *not exist; what exists are wars, in the plural, ranging from tribal skirmishes to World War II.*"[16] We find a more philosophical description of this theory in the words of William James:

> Let us not fall immediately into a one-sided view of our subject, but rather admit freely at the outset that we may very likely find no one essence, but many characters which may be equally important. . . . The man who knows [for instance] governments most completely is he who troubles himself least about a definition which shall give their essence.... let us make our acquaintance with all their particulars in turn, he would naturally regard an abstract conception in which these were unified as a thing more misleading than enlightening.[17]

These arguments against defining the concept of "war" need to be refuted. Gallie's comments can be rejected on the grounds that nothing can be gained unless an effort is made to consider what "war" is. Frondizi's point is plausible and seemingly trivial, yet it belies a fundamental epistemological error, namely that abstract concepts, or "universals", do not exist.[18] James invokes this anti-conceptualism, which is at the heart of this issue.

Anti-conceptualism is trivially correct in noting, for example, that the Peloponnesian War (431-404 BC), the Zulu War (1879), the Gulf

War (1990-91), and the Napoleonic Wars (1793-1815) are different *entities*, just as it is valid reasoning to state that the two letter f's in the word "different" are not the same entities. What are philosophically called "numerically different objects" cannot occupy the same space at the same time, hence individual wars are different in the numerical (trivial) particular; yet it is absurd to deny that commonalties, or even — at least, if we may be bold enough to employ a notion of the great anti-conceptualist thinker — Wittgensteinian "family resemblances" (see below), exist which enable us to refer to each phenomenon as part of the collective concept, "war". What is being pointed out, though, are the *numerical*, or concrete, particular differences between wars. Anti-conceptualism denies that wars can be sufficiently *qualitatively and conceptually* similar to warrant inclusion into a higher abstract concept. But we need abstracts for thinking — without them our minds would quickly exhaust themselves by attempting to comprehend the nature of war on the concrete level: "what exist are wars, in the plural." Yet what provides the subject of the sentence is precisely an abstract term, "wars", which permits us to distinguish Frondizi's "wars" from Frondizi's entities that are not wars.

It is true that each war will have its own particular combination of unrepeatable *causes*, either in the trivial sense that different people are involved, or in the broader sense that wars necessarily have different causes if they are chronologically separated (but that is not to deny that the particular causes of war can also be abstracted[19]), yet it does not follow that the resulting phenomena are intrinsically and sufficiently different to warrant a conceptual scepticism.

An analogy provides a useful counter-argument: deafness can result from a variety of causes and may possess a host of types, but to deny the usefulness or even the existence of the concept "deafness" is nonsensical, and, arguably would not get medical science far! In this sense, universal terms are useful for forming an understanding of war, but as with the sciences, the definition is open to change as understanding of the phenomenon expands. For example, malaria is the name given to a condition caused by a protozoan parasite called plasmodium, but the original conjecture was that it was due to bad air, hence its name; fortunately, the humanities are less vulnerable to the revolutionary conceptual changes that science undergoes with insights and technological advances that radically open up new vistas — but they are not immune, either. Pride is something that both our society and the ancient Athenians would recognise as a human disposition, yet we would draw different ethical conclusions on being proud.

Anti-conceptualism should be refuted from the start, for underlying the refusal to consider what "war" means sits an intellectual apathy that is not conducive to understanding anything — this is epistemological scepticism at its worst.[20] Without forming and/or applying a guiding conceptual framework, we cannot compare wars, and we cannot apply lessons from particular wars to other wars or to war in general.

War, it shall be argued in the following chapters, results from a plurality of origins in man's nature — from his biological, cultural, and rational aspects — and these need to be incorporated in the general definition of war. Focusing on man's rational aspects only makes the invalid presumption that war is a wholly rational activity, one whose various motivations, means, and ends can be articulated fully and considered from, say, a utilitarian cost-benefit examination. War inherently involves the pursuit of values, as all human activity does; but it is not the sole means of acquiring values, for production and trade are alternatives. Nonetheless an objective distinction can be made concerning war's method of acquiring values — it is violent. Trade is the exchange of values, which is often mutually beneficial, whereas war involves the threat or actual violation or taking of others' values by an organised collective. War is an open-ended condition of organised violence — it may involve states and it may be declared, but not necessarily; it always involves some form of organisation and it must be considered to involve a condition rather than the existence of violence — for sometimes wars involve no battles or clashes of arms.

Given this general definition of war, we can explore various types of war that are useful for historical and political research.

Notes

1.   Original emphasis. Also: "'War' is a generic form that applies to certain bellicose acts that have in common the use of force and violence. If war is not a unique event but a multiplicity of events, or of types and classes of events, it seems logical that they are initiated by different causes. A diversity of causes must correspond to the diversity of phenomena." Frondizi, "The Ideological Origins of the Third World War," p.80

2.   Liddell Hart, *Thoughts on War*, p.24

3.   E.g., consider the grey areas of "war" between a "riot" and a "civil war" or between "banditry" and "guerrilla war".

4.   One of Hobbes's definitions of war is that it is a state of no rules, morality, or laws, cf. *Leviathan*.

5.   E.g., Anti-capitalist riots that target international meetings by new socialist movements. Cf. My "The Anti-Capitalist Capitalists" in *Ideas for Liberty*, March 2001. Or the Rabulist riots of Sweden (1838) whose target was government censorship of the press.

6.   A distinction needs to remain between a riot and a rebellion. A rebellion is an act of war (against a presiding polity) in the sense that it is organised and open-ended it may peter out or gather a momentum that draws in other nations and causes (e.g., the ripples from the American rebellion of 1776-83 into the French Revolution of 1789 and into the United Irishmen rebellion of 1798.) A rebellion may be peaceful in the sense of no physical clash of arms takes place, e.g., the peaceful "fuel tax rebellion" that took place in September 2000 in the UK. But that is possible of war too. The Glorious Revolution of 1688, a rebellion overthrowing King James II, was nominally bloodless (in England at least), but the threat of violence was present, since William and Mary landed in Devon with a Dutch army. On the other hand a riot is generally an unorganised affair, it is a sub-war form of collective violence, although the differences in the particular may be blurred at the edges.

  Interestingly, the phrase "reading the Riot Act" stems from the Riot Act of Britain, introduced in 1715 as a law to disperse groups of more than twelve people. It was designed to dissemble Jacobite support (supporters of James II and his descendants) following the controversial Hanoverian accession to the throne.

7.   Language is a tool for referring to entities: concrete entities such as "the War of the Roses" and abstract entities such as "civil wars"; "war" indicates a sociological category, and if it fails, or if the definition escapes the concrete entity it is attempting to describe, it becomes useless philosophically speaking, and dangerous sociologically speaking.

8.   Tim Allen rightly comments: "However ambiguous the term 'war' may be, there seems no point in conflating it with other forms of violence. We may lose capacity for specificity if aggression, force, killing, and war are all perceived as interchangeable terms." Allen, "Perceiving Contemporary Wars", in *The Media of Conflict*, p.16.

9.   A problem discussed by Kant in his *Critique of Pure Reason*, pp. 586-589

10.   Cf. Rand, *Introduction to Objectivist Epistemology*, p.6

11.   This is a particularly wonderful description by Theodore Zeldin: "I see thinking as bringing ideas together, as ideas flirting with each other, learning to dance and embrace. I appreciate that as a sensuous pleasure. Ideas are constantly swimming around in the brain, searching like sperms for the egg they can unite with to produce a new idea. The brain is full of lonely ideas, begging you to make some sense of them, to recognise them as interesting. The lazy brain just files them away in old

pigeon-holes, like a bureaucrat who wants an easy life. The lively brain picks and chooses and creates new works of art out of ideas." *Conversation*, p. 85.

12. Cf. A.J. Ayer. "Consider, for example, the simple action of drinking a glass of wine. As performed by different people in different circumstances, this may be an act of self-indulgence, an expression of politeness, a proof of alcoholism, a manifestation of loyalty, a gesture of despair, an attempt at suicide, the performance of a social rite, a religious communication, an attempt to summon up one's courage, an attempt to seduce or corrupt another person, the sealing of a bargain, a display of professional expertise, a piece of inadvertence, an act of expiation, the response to a challenge and many other things besides." *Metaphysics and Commonsense* (1967), from Almond, *Ethics* p. 7.

13. A note should be made here on relating the definition to morality: that concepts relating to human nature and actions are contextual is not to imply that moral judgements are relativistic, which would entail, for example, that waging a particular war in one era is morally justifiable yet in another era morally unjustifiable. What is implied is that the particular meaning of a concept may differ over some time and place — this still allows the production of a universalist morality concerning war. Contextual conceptualism admits that "war" to one group may imply a ritual, to another suffering, to another glory, and this has repercussions not so much on the nature of war as on the beliefs groups may have — beliefs that drive war. But that does not obviate the need to form a conceptual denominator between two groups — especially in the case of war where so much may be at stake over how one group defines war.

14. Gallie, *Understanding War*, p. 60.

15. Gallie, *ibid.*, p. 67

16. Original emphasis. Also: "'War' is a generic form that applies to certain bellicose acts that have in common the use of force and violence. If war is not a unique event but a multiplicity of events, or of types and classes of events, it seems logical that they are initiated by different causes. A diversity of causes must correspond to the diversity of phenomena." Frondizi, "The Ideological Origins of the Third World War," p. 80

17. William James, from *The Varieties of Religious Experience, quoted in* Brenner, *Logic and Philosophy*, p. 29.

18. This anti-conceptualist position is reflected in Berkeley's criticism of Locke's epistemology; "in truth, there is no such thing as one precise and definite signification annexed to any general name, they all signify indifferently a great number of particular ideas." *The Principles of Human Knowledge*, p. 58. Berkeley would agree with Frondizi, that 'war' does not exist, for his epistemology entails that when we think of war what we envisage individual wars we know of.

19. E.g., motives of fear, economic gain, aggrandisement, alleged destiny and so on.

20. Why such radical scepticism is not only illogical but unproductive of any useful mental activity, think of one's friends — to learn about them, it is worthwhile considering each of them in turn, and such a method is highly useful and rewarding. One may focus on their particular traits and habits; yet to deny the next step in considering common factors is to handicap research: what makes them friends, what differentiates them from pets, hobbies, etc. The same pertains to examining war: much can be gleaned from studying individual wars (e.g., the strategy, technology, and repercussions, etc.), but abstract, data-encompassing terms are required for protracted research.

CHAPTER THREE: Types of War

The general definition of war as *a state of organized open-ended collective conflict* allows several sub-definitions that try to incorporate different levels of war's complexity — such as the extent and involvement of cultural ideas, technology, and weaponry, as well as varying levels of political and economic organization. The hierarchy of war echoes the hierarchical nature of man's values that rise from first order biological values, second order cultural values, and third order rational values.[1] Accordingly, types of war reflect the increasing complexity of cultural and political values and ideas that converge in a particular war. In modern warfare — of states and professional armies — instinct is supplanted by cultural forces that form the nature and face of battle, which are in turn supplanted by the machinations of explicated reason — or as Clausewitz terms it, politics by other means. However, what is important to note is that the lower order values — instinct, self-preservation, fear — are never fully superseded by higher values: they remain necessary conditions of higher action and development. Just as reason cannot annihilate emotions, so highly-political wars — those characterized, for instance, by balance of power games — cannot sever the ties to deep cultural structures or even the underlying nature of human biology. Hence, while the types of warfare can be conceptually distinguished for ease of study, the manner in which they relate to man's nature is a more complex matrix that has overlapping and mutual interactions.

This chapter surveys the various sub-forms of war, beginning with the simplest types and proceeding through more complex forms and recent developments in the theory of war.

ANIMAL WARFARE

Quincy Wright employs the term "animal wars" to make the distinction from "human wars".[2] What can be called "animal warfare" exists as an instinctive collective defensive mechanism for many biological entities, who at times fight in organized patterns to defend territorial or reproductive rights[3] in which the stronger of the species will win out over those less able to adapt.[4] Such organization that may occur arises predominantly at an instinctive level, which implies that the actions of attacking and defending are already genetically preprogrammed responses to threats.

Such instincts are apparently stronger in animals protecting their immediate kin,[5] and some species (e.g., ants) even have evolved separate castes specially for war purposes. What we can glean from this is that the waging of war on this level is not a matter of choice; it is a matter of instinct. Incidentally, it would be wrong to extend an ethical discussion of war into the non-human animal arena, for animals are not ethical creatures; however, there is nothing wrong in describing the phenomenon of war as it arises in the animal kingdom

Nonetheless, endemic violence between members of a species, or between mutually dependent species such as parasites and hosts, is ultimately biologically illogical.[6] If violence were endemic, it would result in a specie's self-destruction — or the destruction of parasites' hosts. Wars in the animal and human kingdoms often involve only a part of the population that may, numerically speaking, be sacrificed; hence whole scale extinction of animal species is more likely to result from external changes to the environment than a total war of all against all. (Incidentally, this ultimate limit to warfare provides us with an excellent economic model to examine human warfare — how and why particular wars have arisen and how and why they have eventually ended.)

The extent and duration of animal warfare is limited according to evolutionary principles governing self-preservation and the preservation of immediate kin. Animals fight to defend territory or resource use — especially at times of great distress; but the natural kingdom cannot be said to be caught up in a spiral of violence or endemic warfare. Neither is it a romanticized, untouched kingdom — a garden of Eden which, were it not for man's presence, would be an idyllic, prelapsarian world of peaceful interaction. The natural world is dangerous and predation is common, although the evolving balance often converges onto forms of mutual reciprocity in which parasites or aggressive species do not eliminate their valued prey.

Since humans are also animals, arguably much can be gained from learning about the nature of animal warfare — especially the roles of sex, dominance, and activity. Much research has followed close observations of humanity's closest relatives, the primates,[7] but that does not imply that all that can be learned from animals applies to human action. Similarities and analogies can be applied, especially in the tactical methods of warfare, the chase, deception, camouflage, encirclement, reconnaissance, and so on, that animals have evolved and which humans try to mimic; but the human mind also generates purposes, intentions, concepts, and explicit understandings unknown in the animal kingdom (e.g., the suicide bomber), even if trial and error processes in man's army strategy converge on or mimic strategies that have evolved in the natural kingdom.

All forms of collective animal violence may be resolved as territorial or reproductive competition, or clashes over resources that do not involve motives, beliefs, and tacit knowledge. Hence, just as there is a gap between the animal and human kingdoms, a gap arises between animal warfare and human warfare. This reduces the explanatory content or possibility of strong causal analogies between animal behavior and human behavior. To some extent we are glorified primates, but humans are vastly more intricate social creatures capable of complex speech, extended reason,[8] self-reflection, conscientious activity, and ethical behavior which complicates the nature of war above the level of animalistic behavior.

Ethnological research may provide indicators as to how human warfare evolved out of proto-human species and the nature of instinctual reactions that have evolved over countless generations, but it cannot provide an exhaustive account of human warfare we know today.

PRIMITIVE WARFARE

Primitive war begins with the emergence of culture and its patterns of learned behavior and organization. The higher aspects of primitive war are characterized by the increasing role of articulated goals,
motivated by increasingly complex invoked values such as honor, prestige, revenge, and glory — the so-called "martial values".[9] "Primitive
war" is a term that should only be used for pre-historical studies, for
this kind of warfare belongs to humanity's distant ancestors, those who
were slowly emerging from a purely animalistic state.

Nonetheless, overlapping between types must be admitted — indeed, it is crucial if we are to understand war's complexity. That is, animal warfare should be seen as dovetailing into primitive human warfare
alongside the evolving complexity of the human mind and cultural interaction. Similarly, some of the higher primates may exhibit learned
modes of behavior similar to those of younger humans, or to the more
primitive ancestors of *Homo sapiens sapiens*. Yet the violent implosion of
human morality in which all manner of violence is unleashed in close
combat or in war generally is something peculiar to our species. This
intensification begins with the emergence of primitive warfare.

But there is no grandiose and instantaneous leap between being a
biological species and becoming a cultural species; hence we should not
ignore the biological roots of warfare in a general study of why man
wages war.

While the reactions of men in war can revert to primal instincts
that warrant no luxury of conscience or reflection, or whose reflection
is forged by extremity[10] or by intensive training, the general organization of primitive war is nonetheless a step above the instinctive actions
of animals. This is because it involves articulated actions and reactions
as well as tacit and explicit agreements between men — that is, forms
of behavior that are.

Primitive war is surrounded by ritual in which all aspects of war
are accompanied by magic and taboos, rules, and rites governing the
initiation of combat, the transformation into warrior, the burial of the
dead, the purification of the group and its warriors in peace, and so on.[11]
We see echoes of it in the historical ancients' accounts of war-myths
and beliefs. Interestingly, the modernization or civilization of man does
not diminish the need for such rituals. Man can never become a being of

pure reason, a disembodied Cartesian rational animal unconnected with subtle cultural demands for recognition, status, and security: and this is especially evident in times of war or great distress, when the great existential barrier between life and death is prominent. It is then that man often turns to the "Gods" (religion, or an all-encompassing philosophy) for security and for penance — a phenomenon characteristic of the modern soldier under fire as well as the Homeric.

The organization of primitive war exists on a rudimentary level of sporadic teamwork, perhaps identified around specific individuals. Such tacitly or crudely organized affairs mimic the hunting patterns of animals or indeed hunting strategies themselves. "Among nations of hunters", writes Adam Smith, "the lowest and rudest state of society . . . every man is a warrior as well as a hunter."[12] In such societies, hunting and fighting overlap, for the division of labor is not yet broad enough to raise a standing army. Such wars may be at first bound by strict rules and rituals and involve few casualties; they may then escalate to a total war in which victory can only be gained through the whole scale dispersal of the defeated tribe.[13] Whether primitive war *inevitably* escalates or not is at this point a matter of conjecture; population pressures on the resource base may promote war (or dispersion) as a resolution, but so too may the particular stubbornness of the warriors in their pursuit of cultural status — of their honor, or demands for revenge.

In the Age of Enlightenment, when reason was held to be the guiding judge, the primitive and basic cultural response did not fade from the battlefield. It was heard whenever dying or cornered men would cry out for revenge or for honor, the group's identity being at stake: "Push on, old three tens — pay'em for the 44th — you're much wanted, boys; success to you, my darlings," called the wounded of the 44th to the 30th at Quatre Bras, 1815,[14] stirring primary, deeply held values for revenge and honor that echo on all battlefields over the centuries. Indeed, the very regimental system that evolved from the 17th century mimics the ethic of early tribes, in which the individual loses his identity in the group's.

As the level of cultural complexity increases, primitive war can in turn be distinguished between higher and lower types. "Low primitive war" is exemplified by the wars or collective disputes of proto-humans, whose reasoning capacities are small, yet who were capable of concerted action that echoed hunting and foraging strategies. Many animals are capable of cooperation, and perhaps the dividing line between, say, the hunting strategies of wolves and those of early hominids did not differ too much.[15] And apparently such wars may have involved both men and women warriors, for both genders would have been used in the hunting of big game.[16] Indeed, the Germanic etymology of war, *werre* — meaning confusion — hints at the ancient conceptual as well as literal chaos these collective clashes evoked in the minds of early men.

"High primitive war" develops with *Homo sapiens sapiens* and the evolution of articulated expression and coordinated and reasoned planning. Reasoned argument supplements and complements the culturally evolved and biologically inherited reactions and structures of early forms of warfare and organization. Here we find the beginnings of rationally organized warfare: the employment of specific weaponry and the advent of military transport, and the evolution of rituals surrounding slaughters and battles that invoke the gods or ancestors — i.e., some moral and ethical rules — for war's justification. The military writer Basil Liddell Hart noted in 1944 that "armies are temples of ancestor worship",[17] which unwittingly captures not just regimental atavism but also a recognition of the deeper cultural roots to war that puts the private on the same historical plane with all those warriors from the distant past. In bearing arms, the warrior enters a historical stream of heroes whose valor, glory, and sacrifice in battle is recalled.

Although high primitive warfare is characterized by a lack of systematic strategy and by more private and personal considerations rather than public interest policies,[18] the values fought for become more complex and include attempts to impose social or ideational systems. But essentially the pursuit of others' territory and resources may still dominate belligerent motives, while the latter may complement, vindicate, or rationalize economic motives: the explanation must remain ambivalent here, for we are no longer in a world of simplistic material cause and effect but in a cultural world exhibiting a plurality of values and hence of motives. It would be wrong to suggest that waging war to revenge previous casualties or to reinstate a chief's or tribe's honor excludes economic motivations, just as it would be wrong to suggest that primitive wars are solely motivated by economic reasons and that a tribe could not wage war for the sake of its honor in the absence of economic considerations. It would also be wrong to infer that the ability of primitive tribes to articulate their reasons for war disengages them — or the more civilized groups — from the biological or deep cultural structures that produce or sustain warfare.

Concomitantly, the move to a sedentary existence generates a more complex set of values that wars can be fought over, and in turn the advent of agriculture increases the possibility of consistent economic surpluses both in terms of resources and labor time. This suggests to many that unemployed hunters turned their blood thirst against their neighbors in emulation of pre-agricultural cultural rituals.[19] Such rituals that spill over into warfare created systems of honor and virtue that became embedded in cultural as well as political notions of identity. As war became increasingly common, such values in turn become indistinguishable from the martial values .

Arguably, the motivating structures that existed in our deep history do not suddenly disappear as we become cultural and then political beings. Philosophically, man's maturation into a thinking and rational being does not involve a process of shedding of elements that formerly motivated his behavior. Instead, cultural norms and reasoned beliefs supplement what is already there.

CIVILIZED OR POLITICAL WAR

With the oxymoronically entitled "civilized war", war's organization expands and intensifies with the complexity of political organization.[20] Particularly, this is characterized by the advent of orders, which initially are verbally expressed and in more advanced societies are committed to writing.[21] This usually (but not necessarily) involves the formation of states and the rise of permanent governments that centralize administrative powers and which are hence capable of a greater exploitation (through forms of taxation) of the evolving divisions of labor and expansion of production that is characteristic of sedentary civilization. In other words, the rise of government presents the chance for an intensification of economic growth through the forging and defending of its jurisdiction — yet this also presents an opportunity for governments to cream off the profits of trade and production for ulterior purposes.[22]

Material progress brings untold benefits to humanity in terms of higher living standards and widening choices, but like Milton's "good and evil as two twins cleaving together,"[23] the simple fact that a society is able to produce more than it requires implies that some of that economic surplus may be channeled into a war machine,[24] *if the beliefs of that society so demand,* which is, of course, not necessarily the case. The growth of the state does not necessitate aggressive war — or an increase in war's probability — without a corresponding generally held belief among the population that such war is to be valued. It is, however, likely that a tolerance of increased state powers will lend itself to a more obedient population who are willing to put up with aggressive war policies promulgated by those who seek to exploit the available power for their own ends.[25]

The physical possibility of economically exploiting economic surpluses for war necessarily expands with the growth of the economic base. So it is not surprising that with the advance of agriculture — where war is common or becomes so — fortifications become more elaborate and weapons more intricate and longer ranged. Concomitantly, wars become increasingly sustainable over longer periods of time and across greater distances. Standing or professional armies may be maintained either seasonally or permanently, and battles become more organized, reflecting a greater intellectual input into strategy and tactics.

The costs of war also increase with the complexity of civilization, for employing an army involves an increase in opportunities foregone for society. "A shepherd has a great deal of leisure; a husbandman, in the rude state of husbandry, has some; an artificer or manufacturer has none at all," notes Adam Smith, on the increasing costs of sustaining defenses.[26] The recipients of these incomes have typically been the warrior, land-owning élites in Western Europe and Japan — societies that echo the ancient Spartan practice of living off the *helots,* who tilled the lands for their wars. Aggressive civilized war is certainly an economically *luxurious* pursuit, which is reflected in the nature of the classes controlling and dispersing the armies and weapons as well as in the poetry and chivalry of the orders of the knights.

The nature of civilized war remains predominantly unchanged until the invention of gun-powder and of printing.[27] This again intensifies the complexity, potential duration, violence, tactics and ethics of warfare. It also "democratizes" the art of warfare, so that the "common" pikeman or archer could stop an aristocratic cavalry charge. At the battle of Crécy, in 1346, one of the greatest concentrations of knights on the medieval battlefield charged an English army predominantly made up of common folk: out of 12,000 soldiers, 8,000 were archers; they faced 60,000 French, of which 12,000 were heavy cavalry. The French knights and their allies refused to charge the peasants, who rained 60,000 arrows per minute on their heads, preferring instead to seek battle with the socially equal English knights.[28] The English lost about 200 dead and wounded, compared to the 1,542 French knights killed and between 10,000 and 20,000 commoners-at arms. Such expensively maintained ranks of cavalry were being surpassed by the less expensive, cost-effective infantry; later, in the 20th century, the mass production of arms further transformed or "democratized" the battlefield, removing the technological supremacy that the West had enjoyed throughout the 19th century against African and Asian opposition.

The modern era emerging from Western Europe in the 16th century heralded revolutions in science, humanism and liberalism with the ideas of toleration, rights, justice, and liberty. Nonetheless, the accompanying economic expansion also meant that a belligerent state could tax more resources for its war-machine — and for longer periods of time. War certainly became more expensive and complicated, but this was because a complex and extended economy could support it: where it could not, an economy would collapse inward as the specialization of labor de-intensified, since war necessarily usurps production for destruction, and that is a drain on any economy.[29]

MODERN WARFARE

Modern warfare is characterized by a further intensified capacity to channel resources for war from increased mechanization, mass production of weapons, speedy communications, and the extension of the division and specialization of labor to professional or standing armies. However, a complex economy generates a more intricate division of labor with corresponding increases in production, and each activity becomes relatively more costly, so the opportunity cost of war increases with economic complexity. The key for militant leaders has always been to harness as much as possible of the expanded economic output for war purposes without undermining the economic base from which wars can be fought — and this becomes more apparent with the rise of modern warfare. Fighting a modern war thus becomes increasingly difficult because countervailing economic and political powers arise in the marketplace to check the belligerence of leaders.[30] Again, it must be emphasized that it is not the economic surplus or existence of methods of mass production that promote war but the ideas that society possesses on who should use those resources and how; arguably, the more control given to the state by a populace over the dispersion of resources, the more likely it is to usurp those resources for war.

Warfare since the 16th century divides, especially for purposes of military history, into pre-industrial and industrial types. Wars prior to the mid-19th century were characterized by a reliance on predominantly agrarian economies with little diversity of production, but the onset of the industrial revolution altered the nature of war through the intensive mass production of arms. The new character of war was witnessed in the American Civil War (1861-65), which involved the might of the industrial North against the predominantly agricultural South, and this type of warfare was experienced in its most horrific form in the First World War (1914-18), involving the industrialized economies of Britain, France, and Germany, Russia, and the Austro-Hungarian Empire. World War One was a feudal battle infused with modern nationalism writ large with industrial products — a fearful combination and a bloody result.

NUCLEAR WARFARE

Nuclear war is at once as different from modern war as modern war is different from pre-modern war. Again, it represents an intensification of the use of technology in war. The invention of nuclear arms alters the form but not the definition of war. The recent Cold War (1945-89) between the United States and the Soviet Union exemplifies this new era of war, in which implicit threats of total destruction overhang international incidents such as the Cuban Missile Crisis (1962). Nevertheless, the more conventional modern wars that involved the big Western powers in "containment" in Korea (1950-55) and Vietnam (1945-75), and wars against aggression in the Falklands (1982) and against Iraq (1991, 1996), Serbia (1999) and Afghanistan (2001), did not involve any explicit or publicized threats of nuclear war. However, perennial skirmishes between India and Pakistan (1999) have caused concern for the use of nuclear weaponry over their rival claims to the Kashmir province.

Unlike other types of war, the potential nature of nuclear war practically renders obsolete any possibility of limited warfare involving discrimination of targets and proportionality. It thus has grave implications for ethical thinking on war. A nuclear war would effectively be a total war, as defined by an absence of proportionality and discrimination.[31] The Russian marshal, Sokolovsky, argued that "[t]he appearance of rockets with nuclear warheads radically changed previous concepts of the nature of war"[32] and that the unlimited capacity to deliver nuclear weapons creates unlimited modern warfare. Trivially, an unlimited capacity to wage any type of war is impossible,[33] for resources are scarce, but the existence of a quantity of weapons that has the capacity to destroy the world many times over does not diminish Sokolovsky's point. Nonetheless, nuclear war — although its prospect is thoroughly mortifying — does not alter the common conceptual denominator of war that has been proposed. It certainly expands war's dimensions and perhaps reduces the time-frame of engagement, but it does not alter the nature of war itself, only its particulars.

Admittedly, a nuclear war would extend warfare beyond any controllable limits of proportional response and discrimination between targets, and the speed of the delivery of warheads potentially reduces the temporal element of war below the level of traditional strategic thinking involving troop and supply movements. That is, the time involved in declaring war and firing missiles is reduced to extraordinarily minuscule levels in comparison with conventional wars in which time-consuming troop movements are common. But, apodictically, it remains on the same standard of temporal comparison, that is, the logic of delivery and response remains unaltered, despite the compressing of the time scale. A timeless war, a war of Cartesian minds which exist atemporally, cannot occur.

Post-Modern Warfare

A sixth type of war that has entered recent parlance is "post-modern war", which can incorporate "cyber-war", "info-war", or "virtual war".[34] Cyber-warfare involves attacking the electronic communications systems of an enemy through the use of computer viruses or electromagnetic blasts in the atmosphere designed to disable computer systems. The definition should not include the isolated events of single hackers, just as an act of robbery or of vandalism, although malicious and violent, does not constitute a war. Cyber-warfare has to be organized in some manner and it deals with a particular strategy of fighting, i.e., targeting communications. Virtual warfare involves the abandonment — perhaps total — of face to face combat, in favor of wars fought from safe shelters hundreds and even thousands of miles away from the actual "battlefield". There pilot planes and guided cruise missiles hone in on targets.[35] Virtual war constitutes the next progression in battlefield technology, a path that began with the first thrown implement.

While the particular media and technologies involved in cyber and virtual wars are new, attacking communications does not constitute a new form of war; it therefore does not re-define war. The target reflects the dependence that modern economies have on communication; but tactics to disable communications also belie an ignorance regarding the complexity and flexibility that enable complex economies to circumvent such attacks. For example, disabling satellite communications systems, while strategically important, would not destroy the potential lines of communication for, say, the American economy, whereas for nations that focus energies into producing satellites, and which do not possess alternative methods of communication, the loss would be devastating. The destruction of the World Trade Center Towers in 2001 generated economic repercussions, of course, but isolated attacks on economic centers cannot disrupt what is essentially, on a deep cultural level, an open, and complex society. Trade quickly re-routes its channels: the destruction meted out by the Allies and the Luftwaffe in World War II on Germany and Britain respectively show the resilience of vastly complicated industrial nations to rebound, unlike the more shallow economies of poorer countries whose relationship between the population and the economy is much more fragile.[36] The 2001-2002 campaign in Afghanistan highlights the differences between fighting virtual wars against a country that is thoroughly poor in economic terms and dropping bombs onto economically advanced Serbia in 1999. Hitting the power stations certainly shut down Milosevic's communication centers,[37] but it did not destroy his army's ability to conduct delegated operations in an old-fashioned way.

Post-modern warfare may be also a slight misnomer, although it is an attractive term in some respects. It attempts to describe a low-intensity warfare that may exist under the nuclear umbrella of the superpowers, as well as new strategies and tactics (especially since the prevalence of inexpensive machine guns) such as incorporating children into armies,[38] who are exploited for both their cheapness and their lack of any higher-level moral restraints. Such developments require the attention of anthropologists and military historians — never mind humanitarians and philosophers — but such warfare does not alter the overriding conceptual definition of war. Similarly, Ignatieff's concerns in *Virtual War* over the ethical impact of the use of projectiles in war has a long history; famously, the Japanese warrior cult of the *samurai* prohibited the use of guns because of their dehumanizing effect — and the leveling of classes that the musket afforded. But even when wars are fought by computer operators guiding missiles and robots from a safe location behind the lines, the nature of war does not change.

CONCLUSIONS

Arguably, in all of the types of war examined above, the organization or the nature of the violence alters, but the essence of war as *a state of organized open-ended collective conflict* endures.

What is important to remember is that the types of war overlap. There is no complete ecdysis of previous forms as the complexity of war increases — rather, previous structures remain incorporated in the new forms that emerge with technological or social developments. Secondly, it should not be assumed that war's nature inevitably tends towards increasingly complex forms, for human progression should never be apodictically assumed.[39] Societies may regress — forgetting or squandering the knowledge learned by previous generations — and the art and complexity of war may correspondingly decline. War can be the cause or the symptom of that decline — if one considers the decline of the Roman Empire, for example, in which over a few centuries technical understanding began to diminish and the Empire's weakening political and economic structure attracted incursions from Eastern hordes.[40]

The next chapters turn to consider the causes of war.

Notes

1. Quincy Wright's taxonomy is useful as a starter, but it requires adaptation to include new types of war that have entered the vocabulary since the publication of *A Study of War* in 1965.
2. As humans are animals, defensive instinctive reactions shared with other animals may generate war at the pre-rational level of action, and wars may tap back into such reactions.
3. For individual organisms, the instinctive act of violence is motivated by sex, territory, dominance, and activity between members of the same species. For the more social creatures, the act of violence can be motivated by the group's needs for territory, food, migration or parasitic dominance. Wright, *op cit., p.44*
4. As Quincy Wright observes: "Animal fighting . . . must ordinarily be interpreted functionally in relation not to a society or a specific culture but to a race or species. A tendency towards deadly intra-specific fighting would be a serious disadvantage for the race and would usually be eliminated by natural selection." Wright, *A Study of War.*, p.45
5. Cf. "The Origins of Altruism" in Peter Singer's *The Expanding Circle.*
6. Cf. Richard Dawkins's *The Selfish Gene*, p.243, where he argues that in evolutionary logic, a parasite acts to ensure the host's survival (or the host specie's survival, for the parasite could terminate an individual life but still flourish if it passes on to others); ultimately the two may interrelate symbiotically and co-operatively.
7. Wright, *op cit.*, p.51—a proposal certainly reflected in the works of Robert Ardrey and Konrad Lorenz.
8. By "extended reason" I mean the capacity to imagine, conjecture, formulate beliefs and arguments. Animals are rational beings too in the sense that they behave in a rational manner according to their preferences; hence the distinction here between rationality and extended rationality.
9. Dawson, *Origins of Western Warfare*, p.17
10. Culturally evolved rules and mores of conduct help us to decide between competing emotions, motives, choices, and so on, and reasoning in turn prompts the search for consistency, Midgley argues: *"What makes rules necessary is the fact that motives clash, and clash in the context of mental life that badly needs to work as a whole."* Mary Midgley, *The Ethical Primate*, p.138 (original emphasis). When pressed by extremely violent circumstances, the ability to hold on to that mental life of learned rules and codes of conduct becomes tenuous, as is described anecdotally in various memoirs: "A very sad thing happened while we were there—to everyone. It happened slowly and gradually so no one noticed until it happened. We began slowly with each death and ever casualty until there were so many deaths and so many wounded, we started to treat deaths and loss of limbs with callousness, and it happens because the human mind can't hold that much suffering and survive." Jeff Needle, Vietnam War veteran, quoted in Glover, *Humanity*, p.50
11. Dawson, *Origins of Western Warfare*, p.15; Ehrenreich, *Blood Rites*, pp. 10-11
12. *Wealth of Nations*, V.i.a.2.
13. E.g., the Maring peoples. Cf. Dawson, *The Origins of Western Warfare*, p.15
14. Quoted in Longford, *Wellington*, p.287.
15. Until the proverbial moment captured symbolically and artistically in

Stanley Kubrick's film of Arthur C. Clarke's *2001* when a hominid picks up a tool to be used for killing.

16. Ehrenreich, *Blood Rites.* p.103
17. Liddell Hart, *Thoughts on War.*
18. Dawson, *Origins of Western Warfare.* P.13
19. This is picked up by Ehrenreich in *Blood Rites*, although not original to her, for it appears in the writings of the physiocrat economists of Eighteenth Century France, who argued that war is generated by the existence of a surplus aristocratic class, and later by Thomas Malthus in his theory on demography: excess populations are more likely to wage war (succumb to disease, die of starvation, etc.).
20. Dawson argues that in man's evolution firstly, warfare "escaped from the control of nature and became an instrument of culture...[and then]...By the time the stage of the chiefdom is reached, warfare has begun to escape from the control of culture and becoming a political instrument..." *The Origins of Western Warfare*, p.36 His theory suggests a historicist reading of human development that echoes the Hegelian projects of presuming to discern patterns and epochs in history that man must go through or which man's maturation as a species is judged by but also implies that the previous forms were shed by such developments which I am arguing that they are not.
21. For instance, Keegan comments that it was not the Sumerian tools that made them successful warriors but their superior powers of organisation. *A History of Warfare*, p.126 More complex forms of explicitly co-ordinated organisation are possible with writing, although the greatest and most intricate web of organised action is committed through market processes.
22. Balancing the two is the subject matter of much political philosophy of course.
23. Milton, *Areopagitica.*
24. The father of economics, Adam Smith, notes how warfare becomes increasingly expensive though the more complex and advanced a society is. In terms of capital consumption, primitive weapons can be re-used several times (a thrown spear for instance can be thrown back), where as with the advent of gun powder, the firing of a missile becomes an act of consumption, which entails a higher cost of waging war. Similarly, the opportunity cost of leaving farm lands outside of the harvest and sowing seasons is minimal to an agricultural society, while taking a factory worker away from the factory involves a much higher cost of opportunities forgone. Cf. *The Wealth of Nations*, Book V.i.
25. This is especially the case when the costs of war are not directly born by the population but are ameliorated or hidden by credit expansion, monetary debasement, or are deferred through the raising of a national debt (in which case future generations end up footing the bill).
26. *Wealth of Nations*, V.i.a.15
27. Keegan notes that Alexander the Great's army would not have been unduly surprised by a Fourteenth Century European army.
28. Regan, *Military Blunders*, pp. 83-4.
29. Ultimately war destroys the extended economy and reduces it to a state of barter and parochial commerce—the air attacks on Iraq in the Gulf war reduced its infrastructure to medieval levels according to UN sources.

30. Consider the attempts of the Western economies in the twentieth centuries to produce what has been called "war socialism" or a "war economy". Cf, Mises, *Nation, State, and Economy*, p.141.

31. Its nature is aptly elucidated by Sakharov (1921-89), the dissident Russian scientist and Nobel Peace prize holder (1975): "[T]he absorption of the radioactive products of nuclear explosions by the billions of people inhabiting the earth leads to an increase in the incidence of several diseases and birth defects of so-called sub threshold biological effects -for example, because of damage to DNA molecules, the bearers of heredity. When the radioactive products of an explosion get into the atmosphere, each megaton of the nuclear explosion means thousands of unknown victims." From "Sakharov Speaks', Andrei Sakharov, in *Continuity and Change*, ed. Philip C. Ensley, p.168

32. Marshall V.D.Sokolovsky, "Soviet Strategy', in *War*, ed.Freedman, p.235. (bibliography: pp235-238)

33. This is one of obvious constraints to Clausewitz's concept of "total war".

34. For a useful description of these types of war, cf. Gray *Postmodern War*, and Ignatieff's *Virtual War*.

35. Glimmerings of virtual war were seen in the Gulf War (1990-91), but truly it came into its own in the Kosovo conflict (1999) when a casualty-free action was waged by the USA through the assistance of remote devices.

36. Economically, the terrorist attacks did not "push" the USA into a recession; the recession was already inevitable given the misallocation of resources produced by preceding monetary expansion. What the destruction and disruption did was to channel and intensify the nature of the downturn that was unfolding. For explanations of trade cycles, booms, and recessions, cf. the writings of Ludwig Mises and the Austrian school of economics.

37. Cf. Ignatieff's *Virtual War*.

38. Cf. Ignatieff, *The Warrior's Honor*.

39. Progress depends on our willingness to invest into the future, and the conception of the future depends on beliefs concerning on the nature of time. Up until the Seventeenth Century, much of man's conception of time was backward looking, that is, today's events were compared to yesterday's and the golden age lay in the past not in the future. Since then it has been "forward looking" in the sense that we see our lives as stretching into an undetermined future that we can create.

40. Gibbon, *Decline and Fall of the Roman Empire*.

What causes war is of course a perennial issue for those interested in peace. If we are able to understand the origins of such a destructive phenomenon, we may be able to dissemble those martial conditions and factors — or at least be in a position to divert man's energies into more peaceful pursuits. However, what we find is that causes — in the sense of antecedent material or environmental conditions — are not sufficient to explain why man wages war. Man is not determined by his environment, so to *explain* war, we must refer to *reasons* — that is, to the contents of man's mind: his beliefs. Man chooses war, and by this is meant that each individual participant chooses war (or has to choose differently, if war is thrust upon him through invasion or conscription). The individual is a volitional being, whose cognition is free to use and direct; and in group activity such as a battle, each individual must contribute his thought and effort — even if only by accepting the orders of others. Metaphysically, such concerted action is always voluntary — that is, it requires the compliance of each individual. War arises when individuals *decide* to aggress or defend values in a group endeavor, either by joining up themselves or by delegating others to fight. The group does not decide, for groups do not think or act — action and thought always pertain to individuals.

Resolving the philosophical confusions here, concerning the nature of action, is the subject of the following chapters, in which a variety of theories are examined for their coherence, strengths, and weaknesses in explaining war. The concluding thread running through them is that the cause of war is intricate and warrants no simplistic solution: man chooses war, and his choice is dependent on theories and beliefs. What is required for peace is a combination of changes in man's liminal and explicit thinking regarding the metaphysical status of his own choice: man is free to choose; therefore he is free to choose war. But he is also "free" to renounce his freedom[1] and to offer his body to others to determine its fate. However, since much of the reason for war is generated by a thoughtless or unthinking acceptance of cultural and traditional ideas — which often denounce man's ability to choose, peace is best secured by the dissemination of a pro-reason (critically rational) mindset *and* the evolution and development of the alternative culture of the market system, in which the use of physical force is renounced in favor of voluntary contracts. That is, the individual should learn to think for himself and the culture of contract should be allowed to replace the culture of status.[2]

Ethically, people should be free to pursue their own ends as they see fit, so long as they do not initiate physical force against others. But war is a collective endeavor — involving hundreds and thousands of people — in which the individual often loses a sense of self in relation to the platoon, regiment, group, or war. Or, put differently, most military thinkers hold that the individual *ought to* lose a sense of self if such collective action is to be deployed effectively according to policies set by others: the world historical leaders — the Kings, the Generals, the Parliaments or Presidents — who perceive individuals as pawns to be deployed in political games. The loss of self is the purpose of basic drill in the army: the individual loses his personal identity and learns to accept the commands as given with an unquestioning obedience. Herein resides a great threat to freedom, which is so dependent on the critical rationality of all members of a society. The more a people blindly accept authority, the more likely they will become puppets and the more likely they will see themselves as undifferentiated from the masses around them — to be used,[3] exploited, and deployed by those in command.

The ramifications of creating a society of unthinking automatons are obviously dangerous to the free world, which flourishes because of its plurality, individualism, and emphasis on reason. The thoughtless become slaves for others' designs, even if they reside nominally or legally free in a democracy. But while such policies are easily criticized, less obvious are the underlying metaphysical and epistemological theories that in fact teach us to believe that we cannot help what we do, that we are merely undifferentiable entities whose nature is forged by what has gone before, or who cannot be but what others (society), nature (genetics), or the economic system has made us. These are the theories of determinism, the metaphysical theories that renounce the possibility of choice.

The relevant philosophical division begins with those who believe that man is subject to forces beyond his control (determinists) and those who believe man possesses free will to effect his own affairs (indeterminists, or libertarians). A third position is provided by compatibilists, who argue that man is both free and unfree, in senses that proponents naturally disagree on: they may accept, for instance, that man is subject to general determining principles of action, but assert that he is free to choose among the values or beliefs if they are compatible with his character, higher values, informed reason, historical context, mental abilities, and so on. Or as Leonard Peikoff describes freedom: "Man is not only free, he is the product of his freedom — which means: of his intellect."[4]

Libertarians — metaphysical indeterminists — claim that man is absolutely free to choose and no prior factors or events force him to choose a particular course of action now. They claim determinism is wrong, for it permits no choice, and since choice is obviously an element of human life it follows that man is free to choose his next action. However appealing the notion is, if choice is not predetermined by something (a value, a decision, a desire, a self), then it cannot truly be said to be a choice — it is a haphazard, arbitrary *event* and not a choice at all. Existentialists propound this conception of choice — and Jean-Paul Sartre produces some very poignant remarks on the topic;[5] but this means that choice for the indeterminist existentialist is rendered a pointless exercise, both morally and metaphysically. If we possess no pre-existing nature, then there is no basis to our judgments and choices:[6] man is "thrown into the world", as Sartre describes it, and is therefore, it can be surmised, as much adrift in a universe not of his choosing as the determinist would have it.

Determinists claim that everything that happens in the universe is determined — every event or action has a prior cause; they emphasize the closed nature of the universe (in terms of the presiding laws of nature). Some determinists — those reviewed here — argue that man is subject to external forces, and accordingly any conception of being free to choose is illusory. This universe is closed in the sense that all events have prior causes, which in turn have antecedent causes *ad infinitum*.[7] Accordingly, war is the product of a concatenation of events, and man is helpless against this surge of forces; so long as the causal conditions prevail, he is therefore innocent of any responsibility for war.[8]

Since determinism is popularly held and resounds through much thinking on the cause of war, this chapter takes issue with the determinist-materialist position arguing that its denial of human choice is not logical and therefore does not explain war's causation. Indeed, to the extent to which it educates people to accept war as something beyond our volition, determinism perpetuates war. Instead, it is argued that war is certainly a matter of human choice.

WAR: DETERMINISM AND MATERIALISM

Materialism is a philosophical theory that explains the nature of the universe as a material entity and which permits, therefore, no immaterial entities such as spirits or minds or any such immaterial entities.[9]

Materialists are often, although not necessarily, also determinists, and it is this combination of ideas that I wish to evaluate here.[10] Determinism claims that all events are caused by prior events: there is no such thing as an uncaused event, and materialism adds that such events and causal connections are physical or material in nature. Accordingly, the theory of deterministic materialism entails that man is wholly subject to the forces of the universe and that he therefore possesses no ability or "freedom of will" to choose his destiny. This entails that war is not of his choosing — man is a mere pawn in a deterministic universe and any conception he has of his own "free will" is illusory; war is not something he can do anything about — but neither is any event.

How would a determinist begin to explain war? One example may be that events in the universe such as the movement of the planets, sun spot activity, and climatic or environmental changes and so on, alter human behavior, changing people from peace-loving, curious folk into ferocious, suspicious beasts. Some claim to see cyclical patterns in such changes; others seek a fundamental, original cause.[11] Although the term is effectively redundant, man is a victim of processes beyond his control: if man is subject to such great matrices of cause and effect, it follows that he is not responsible for business cycles, creative periods, dark ages, or wars. Man is caught in a causally closed material universe in which individuals and people do not forge their own destinies, and war, or its causal factors, is an inevitable event. "The world began with war and will end with war," says an Arab proverb. The logic entails that given a set of necessary conditions, a sufficient causal condition follows: that is, given a change in the weather, war must follow. Accordingly, the freedom to consider what man *ought* to do is rejected by determinists — he can only do what he can do.

But logically speaking, according to determinism, man's intellectual ability to discern patterns or cycles, or his ability to disclose and to teach what he understands to be the fundamental causal conditions of war, does not in itself arm him against war. He can only oppose war, if he rejects determinism. That is, he grasps his own capability to cause — i.e., *choose* — and to direct events himself. Thus, in terms of human action, the causal efficacy of materialism is in fact the extent to which materialists *believe* man may predict war or to the extent that they *believe* the same causal factors can be directed into more peaceful events. If I claim that I must act in a certain manner, it remains true that I believe that I must so act; and hence, if I claim that I cannot change my manner, it remains true that I choose not to alter my belief that I cannot change my manner.

This implies that we must consider how sound determinism is. If a strict determinism is held, man has no control over war or its study, except to the extent that man is directed — again by processes beyond his control — to tame it or study it. In such a universe neither blame nor praise is relevant: life and death, war and peace, sickness and health, action and inaction are events to which we are subject and the extent to which we "think" we can control them is a mere illusion prompted by other material processes.

However, attempts to reduce human activity to strict determinism are in vain. Even if it is a solid principle that external systems like the weather affect the human condition, a strict and predictable[12] determinism concerning human action has to be rejected. Warm and humid weather may induce physical lethargy, but what lethargic humans do with their time is not predetermined by the environment: it is determined by their ideas regarding what they ought or wish to do. They can choose to be indolent or to be active, to cool off with a swim or to lie basking in the heat. Choice is an integral part of human nature, and the choices people make are dependent on the beliefs they have, and those beliefs are not wholly determined by the physical universe — although actions are constrained by it.

Beliefs are conceptual, mental entities that we accept, learn, and ruminate over. Beliefs, although products of our physical brains,[13] are distinct from the operation of neurological networks. That you are thinking may be discernible to the human eye, or more intricately to a brain scan, but what you are thinking is inaccessible. That you are thinking about something that is causing you to relax, laugh, lament, or cry may also be discernible to an observer, but the content again remains inaccessible. However, strict determinism rejects the possibility that man can *think* about the range of options confronting his next decision, which implies that he is an unthinking automaton — a puppet to an infinite regression of prior events.[13]

Strictly speaking, determinists cannot hold wars to be human events, for men are merely reactive materials incapable of choice (in the popular sense of exerting one's will or volition).[14] Wars are thus relegated to metaphysical (or natural) events. In a determinist universe without conscience, beliefs, or purpose, wars can only be an emanation of behavior caused by prior physical processes.[15]

Determinism also rejects the possibility that humans are capable of altering their behavior to remove the seeds of war. Logically, according to determinism, given a set of necessary causal conditions war will happen; knowledge of this set of conditions, however, does not negate the cause. Knowledge, therefore is epiphenomenal — it emerges from human action and intercourse but is completely useless.

As the theory of determinism is weakened, supporters may allow that war's occurrence is necessary but predictable. Others may examine to what extent war is a permanent condition, or a recurring phenomenon, one that emerges in predictable or unpredictable cycles or phases.[16] A gap still exists though between strict determinists, who may claim war to be an inherent phenomenon of human existence, and those who assert the fatalist conclusion that nothing can be done. It is plausible, for example, to assert that in the face of powerful causal factors, the root causes ought to be examined and attempts be made to remove them (if it is philosophically permitted that we are free to affect such causes).

Depending on the particular causes elaborated on, the attempt — in the eyes of supporters — may or may not be futile.[17] If the determinist theory accepts the causal power of ideas — of belief systems — then the attempt to abolish or control war becomes theoretically possible. However, most determinist theories retain the claim that man's ideas, his thoughts, are the product of external forces: brain pushes mind, body pushes brain, the world pushes body.

A weaker version of the permanent war thesis is the "cataclysmic view" of war, which describes war to be a periodic disaster encumbering human life, a necessary albeit unfortunate part of life. Proponents may describe war as a thoroughly predictable event (or at least theoretically predictable), or as the product of chaotic or complex forces akin to meteorological systems, which man may not predict accurately but can at least be prepared for.[18] For example, if war is like a hurricane that periodically rises to destroy human communities, authorities may seek to protect communities with better defenses: bomb shelters, missile defense systems, a standing militia, and so on.

Cataclysmic war theories are internally contradictory, however. If we can establish that war is like a contagious disease or like a tornado, which implies that we may ameliorate its effects,[19] then we are free to seek its abolition, just as diseases may be eradicated or inoculated against.

Behind both the permanent and the cataclysmic theories of war lies a conceptual error: the reduction of war to a metaphysical (in the sense of unalterable) fact rather than a set of beliefs. To assume that war is an inevitable, metaphysical fact is like confusing a lightning bolt with arson when a barn has been burned down — a dangerous conceptual error.[20] In turn, this has grave implications for policy, for if people believe that war represents the natural state of things ("war is the father of all things," noted Heraclitus), or if people believe that wars are unpredictable phenomena that suddenly grip humanity, then policies, laws, and responses will reflect such determinist thinking — and our understanding of war will remain at a dangerously pre-philosophical, unscientific level similar to our understanding of the natural world prior to the 16th century.

A sounder proposition is that man forms ideas and beliefs. He reflects on how to act. It remains true that the nature of the universe is fixed, as are the physical laws that must be obeyed for the successful adaptation of any species (and similarly certain social laws constrain activities — the laws of economics, for example), *but the values people pursue within the universe are functions of the ideas they hold* and may be inimical or beneficial for adaptation and hence cultural and biological evolution. Every action we take is dependent on an explicit or implicit plan of action that we formulate in our minds, and this is equally true for the purchases we make, the candidates we vote for, the greetings we give, and manner in which we stand, sit, drink, play, laugh, sing, fight, and love.

War is not a metaphysical certainty — that is, a fact that humanity must learn to live with.[21] One element of determinism can be accepted, though — for wars that exist far below the military horizon, wars that evolve as purely cultural or biological solutions to inter-societal problems for dispersing populations or ensuring proprietary rights are — initially at least — beyond the scope of humanity to alter.[22] But with the rise of reason and complex society, war rises above the unchosen or unarticulated response to inter- and intra-social conflict to a deliberately invoked enterprise.

Although the reasons and justifications for waging war may remain couched in atavistic terms — see later chapters — war remains a product of choices. This is true even when the choices work on the assumption that war is not a choice: that is, determinists believe their choices are determined, hence their choice to go to war is similarly determined. "I cannot help doing what I am doing" should be read as "I choose to pretend that I cannot help what I am doing." But, if we can ascertain that war is a product of choice, it follows that war can be avoided and even abolished; nonetheless, the ambition of perpetual peace will certainly be difficult to achieve, as the rest of the book argues. Man is free to choose, but not so free as to be removed from the physical, social, biological, and cultural worlds he inhabits. Ideas can liberate thinking and expand the realm of choice, but man also remains a biological and cultural entity subject to laws, the actions of others, and ideas that are not always of his choosing and sometimes are not accessible to his reason.[23]

The unfolding philosophy of war is thus much more complex than asserting that "man is free to choose war and therefore he is free to not choose war." We need to explore the causal relationships between his nature and his thinking, and in doing so we need to explore the realms of ideas that motivate and restrain him. The status of ideas become increasingly important, but their causal value only makes sense when determinism and indeterminism are rejected. Action follows from choice, and choice follows from the exercise of reason. In turn reason is the product of induction and deduction, of experience and *reflection* upon that experience, and, of course, of conjecture and imagination. The individual determines his own choices by virtue of the decisions he makes — to the question what determines the decisions he makes the only answer can be: he does. "Reason *is* will, and therefore the power of choice is the power that rules man."[24]

The next chapter raises the intellectual stakes from the generally metaphysical to complex theories of human nature — it can be claimed that war is a product of "human nature", and what is meant by that and how a theory of man's nature can relate to war requires investigation.

Notes

1. That is he can deny that he chooses anything: of course this is a choice, and an active and continual one at that.
2. Since the open market system explicitly operates through individual decision making, it can act to counter slavish cultures. A proper market system cannot thrive without a government, whose remit ought to be rationally and strictly controlled. When government expands its influence in our lives — through economic and political interventionist measures — individuals lose both their freedom and their habits of choice. Interventionism often precedes war or becomes an acceptable element to war. De Tocqueville warned of the implications in 1803: "If [war] does not lead to despotism by sudden violence, it prepares men for it more gently by their habits. All those who seek to destroy the liberties of a democratic nation ought to know that was is the surest and the shortest means to accomplish it." *Democracy in America*, Volume II, p.269
3. Peikoff, *Objectivism*, p.205
4. Cf. Sartre's *Existentialism and Humanism* and *Being and Nothingness*.
5. Scruton, *Modern Philosophy*, p.310
6. Although it can be consistently held that the laws may change or that elements of the universe are chaotic or complex.
7. The strongest philosophical position presented in this vein is a materialist form of determinism, whose proponents claim that man exists in a thoroughly material world — there being no spirits, souls, minds, or immaterial entities of any sort. For reviews of these positions, cf. Stephen Priest, *Theories of the Mind*, and Timothy Sprigge's *Theories of Existence*.
8. In the philosophy of the mind, for instance, materialism asserts that the mind is the brain. For instance, the common conception we possess of ideas in the mind are reducible to statements regarding the physical activity of the brain, and are resoluble into prior determining structures. There are several versions of materialism, ably explored by Stephen Priest in *Theories of the Mind* (1990), chapter 4.
9. Materialism does not exhaust determinism though. Idealists argue that the world is constituted by nothing by Ideas, in the Platonic or Berkeleyian sense of immaterial objects — everything is mind or soul, they claim. Idealists too can be determinists, with every immaterial event possessing a prior immaterial cause. Materialism is the more popular form that determinism takes and will be dealt with here. The materialist may be an indeterminist, arguing that all events in the universe may indeed be physical, but resolving the causation is more problematic or unpredictable. The Ancient Greek Democritus (460-370 BC), for example, argue for the existence of atoms as constituting the primary structure of the universe, but he conjectures that the resulting collision between atoms produces unpredictable events and hence uncertainty. Priest, *ibid.* p.99. Democritus' theory is a forerunner of Heisenberg's "uncertainty principle" (proposed in 1925) that it is impossible to ascertain both the momentum and the position of a particle.
10. Kondratieff and his followers for example pursue a cyclical research of human endeavors. Interestingly, Nikolay Dmitriyevich Kondratieff (1892-1938), who pro-

posed that human technological growth is cyclical every fifty years, opposed Stalin's collectivization of agriculture and was executed.

11. Although logically these two can be distinguished: to have a materially closed universe does not necessarily entail that it is a predictable universe as Karl Popper has argued, cf. "Of Clouds and Clocks" in *Objective Knowledge*.

12. Possession of a brain is a necessary but not sufficient condition of thought.

13. Peikoff argues that; "because man has free will, no human choice — and no phenomenon which is a product of human choice — is metaphysically necessary." "The Analytic-Synthetic Dichotomy", p.149

14. The materialist-determinist theory of war also removes any responsibility from humanity to deal with war, since its causes are assumed to be outside human jurisdiction. But humanity is responsible for its actions, since it possesses free will.

15. The psychology theory of behaviorism is quite akin to strict materialism, since it too denies the possibility of consciousness.

16. Such theories fall foul of Popper's critique of historicism—that man walks a destiny not of his own choosing and what therefore befalls him is likewise not of his own choosing.

17. If the roots of war are to be found in the very structures of the human mind, as Hegel argues, could the mind's manner of thinking be altered in a similar manner to the intervention enacted on a domesticated species — i.e., to remove the belligerent gene in modern parlance through selective breeding (a pacifying eugenics)? From the viewpoint of *immaterial* determinism (idealist philosophies), if the origins of war are to be found in a bipolar dualism in men's souls, in effect a Manichæan struggle between good and evil, then war may be ended with the renouncing of evil deeds and a strict supervision of the evil in men's souls.

18. Theories of complexity or of chaos being deployed here.

19. Only a thorough skepticism or radical epistemological nihilism could deny that knowledge could never be put to some use. A man may know a bridge is unsafe and still choose to walk it, either with the intention of enjoying a risk or ending his life, or because he has no other acceptable means of escape. Some philosophers do deny the efficacy of knowledge but thereby contradict their own imparting of such wisdom!

20. Nuances can of course be played with here — that a farmer builds a barn on top of an unsheltered hill is to increase the risk of it being struck, as it would in building a barn in a community of anti-farmers or arsonists.

21. The fallacies of determinism are constant: for if we can learn to live with war, then we can learn to live with out it — we can prepare ourselves either way.

22. But they are too much like animal wars to be considered a part of the human realm of explicitly reasoned choice.

23. Although the conscious mind can, in principle, access all the reasons for doing something in a particular manner, its high marginal cost precludes most people from considering their every day actions. Nonetheless, our every day actions, reactions, movements, postures, etc., can be the subject of our conscious mind. Cf. F.M. Alexander, *Man's Supreme Inheritance*, ch. "Habits of Thought and Body", pp. 46-66

24. Peikoff, *Objectivism*, p.204.

CHAPTER FIVE: Human Nature and War

What constitutes man's nature is one of the most important philosophical questions and one that directly relates to how war is viewed. Is man naturally or essentially pacifistic? Or is he naturally belligerent? Theories which suggest that the environment causes man to take up arms were rejected in the previous chapter — man *chooses* war; but what if the cause of war is to be found in his own breast or in his own mind? What if man cannot help but wage war, for that is the kind of species that he is? Logically, such theories are deterministic, except here the causal factor that provokes man to war is shifted from the external environment to internal genetic or psychological makeup. But the same logical refutation follows: man acts upon choices and those choices are the products of his belief system, as he himself has learned and reflected on them. Nonetheless, the relationship between beliefs and choices is complex and is a theme throughout this book's exploration of war. But to clear the decks for a more thorough and sound understanding, competing theories of human nature ought to be considered; after all, as they become belief systems — embedded in cultural expectations or espoused by philosophers — they become causal factors in why man wages war.

Various theories on man's nature are popularly held: they are easily proposed in conversation, and often are heard in laments of man's decrepit nature, his original sin, his love of cruelty and of evil, and, of course, his love of war.[1] Man's very nature is often castigated as being the cause of war by philosophers and writers of great literature, pamphlets and poetry,[2] whose thoughts trickle down into popular speech and cultural conceptions, to be picked up and recycled in conversation and argument.

The range of human nature theories should not imply that they do not affect our choices, for in becoming beliefs, either popularly held or held by those who form opinion, they provide guides or ostensible constraints on what is possible for man. And man acts on his beliefs. Do we believe that war is man's lot? If we believe so, then we will never abolish it, for we will not believe that it is within our command to end. Or is war a symptom of man's general pugnacity — regardless of his beliefs — which could be trained into ulterior channels? Then let's provide for those alternatives. If war is not of man's choosing, then he can be excused to some extent or other, but if it is fully a product of his free will — and hence of the beliefs that he acts upon — then he stands judged for his actions prior to, during, and after war.[3]

Let us begin, though, with the determinist position that seeks to explain war as being caused by man's inherently bellicose nature.

To suggest that war is a product of man's nature is to suggest that it is an inherent element of his behavior. This implies that his being is determined by connate genetic elements, or by the permanent psychological structures of his mind, or that war is a necessary product of his sociability (that living a social existence provokes man into defending, for instance, his territory and values). Against such variants of determinism others, most notably Jean-Paul Sartre, have denied all forms of determinism implicit in theories of human nature. Man, he claims, is free — absolutely free — to choose his next action: to fire a gun, to surrender, to join the resistance, to betray the resistance, to scream on the torture rack.[4] Sartre's libertarianism, though, as we saw in the previous chapter, also reduces man to a helpless albeit volitional being for whom choice is as arbitrary as the world into which he is thrown. Most theorists of human nature prefer to seek an all-encompassing variable or factor that *explains* war, that provides us with the solution for our persistent belligerence in the face of reasoned demands for peace.

JEAN-PAUL SARTRE'S EXISTENTIALISM

On the far side of philosophy are the writings of Jean-Paul Sartre, which offer a useful foil to many theories of man's nature. Sartre categorically denies the possibility of a human nature — or rather implies that it is infinitely pliable. There is no set nature, no predetermined sense of action, he argues, and hence, no excuse for what we do. Man's "existence precedes his essence", writes Sartre, which means that we are completely free to determine who we are. "Man first of all exists, encounters himself, surges up in the world — and defines himself afterwards."[5] Accordingly, any attempt to resolve our actions into determinist structures such as the environment, childhood, id, culture or society, divine purpose, or genes is not only bad philosophy, but constitutes an attempt to deny our metaphysical freedom in preference for living in what he calls bad faith", or to live "inauthentically".

Since man is free, and hence possesses no nature, he must be said to choose everything; thus he thoroughly can be said to choose war. The question for Sartre is whether he chooses it authentically or inauthentically,[6] that is, in full knowledge of his freedom or in excusing his actions as being predetermined.

Les Liaisons Dangereuses by de Laclos provides a wonderful literary example of inauthenticity used to end a relationship. The Marquise de Merteuil instructs the Vicomte de Valmont to give up his mistress, using such dialogue: "One grows weary of everything . . . it is a law of Nature; it is not my fault. . . . Farewell, my angel, I took you with pleasure, I abandon you without regret; perhaps I shall come back to you. So goes the world. It is not my fault."[7] The dramatic twist in the story is prompted by this recourse to determinism: so far as the Vicomte is fully cognizant of his treachery and his excuses, he lives authentically, but not if he believes that it is not his fault. And so nations excuse their going to war authentically and inauthentically, sincerely and superficially sincerely with apologetics to human rights or the public interest, as if they could not but go to war.

Sartre's existentialism denies that human nature may determine action; thus it leaves war solely the product of man's choices. It is an appealing position that seeks to dissemble excuses and rationalizations for those consequences that could have been avoided, but even Sartre accepts that man is constrained in what he can do by what he has done and by the physical limits of his body and of the universe. He names this totality of constraints man's "facticity". On a first reading this apparently entails that man is not "free" to become a plant, or a crook is not "free" to ignore his sentence (although he may authentically acknowledge his guilt); but on further reflection one has to consider the extent and strength of such facts that man has to accept or bend his will to. The free man is still restrained by the actions of others — if he finds himself in a war not of his making, his choices are somewhat curtailed. Similarly, what has happened in the past cannot be altered; the conservative existentialist writer, Ortega y Gasset, writes: "Man is what has happened to him, what he has done," but the next moment is fully his: "it is accordingly meaningless to set limits to what he is capable of being."[8]

`Yet, the fact that many people do live inauthentically, ascribing determining causal factors to their actions, does provide a useful explanation of why war occurs. For example, the refusal to accept personal responsibility in deferring to the wishes of the majority, government, tradition, and religion, etc., does not absolve the individual from the ensuing sequences of events — and arguably it is precisely because so many flow with what others do that war is sustained in the modern world.

However, existentialism does not sufficiently explain war; it may applaud the man who *authentically* claims, "I know this is war and I choose to fight", but it does not provide an explanation as to why man seeks war as a value — nor why it is such a perennial human institution. "Man has to be himself in spite of unfavorable circumstances," advises Ortega y Gasset,[9] but which circumstances are unfavorable or favorable is a product of his belief system; and that belief system is a complicated matrix of ideas and notions accepted implicitly and explicitly by the individual as he proceeds through life.[10] Is that belief system pro-man or anti-man? For the existentialist it seemingly does not matter: man is what he makes of himself. Yet what *ought* he to make of himself? Sartre does not provide much of an answer — in his ethics, he reverts to a Kantian position that one ought to do that which will be universalizable. But without a standard, that does not give humanity much to go on — which implies that war could be a universal good. Alternatively, the existentialist could accept the proposition that war is something that happens to man, and the individual, thrown into war, must simply decide how to live within it: certainly a great premise for novels and plays, but it does not get us to the origins of war.

Another limitation to existentialism is the emphasis on the conterminous mind — that is, the mind as it thinks *now* — to capture knowledge and meaning. This means that the existentialist's decision to fight or to lay down arms is derived from an exhaustive, explicated review of knowledge; but explicated reasoning for the existentialist can only be a shallow act, since all words and all meanings are ultimately absurd.[11] As long as the individual genuinely accepts his choice as his own, he lives authentically — it really does not matter what he chooses, as long as it is sincerely chosen.

Words and beliefs are not arbitrary, however; they present visions and claims to man's life and actions that have often evolved and/or been developed by generations of thinkers. Our judgment concerning them can only be on their appropriateness for living, and insofar as existentialism undermines the reality of the universe — for existentialist entities gain their identity from subjective perception — then existentialism undermines any human activity and any understanding of that activity. It is unsurprising that existentialism results in an extreme form of epistemological subjectivism in which — relevant for our purposes here — one man's terrorist is another man's freedom fighter (or, alternatively, terror and freedom are subjective concepts whose meanings are arbitrarily given): the world is lost and so too, as existentialists emphasize, is human nature.

What this means for war is that it is something that is inexplicable — an event that arises every now and again to throw individuals into poetically existentialist dilemmas, when death is brought to the fore and the power and meaning of choice come into strong relief. Beyond that, a theory of war based on the existentialist critique of human nature can be constructed, and one that is of use to some extent. The conformity of the majority, who blandly obey the customs and mores of their society, will act to perpetuate traditions and institutions that are inimical to the life of authenticity; war's persistent grip on the human imagination cannot be explained away solely by its economic benefits (perceived or real) or by the existence of ruling warrior classes — it persists because people continue to believe in it, regardless of whether they believe in it because it offers material, cultural, or spiritual advantages. Reason properly used clarifies the benefits to be gained from cooperation over conflict, yet many choose to remain ignorant of its claims. Later chapters explore why this is so, but here we may give Sartre a nod in partial agreement: the appeal of war is often inauthentic.

Sartre's position is diametrically opposed by those who claim that humanity does indeed possess a nature, although they disagree as to what that nature entails.

PLATO

Plato's writings present the first thorough philosophical theory of man. He believes that human nature is divided into two general elements — the immaterial mind or soul and the physical body. The soul is the source of knowledge, and is in turn divided into reason, spirit, and appetite. Appetite can tell a man he is hungry, and reason that the food in front of him is off, while spirit is a form of self-assertion or will that often allies with reason against appetite to control man's baser desires. Reason, Plato advises, should maintain absolute control over will and appetite.

Analogously, since we are social creatures, reason should rule our political affairs and keep in control the lusts for war and glory. Thus the best people to manage our political affairs are, accordingly, those who are most reasonable — namely, Plato's philosopher kings.[13]

For Plato, peace and harmony ensue for the individual who is able to live justly and who maintains a proper balance between reason, spirit, and appetite. Similarly, peace and harmony will follow for the society that maintains a balance between the corresponding social classes of philosopher kings, auxiliaries, and workers: classes of people that conveniently mirror Plato's view of their own dominant elements. Workers, it is implied, are motivated by their appetite, while the auxiliaries, who form the police and civil service, are governed more by their spirit. Only an élite may rise to become philosopher kings, for they are sufficiently infused with reason to raise themselves above instinct and appetite.

Plato presents a description of the perpetual psychological struggle within man and how it spills over into war; this, however, also takes place in the context of a gradual and perceptible decline in man's moral nature, which Plato, in *The Republic*, hopes to stop. Following many Greeks, Plato believed in an earlier golden age in which peace reigned, "the fall" from which set into motion *change* and hence further degradation. Man must therefore do all he can to retard his fall into chaos, and that requires a strong state to curtail all potential sources of change.[13]

Plato's vision of human nature relates to a particularly prevalent doctrine of war in which war emanates from the lower elements of the soul rising up to dominate reason (or in Platonic revolutionary thought the disposition of the workers to rise up to overthrow the philosopher kings!). War is therefore irrational (as is revolution); but, because of the troublesome nature of the soul, it is not likely to be abolished. Although Plato goes on in *The Laws* to describe economic and political *motives* for war, it is in his version of human nature that we find its ultimate cause, namely in the tripartite division of the soul.[14]

Both Plato's psychological and political theories have enjoyed and continue to enjoy a strong intellectual following. Yet the consequences of the belief that have filtered into the broad spectrum of academic fields from politics to economics to psychology to theology and so on have been disastrous for humanity.

The belief that one or more elements of man's nature is naturally at war with the others promotes the acceptance of an internal psychological war within man, which spills over into a war between the various orders of society. In the individual, the mind should maintain a strict control over the wandering, lascivious appetites of the body. In the social sphere, ascetics should impose an authoritarian control over those who are more apt to be lustful. Although the benefits of self-discipline and emotional and physiological control for an open, civil society cannot be underestimated, they do not have to be explained in separatist terms, i.e., from any assumption that man possesses mutually exclusive psychological spheres.

The individual is a complex entity, whose internal psychological elements — aspects of the mind — are conditioned by inherent capacities, and by the exercise of those capacities, experiences, and beliefs. And beliefs cascade over the implicit, non-verbalized conceptions we possess from experience or from implied conclusions we have drawn, as well as over the explicitly verbal arguments, prescriptions, justifications, excuses, lies, fables, anecdotes, and conversations in which we partake with others and with ourselves. The 19th century historian Jacob Burkhardt notes that, "All human knowledge is accompanied by the history of the ancient world as music is by a bass chord heard again and again; the history, that is, of all those peoples whose life has flowed together into our own."[15] No demarcation is possible, and attempts to sever our nature — or our history — into convenient parts results in an unhealthy imbalance in man, often resulting in destructive or debilitating guilt complexes.

Yet as a theory of war's causation, such a view of human nature is not without its merits. Civil society requires moral restraints. The codes of conduct appropriate for a society have evolved and continue to evolve to provide guides on how an individual behaves within the group, and likewise how he should behave towards members of other groups. Such codes are far from being the product of reason — in fact rationally created codes or laws rarely work well, unless they reflect and/or emanate from well-established principles of behavior that have evolved over generations. Some, however, prefer to not to abide by the rules, or cannot by themselves learn mastery over their immediate needs. Children, for example, often need to be taught some of the rules conducive for their own flourishing in society, while they learn through play and interaction such a variety of rules that could not be taught explicitly. Adolescents often challenge the rules they have learned, and to some extent are merely adding to the eternal experimenting and adapting to life — and their role in history and war cannot be ignored.[16] But more often than not they are coming to terms with their conception and understanding of present versus future interests — expanding their inter-temporal comprehension — in the context of learning rules that they did not create and which they may not understand.

The most useful principle that may be drawn from Plato's theory of human nature is the emphasis on the mind's important role in prioritizing present and future values. But its downfall is to assume that the mind can be separated from its body,[17] and hence explicitly reasoned argument can be separated from implied knowledge — the latter providing man with more understanding than he often realizes.

Yet Plato's teacher Socrates' lesson on his own ignorance is of perennial use. Man cannot know everything — or even much in relation to what could be known — hence any attempt on his part to rationally plan his life (in the sense of explicitly forming all the plans and contingencies in advance) is bound to fail. This also means that utopian designs[18] to rid the world of war and poverty are similarly futile. Platonic utopians are the creation of single minds and subject to the individual's own particular prejudices, but, more importantly, are restricted by the individual's own particular knowledge.[19] They are in turn, insofar as they become politically and culturally held beliefs, *causes* of the most violent warfare: many of the wars of the 20th century were the product of attempts — under the guise of social engineering — by some men to impose on others their particular vision of what life ought to be like. The results are plain to see in the millions that died or were killed in or because of the Soviet Union, China, Nazi Germany, Cambodia, and so on.[20]

Society, however, results from the constant interaction of millions of individuals, all pursuing their own good as they see fit, learning from their mistakes, forming and breaking habits, friendships, and romances, laughing and forgetting — in a word, changing. Plato desired to stop the world so it would not decay, for man's innate curiosity would lead him further from the peaceful bliss of the golden age into a world of strife, but "as rational beings we are also progressive beings;"[21] for our desires will always be one step ahead of our abilities to satisfy them: hence the unsatisfying nature presented in utopias which are ably explored in the satirical dystopian novels of *1984*, *Brave New World*, and so on.

The underlying contention that war originates from man's curiosity or desire for progress (i.e., lack of control over his alleged baser instincts) is one that is mirrored in Christian doctrines that have so effectively influenced Western thinking.

CHRISTIANITY

While fourth century Christians imported much of Plato's model of the soul and body into their political theology (notably through St Augustine), properly speaking Christians possess a different conception of human nature than Plato. For Christianity, man is made in God's image and stands at the top of the hierarchy of living creatures. Man's obedience is to God, but the animal kingdom is his to control as he sees fit. Man's body may be resurrected after death, but he is born with original sin *and* with free will. But following Augustine, most Christians do see human nature as the cause of war and suffering, for humans, not being perfect, are apt to err;

> This [earthly] city is often divided against itself by litigations, wars, quarrels, and such victories as are either life-destroying or short-lived . . . they war to this extent, that every good man resists others in those points in which he resists himself. And in each individual "the flesh lusteth against the spirit, and the spirit against the flesh." [22]

Man may thus choose to live a life of obedience to God, but more importantly, he may choose to redeem his sins through accepting Christ, a sin being committed in man's erring in obedience, or in his alienation from God.

Christians debate the nature of these fundamentals, which impinges on how war is viewed by them. Some, such as Calvinists, have claimed that only a predestined, select few, are chosen by God, and that the rest are damned to hell, regardless of either group's actual morality. Similarly, some Christians have divided the human world into a hierarchy that the original universalist message did not intend — often such social divisions conveniently mirror pre-existing social prejudices. Some have denied free will; others have asserted it. The political and moral message of Christianity therefore splits into a variety of interpretations.

Nevertheless, one of the most important strands running through much Christian thinking is the humanist message.[23] This asserts that we can choose not to fight one another (i.e., to turn the other cheek) and to seek peace. The Christian view of human nature can be thus optimistic: man can renounce violence, even though man's origins are assumed to be defective. Such is the importance of the forgiveness of sin in the doctrines.

On the other hand, the ancient division of peoples into the saved and the damned has motivated many crusades against heretics and non-believers. Bernard of Clairvaux exhorted in 1128:

> Rejoice, brave warrior, if you live and conquer in the Lord, but rejoice still more and give thanks if you die and go to join the Lord. This life can be fruitful and victory is glorious, yet a holy death for righteousness is worth more. Certainly "blessed are they who die *in* the Lord", but how much more so are those who die *for* Him.[24]

And so began a history of aggressive actions against non-believers that started with wars against Islam before turning Christians against

Christians in the 16th and 17th centuries.[25]

The humanist vision of Christianity draws on Stoic cosmopolitanism, but the moral definition of personhood — of who should be included in the humanist vision — has not always been inclusive in Christian thinking. Vitoria's writings in the 16th century[26] offer a glimpse of the modern path that most Christians have taken: that of deeming the native South American Indians to be potential converts who lacked the history and knowledge that Europeans had been blessed with, so that evangelism rather than force ought to be employed to bring God's children into the fold. However, ancient divisions and prejudices run deep in men's beliefs and the 20th century witnessed such barbarity that would have embarrassed the Renaissance world.

There is not the space here to delve into the nuances of Christian thinking on war: the literature and controversies both are vast areas. Its more dominant forms — as having been passed on, for example, by the explicated just war tradition of Augustine and Aquinas — continue to impress on the modern mind. Its main institutions and thinkers have left the belligerent mentality of the medieval church behind and today Christians are often at the forefront of attempts to enable peace between disparate and fighting groups. Its theories of human nature are divergent, however, which implies corresponding divergent understandings of war and hence policies to seek peace. Each vision deserves attention, but what I wish to draw attention to here is the close connection some Christians make to socialism, and the writings of the atheist Karl Marx that have influenced the philosophy of some Christians in their explanations of poverty and of war.

MARXISM

In contrast to the dualist theory of Plato and the humanist vision of Christianity, for Karl Marx man is subject to a closed material universe. Man is not divided nor is he a spiritual entity — he is what society makes him. Indeed, man's nature, for Marxists, reflects the governing economic and material conditions of a particular period. Man is a product of his class, and in turn his class is a product of the economic system; this system governs the manner and content of his thought. Therefore to understand war from a Marxist perspective, one must consider the presiding economic conditions, and the role that the dominant classes play in the system.

"The history of all hitherto existing society is the history of class struggles," begins *The Communist Manifesto*.[27] War is therefore a product of class antagonism, and Marxists have spent much energy and literature to examine and describe the class interests governing the origins of particular wars. The abolition of war can only come once the class system finally collapses in the communist revolution, which will be an inevitable event, according to Marx. If social antagonisms are the product of the clash of classes, once classes no longer exist, violence and war will disappear. Marx presents a theory of history as well as a vision of the future, and as a theory Marxism can motivate activists to bring that vision about; yet at this level of examining war, it must be considered as a determinist-materialist explanation of war's origins. War, for Marx, is not a chosen activity, and thereby man can neither be excused nor blamed for violence.

However, the issue that Marx and his followers face is the extent to which a man is free to bring about the conditions for revolution. Marx himself is ambivalent — he was after all a political agitator, but theoretically his system entailed a closed philosophy of history in which the individual is fated to flow with the impersonal changes wrought in history by changes to the means of production.[28] Those Marxists who believed they could usher in the revolution, or speed up its conditions (Lenin[29]), obviously employed revolutionary means to the end, but thereby seceded from pure historicist Marxism. Morally, they were enthused by the glory of "waging war on (class) war" itself; theoretically they were caught between pure Marxism with its determinism and political Marxism with its powerful rhetoric to break the chains of oppression.

The gravest error in Marxist thinking is to accept that man's beliefs are a product of his social system. For this raises the question of what produced the social system in the first place, and the only coherent explanation is that prior beliefs (some stretching back over millennia) forged the present situation. A man makes a new tool because he has a belief that it will be efficacious, that it will be of use; its production is successful because others believe it will make their lives better. Indeed social structures may change as people adapt to a new way of life with their new tool; but they do so because a man had an idea that passed into the general currency of thinking.

If the circumstances and nature of economic production can be reduced to the choices made by individuals (and if, in turn, those choices are the product of their beliefs), then war must similarly be the product of choice. But the most dangerous intellectual aspect of Marxism is its annihilation of the individual into the collective. Collectives are nothing but groupings of individuals, who each act and think of their own accord, sometimes in agreement with others and at other times not. Yet for Marxists, the individual is nothing without the group — it is from the material circumstances of the group that he gains an identity and a destiny for, according to the Marxists, one's position in the economic system determines what one will do next. There is no choice: only fate. Since Marxist theory dictates that the masses are fated to rise up and take control of the means of production and thereby bring in the communist revolution, it is unsurprising that Marxism has been the excuse for much of the violence and warfare of the 20th century.

BEHAVIORISM

Although far removed from an overarching philosophy of history, behaviorism also asserts a closed determinist universe. Human nature, for the behaviorist, is conditioned by events and situations. Again, interesting paradoxes arise as to the extent of man's ability to change his own conditions, for the proponents often imply that they are somehow not subject to the same causal rules as other mortals. J.B. Watson argued:

> Give me a dozen healthy infants, well-formed, and my own specified world to bring them up in and I'll guarantee to take any one at random and train him to become any kind of specialist I might select — doctor, lawyer, artist, merchant-chief, and yes even beggar-man and thief, regardless of his talents, penchants, abilities, vocations, and race of his ancestors.[30]

Of course, he may reply that he was conditioned to develop into such a programmer; but the freedom to command and control that exudes from such writing belies the theory's weakness.

Behaviorists perceive war as the product of certain human traits that are stimulated by the environment (however they define environment, here). Watson's disciple B.F. Skinner claims that human and social problems can be solved through the technology employed by behaviorism — of altering response mechanisms and providing the right responses for the appropriately desired ends. Since our behavior is thoroughly conditioned by environment, any anti-social behavior can be eradicated. Wars can therefore be abolished through changing the human environment.

The optimism is appealing, yet it rests on some very dubious premises, especially its rejection of mental states and the possibility of internal beliefs causing human action. Secondly, it should be emphasized that the theory implies that some are not subject to the conditioning environment to which humanity is subject, for they seem able to transcend the determining structures to envisage the system as a whole (*de haut en bas*) and how it can be bettered. Arguably, this is an echo of Plato's philosopher kings, who are to rise to the pinnacle of power to impose their vision of how life ought to be. Finally, the very fact that behaviorists can speak of generating *better* conditions implies the existence of beliefs, values and comparisons, and thereby of an internal, mental world of wishes, aspirations, imagination, and dreams that may affect our behavior — as it affects theirs to produce a *theory* (a hypothesis) of behaviorism.

CONCLUSION

There are other theories of human nature; each in turn is derived from metaphysical conceptions of the universe and of man's place in it — whether he is a completely free independent consciousness as Sartre sees it, or thoroughly the product of his time and occupation as Marx sees it.

In human nature theories, war is rendered a peculiar aspect of our nature or a necessary product of it: it is our nature that fates us to fight. Such overarching theories fail in recognizing the causal belief these theories in turn possess. If one believes in the innate evil of human nature, or in its inherent predisposition to violence, then one certainly will not attempt to abandon violence or war — i.e., an ideologically induced fatalism is thus possible.

But if we are curious about the root cause of war, we must go be-

yond simplistic explanations that excuse war on an element of our nature, and again we find that the cause lies in the beliefs we possess and
act upon. This leads up the path that Sartre walked, but we do not end
in his nihilism of subjective nothingness. On the contrary, the values
that we seek can be objectively evaluated and judged, either with reason or through the test of time. Accordingly, the theories of human nature that we do uphold and which become implicit in our varied and
broad thinking on life and its problems are, after all, *beliefs* that we hold
of ourselves and how we relate in the grand scheme of things.

To blame human nature for war is philosophically trivial: if human
nature were different, people would not fight one another. But we must
be wary that implicit in the trivial proposition sits the determinist implication that war is an *inevitable* product of man's nature. Hence war
can be described as being as natural to human existence as breathing or
sleeping. In a strict deterministic theory of human nature, the maturation or even birth of the species *necessitates* war; weaker versions admit
that war can be controlled but never abolished. Yet beyond a few automatic violent responses that humans possess in common with animals,
war *is* a choice and not an inexorable or cataclysmic fact of human existence.

Nonetheless, war is a choice that expresses something peculiarly
natural to man. Wars are chosen, but choosing is a complex process
that admits man's thoughts on the present, the past, and the future, as
well as that which is embedded in his physical and emotional being and
dispositions. The present can never be cleanly broken from the past,
and therefore, what we choose to do next can never be broken from the
present or the past. As Coleridge puts it in his "Kubla Khan":

> Five miles meandering with mazy motion,
> Through dale the sacred river ran,
> Then reached the caverns measureless to man,
> And sank the tumult to a lifeless ocean:
> And 'mid this tumult Kubla heard from far
> Ancestral voices prophesying war![31]

Man is free to choose, to make the next step; but his choices are
framed, not predetermined, by previous choices — indeed by the ances-
tral voices that still echo not just in texts and songs but also in the

meanings, implications, and expectations of language. Choices are the product of man's beliefs, explicit, liminal, and subliminal.

That war is a chosen endeavor makes it tragic, but neither tragedy nor war betoken simplistic explanations. Tragedy is not tragic because men die, or because their ambitions are thwarted; tragedy results from a combination of facts and understandings strewn across an unending field of comprehensible reasons and uncomprehended intuitions that point to the ineffable. Take a man raising himself from the ground to charge the enemy: potential explanations run riot in our minds, leaving the poet, composer, or artist to capture some essence of human nature that our normal modes of communication can only barely hint at; a complete explanation is beyond our abilities. It may be beyond the ability of the man on the ground to explain his reasons fully; hence we admit artistic license in describing motivation: but ultimately we may only say that he runs at the enemy, because that is who he is. He is killed in an instant and we call it tragic; and the tragedy is intensified the more we know of the situation and the events leading up to it, but we still cannot access the man's reason for his charge, except in fiction. He is free to charge the enemy, just as he is free to run from it. His human nature hinges upon that: man thinks and believes and then acts upon those beliefs.

The next chapter examines a particular area of human nature theories and war, namely how human biology may be said to cause belligerence or a predisposition to war.

Notes

1. Such writings often miss out on man's passionate nature, his love of beauty, love, and life.

2. See articles in this vein by, e.g., John Nef, "Political, Technological, and Cultural Aspects of War", p.122., Immanuel Kant, "Perpetual Peace" In *Political Writings*, pp.103, 111; and Urpo Harva, "War and Human Nature", p.50 An examination of the literature and poetry is unfortunately beyond this work but beckons as a tempting research project.

3. Historian A. J. Toynbee commented: "As human beings, we are endowed with free-dom of choice, and we cannot shuffle off our responsibility upon the shoulders of God or nature. We must shoulder it ourselves. It is our responsibility." http://www.quoteland.com, accessed September 2001.

4. Or, like Sartre, to drink coffee, intellectualize war, look after his mother, and court occupational officials to stage his plays Cf., Johnson, *Intellectuals*.

5. Sartre, "Existentialism is a Humanism," in Kaufmann, *Existentialism from Dostoyevsky to Sartre*, p.349.

6. There is a friction in his theory concerning self-identification, for he follows the Hegelian examination of the self and the other, accepting that the self and the other attempt to dominate each other — they both try to make the other an object: "one must either transcend the Other or allow oneself to be transcended by him. The essence of the relations between consciousnesses is not the *Mitsein*; it is conflict." Sartre, *Being and Nothingness*, p.429

7. *Les Liaisons Dangereuses*, Folio Society, 1962, p.341-343.

8. Ortega y Gasset, "Man Has No Nature," in *Existentialism from Dostoyevsky to Sartre*, p.157.

9. Ortega y Gasset, *ibid.*, p.153

10. Cf. following chapters.

11. Either they are facts of the world, and hence, according to existentialism existents without essence (as Heidegger asserts in *Poetry, Language, and Thought*), or they are man-made concoctions, and hence revisable according to subjective preference. MacIntyre notes, "For Sartre . . . to live within a ready-made moral vocabulary is necessarily an abdication of moral responsibility, an act of bad faith." *A Short History of Ethics*, p.269

12. Plato, *Republic*, 430

13. In seeking what would halt degeneration, "[Plato] was looking for . . . knowledge, not opinion; the pure rational knowledge of a world that does not change." Popper, *Open Society Volume I*, p.29. Cf. Volume I *passim*.

14. Plato's theory of human nature has influenced many thinkers after him. For exam-ple, one reads echoes of his theory in the works of Freud and his tripartite division of human psychology into the id, ego, and super-ego, and who similarly posits trou-ble between the three as causing social discontent and war. Cf. Freud's "Why War?".

15. Burkhardt, *The Greeks and Greek Civilization*, p.364

16. Barzun reminds us to note the impact of youth on our affairs in his *From Dawn to*

Decadence, passim.

17. An argument expanded on by Descartes in his dualist theory of man.

18. They begin with Plato's *Republic*, re-emerge with Augustine's *City of God*, but truly come into their own during the era of European exploration when we have Thomas More's *Utopia*, Tommaso Campanella's *City of the Sun*, Francis Bacon's *New Atlantis;* Rabelais, Montaigne, and Shakespeare all add to the genre, which again picks up (in English writing) in the Seventeenth Century with Winstanley's *Law of Freedom*, Harrington's *Commonwealth of Oceana*, and in the 19th century with the plans of Robert Owen, William Morris, etc. Most utopias abandon any pretence of economic knowledge.

19. "It is the assumption of ready compliance with rational demands that makes Eutopias [good places] utopian [no place] . . . the common good is achieved by enforcing a uniformity of behavior . . . [and] significantly in none [of the utopias] is there any mention of laughter," writes Barzun, *From Dawn to Decadence*, p.121-125

20. Cf. Johnson, *History of the Modern World.*

21. Reisman, *Capitalism: A Treatise on Economics*, p.46

22. St Augustine, *The City of God*, pp. 53, 55, quoting Gal.v. 17

23. Cf. Erasmus, *The Complaint of Peace.*

24. Quoted in *The Monks of War*, p.1

25. Erasmus reacted to the growing tensions with his *Complaint of Peace* (1517) which set forth a humanist vision for Christianity.

26. Cf. Vitoria, *Political Writings*, especially "On the American Indians".

27. In *A Handbook of Marxism*, p.22

28. Cf. Mises, *Socialism*, p. 249ff.

29. "We cannot know whether in the first or in the second imperialist war between the great nations, whether during or after it, a strong revolutionary movement will flare up. Whatever the case may be, it is our absolute duty systematically and unflinchingly to work in that particular direction." Lenin on the First World War." "Socialism and War" in *A Handbook of Marxism*, p.682.

30. Watson, quoted in Stevenson, *Seven Theories of Human Nature.*

31. Coleridge, "Kubla Khan", in *Poems*, p.145

CHAPTER SIX: War and Human Biology

The determinist project does not end with metaphysical theories concerning the ultimate nature of the universe or of man. Once we take up the vision of man as a distinct entity in the universe, we begin to perceive him first and foremost as a biological being: an entity that lives and dies. But can we perceive in this entity the origins of war? Is there something innate in man's biological inheritance that, in the words of Dryden, "excites us to Arms"?[1] In a more complex form, is there something in man's genetic inheritance that conditions or limits his beliefs — makes him more prone to aggression or to violent collective endeavors? Once again, the determinist position has to be rejected, but that does not imply that all things biological ought to be discarded in discussions of war. Biology forms the first order conditions of man's action: these are necessary but not sufficient conditions of war's origins.

Man is a biological being — an obvious statement, but one often forgotten when we play in the philosophical realms of ethereal notions and concepts. Our bodies are often ignored when the mind begins its ascent into the realm of ideas and the repercussions of dismissing biology are immense. In a pertinent analogy, one of the earliest Greek philosophers, Thales, was reminded of this when he was taken to look at the stars by an old woman and fell into a ditch: "Do you think, Thales, that you will learn what is in the heavens when you cannot see what is in front of your feet?"[2] We should not aim to interrogate human thinking and ideas on war without acknowledging our biological dispositions and instincts role. "The laws of biology are the fundamental lessons of history", note the Durants;[3] indeed we are but one species that has evolved on this planet in its millions of years of existence, and we follow similar patterns to previous and contemporaneous species: we seek food, we eat, we seek mates, we reproduce, we compete, we cooperate, we fight, we survive, we die.

In the previous chapter, war's causation was laid at the door of human nature in general. The various theories proffered insightful but limited views of why man wars; in this chapter we examine theories of war's origins from the biological perspective and again find them wanting, except in the trivial sense that were man constituted differently, he would not war. Nonetheless, components of the biological theses do provide useful explanations that cannot be ignored — we are biological creatures firmly tied into the evolutionary fate of life on the planet, and ultimately our success can only be measured by the successful reproduction of our species.[4]

We turn firstly to instincts and inhibitions, then to theories of human aggression as they are used to explain war's origins. In the next chapter, we examine the biological foundations to culture and relevant theories of war especially territorialism.

WAR AND INSTINCT

Is war an inevitable generation of human biology, of human instincts, or genetically inherited or natural predispositions? "Man has always been unwilling to admit his own ferocity," notes Mary Midgley,[5] drawing our attention to the biological foundations of violence. But is man's ferocity instinctual? The First World War Field-Marshal Haig countered that "men are not brave by nature";[6] that is, they are *taught* to be brave. Yet what belligerent instincts can we be said to possess? — for surely, without any bellicose primary reactive instincts or predispositions, a man could not be taught to fight or to kill.

An instinct is an involuntary response by an animal to an external stimulus, resulting in a predictable and relatively fixed behavioral pattern. War, according to instinctivism, is solely explicable in terms of man's inherited instincts. Some claim that these instincts may once have been highly beneficial for man's populating the earth, but now pose a grave danger. Nicolai, for example, reasons that "although instinct is indeed infallible, which is an advantage, it is also blind and incapable of learning, and this is its doom."[7] And the Durants argue:

> We are acquisitive, greedy, pugnacious because our blood remembers millenniums through which our forebears had to chase and fight and kill in order to survive, and had to eat their gastric capacity for fear they should not soon capture another feast. War is nature's way of eating.[8]

That blood can "remember" is certainly metaphorical language — or should be held as such, for often the "ties of blood" theories are used to forge racist and nationalist ideologies that have been the source of many wars.[9] But what the Durants are emphasizing is the cultural and genetic inheritance of the aggression of thousands of generations. But has war — or collective violence — become instinctual to humankind?

The proposition that instincts cause warfare is divisible into three statements. Firstly, instincts are a necessary condition for war, which implies that wars necessarily follow from automated instinctual urges (although this implies that these same instincts may cause other activities). Secondly, instincts are a sufficient condition for the existence of war — i.e., whenever war occurs, instincts are necessarily operative (but so too may be other causes). Finally, instincts can be held as necessary and sufficient conditions for war: people wage war if and only if instincts are operating; that is, war is a product of instincts.

Instinctive behavior is in turn separable into programs designed for responding to specific circumstances and secondly into predispositions designed for more general circumstances or types of behavior.[10] The capacity for learning, for instance, is instinctive; although some animals are born with relevant content, the human mind is generally considered to be devoid of specific content but to possess prerequisite forms of internal programming that generates action, for instance inquisitiveness (Aristotle) or the biological capacity to recognize abstractions,[11] or to speak languages. General predispositions are innate but they do not produce results by themselves, since the content has to be learned, mimicked, or volitionally engaged for the predisposition to work — in the hierarchy of values here we find the beginnings of human culture.

The "instinctivist thesis" that war is a product of man's instincts is a form of determinism that claims war to be an inevitable product of our nature. In the stricter forms of this theory, war becomes something beyond our capacity to choose. What instinctivists disagree on is whether this tendency can be dissipated by other enterprises; but in admitting this possibility, they weaken the logical strictness of their determinism and thereby permit the ascendancy of culture or reason to ameliorate or even abolish the tendencies they describe.

SELF-SACRIFICE

What can be termed "monistic instinctivism" attests that one instinct leads to war. An interesting disjunction exists between those who believe it is self-preservation and those who believe it is self-sacrifice.[12] Urpo Harva, for example, offers a succinct argument for the latter: "Man possesses a need to sacrifice himself — this is dissipated in modern societies and militarists can easily tap into this repressed desire to sacrifice — not sacrifice for self but for others, ideals — absolute values."[13] This rendition is akin to what Freud terms the "death wish", and similarly, Jaspers's argument that asserts that the instinct to sacrifice leads to the formation of the warrior and war:

> Fighting — risking one's life so as either to meet force with force or else to use force to win power and booty — is a primordial phenomenon of human life. The primordial element is the fierce fighting spirit. Unleashed, it engenders the self-transcending lust of flinging one's life away and the savagery that rates other lives no higher, vents itself in pillage and rape after victory, and finally abates in the climactic feeling of power: to spare the conquered and let him serve as a slave. This abatement led Hegel to interpret the productive meaning of life-and-death struggles. The warrior is a human type, but not everyone is a warrior.[14]

Similarly, Roger Scruton emphasizes the centrality of religion in cultures and the concomitant need for sacrifice for atonement.[15] While this reflects a cultural-ideological theory, arguably it also suggests that the need for sacrifice is an instinctual component of human biology; that when a sin has been committed, then the rites of sacrifice will offer a physical release from the physical burden that a guilty conscience invokes. War, accordingly, emerges from such thinking[16] as a manner in which collective sins can be purged — the sins of failure, of being occupied by foreign forces, of ancestors being defeated, of past glories being tarnished by present decadence, and so on.

However, the argument that war derives from an instinctual drive to self-sacrifice can be disputed.

Firstly, assuming that such a drive exists either in some people or in all of us some of the time, the kind of activity that may be required to purge the instinct for sacrifice is not given as an inherited reaction: that is, humanity does not exhibit frequent and perpetual acts of sacrifice that we all accept as part of our nature. We accept the need to sleep and make no comment on it. But there is no equivalent in the practice of sacrifice: indeed, sacrifice in whatever manner attracts our attention and our critical or appreciative judgment.

Secondly, if we do possess a need for atonement and the concomitant sacrifice of our values either temporally or permanently, as Scruton seems to imply, it does not necessarily follow that such acts have to be in war. This raises the problem of what ought to be considered as recognizable acts of sacrifice – i.e., the ontology of sacrifice. Sacrifice is typically defined as foregoing a lower value in preference for a higher value;[17] however, Peikoff offers a seemingly idiosyncratic definition (popular amongst Objectivists) that sacrifice entails "the surrender of a value...for the sake of a lesser value or non-value"[18] This reflects a commercial usage of the word, namely the "loss incurred in selling something below its value for the sake of getting rid of it",[19] which, if the emphasis is placed on the "loss incurred in selling something below its value" rather confuses the proper nature of sacrifice. Peikoff indeed condemns all sacrifices as the "ethics of evil",[20] since he defines it as renouncing high values for low, but this would imply a grave and perhaps inherent irrationality in humanity. On the other hand, if we view each choice we make as exchanging a state of affairs for one more preferred,[21] we cannot condemn the people who give in to tears or fears as acting irrationally or even evilly: at the moment of their choice they are substituting one state of affairs for another they deem preferable, even if only temporarily so and with hindsight may be regretted. Hence, if we return to the commercial definition of sacrifice and emphasize *"for the sake of getting rid of it"*, the loss incurred on a transaction can be seen as more preferable to sustaining further losses or to not raising immediate cash flows. The sacrifice does indeed entail the giving up of a lower value in favor of a higher value (some cash in the pocket now instead of less or no cash in the future). Having clarified the nature of sacrifice, ethics and psychology can proceed to explore the normative implications involved in issues such as *akrasia* (weakness of will) and low self-esteem that prompt some to give up struggling for higher values (say, self-fulfilment) in preference for the easier life. But of course, that demands an exploration and judgment of what the good-life should entail, which is beyond the remit of this volume.[22]

Thirdly, a phylogenetically inherited instinct to sacrifice oneself is illogical on evolutionary grounds. Darwin, in *The Descent of Man*, noted:

> He who was ready to sacrifice his life, as many a savage has been, rather than betray his comrades, would often leave no offspring to inherit his noble nature. The bravest men, who were always willing to come to the front in war, and who freely risked their lives for others, would on an average perish in larger numbers than other men.[23]

Ultimately, such behavior in a species can only result in its extinction. An instinct to sacrifice the self for lower values is biologically illogical. This has meant that sacrifice historically involved the use of lesser values for the group's atonement; some societies have thus executed prisoners of war, criminals, or children, both to maintain a population balance and to rid the society of undesirables but also to offer the gods a value that did not deplete the group's status. When prisoners of war were eventually seen as presenting extra productive capacity through slave labor, then sacrifices shifted to the use of animals, until they too rose in relative value as to diminish their use for sacrifice. In today's Catholicism the sacrificial act has become a purely symbolic exercise of burning incense, which echoes the ancients' burning of animals and their entrails and, before that, people.

The other instinct that is often blamed for war — that of self-preservation — is a more understandable and readily observable principle. (But recall: whether such an instinct can be said to cause war is a separate question from whether self-preservation ought to be the good.) Two considerations arise. Firstly, again, how self-preservation is satisfied is not necessarily innate: beyond the body's instinctive reactions to fear — the rush of adrenaline and so on — whether a man is prompted to flight, fright, posturing, or fight is predominantly *learned*, and any attempts at diplomacy require even greater mental consideration.[24] Secondly, the instinctivist hypothesis is left attempting to explain the complexity of war from a simplistic solution: the instinct of self-preservation does not explain why one man should attack another beyond reactionary self-defense; neither does it explain why men would be willing to fight in another part of the world for abstract ideals such as freedom, democracy, or religion.

To save the theory from absurd simplicity, it must be recognized that instincts often act pluralistically rather than singularly. This means that, given a plurality of instincts, choices between the competing instincts have to be admitted;[25] but that would impose the need to order those instincts through some learned code and considered thinking: i.e., through reason.

FEAR

Yet it can be countered that despite a plurality of instincts, only one is the root cause of war: fear. Fear is often an easy concept to employ in historical examinations, for most wars can be explained by some element of working fears. However, historical counterexamples negate this move. Fear of Athenian power may have prompted the Spartans to seek war against Athens,[26] but self-preservation motivated the British to fight Nazi Germany and self-sacrifice may be said to have motivated Japanese *kamikaze* suicide pilots and the terrorists who struck the States in 2001; on the other hand, more complex motives including glory, honor, and prestige may motivate men to wage war (all three played a part in the Claudian Roman invasion of Britain). However, those who seek the ultimate *sine qua non* in fear can interpret all other motives in its terms: to fight to preserve oneself emanates from a fear of losing one's life or values; to fight for glory or honor is to be motivated by the fear of losing status; and so on. The problem with arguing in this manner is that fear is a base response to a single object, and while it certainly plays a role in most belligerent or defensive actions, it does not and cannot play the only role. The more information a person has about a situation — and hence the more options that are presented — the further removed from a simple response is a person's motivation and the more ideas concerning what ought to be done come into play. In abstracting motivational causes one can move upwards, for example, from fear to glory to love or duty: glory is invoked by more than just a single object, while love and duty are invoked by a plurality of considerations. Fear may also be present, but it rarely works alone.

THE WEAKNESS OF INSTINCTIVISM

The general thesis of instinctivism is weak. While, broadly speaking, humanity's biological constitution arguably plays a remote necessary causal condition to war (i.e., were man's nature different, he might not war), the instinctivist thesis is beset with logical problems. It asserts that human biology is a proximate and sole causal condition of war, but this is evidently and reasonably not the case.

It can be agreed that men may react violently from instinct and not from deliberation, and may, for instance, instinctively fall in with a mob as it runs amok in the streets. Such actions are ostensibly highly primitive, in that such behavior probably evolved long before intervening rational and cultural standards emerged. In a riot and in the middle of battle, man regresses from a rational being to a cultural being and from a cultural being to a biological being; or, described differently, man regresses from his highest and most complex forms of knowledge to more basic forms that merge with instinctual echoes of ancient responses.

Instinctivists contend that man is not so fully removed from the instincts witnessed in animal studies — a tormented beast will react violently and, they infer, a group threatened by a common enemy will merge together into a defensive herd.[27] It is plausible, however, that humans react at this pre-rational level and can never remove themselves fully from that legacy: the Oxford Union famously rejected to fight for King and Country in the 1930s, yet within a decade all the members of that chamber were in service. But can the reactions of the herd that we witness as temporary aberrations to normal behavior be sufficient to cause war?

Nicolai claims that the instinct for war emerges from two channels. Firstly, from a biological disposition to fighting, and secondly, from a biologically based ideological predisposition glorifying warfare — which complements what he sees as the immanent predisposition to fight.[28] This is a complex but reasonable thesis.

Humanity accordingly possesses a strong instinct for war as "[a] primeval impulse", and people become "intoxicated" for war, falling into a "war fever", he observes. Reason can guide the instincts for war but it can never suppress them, hence the instinct to war remains a dangerous inheritance.[29] Nicolai usefully draws our attention to the overlapping elements of biology, emotions, and reason, even though his emphasis is on the inherited aspects of man's nature.

A stricter version is offered by Raymond Aron: "[m]an, as an animal, is relatively combative — in other words, a slight stimulus is enough to release aggression."[30] A violent act by a person, or an animal, can be explained by a causal chain of events,[31] and reason cannot affect man's biological inheritance: hence combat is strictly a biological act.[32] Generally, Aron believes that attempting to resolve inner urges and demands in a social context inevitably creates an aggressive atmosphere:

> Ambivalence of feelings and rivalry among individuals for coveted goals are phenomena of experience, constants which reveal an element of conflict in most if not all interpersonal relations . . . Physical aggression and the will to destroy are not the only response to frustration, but they are one of the possible responses and perhaps the spontaneous one. In this sense the philosophers were not mistaken to consider that man is by nature dangerous to man.[33]

Nonetheless, Aron does admit that war is one choice among many activities which may act as a displacement for man's pugnacity; this is a theory held by many aggressionists and instinctivists (see below); for example, Lorenz, anticipated by the philosopher William James, proffers sports as a good alternative to war.[34]

Humanity certainly possesses biological capacities for defensive aggression, sympathy, and cooperation, and so on, some of which may even generate animalistic warfare (e.g., the herd mentality of the mob), but none of these alone can explain war's origins in a complex cultural and rational species. In our distant past, instincts may have generated an animalistic warfare, or have overwhelmed cooperative predispositions to secure resources for a population, but once man developed broad cultural structures of morality, language, and laws, war became a chosen, artificial institution, the product of human activity qua cultural and rational beings.

Instinctivism is philosophically unsound, for it circumvents man's ability to make choices between alternative options and to act against immediate instincts. Above the purely biologically reactive level, man forms rules and expectations regarding his own and others' behavior — some tacit, some explicit. Instinctivists who claim that war may be abolished by changing the physical environment to diminish the matrix of potential causes of war are wrong: man's ideas and cultural beliefs must also change before aggression is wholly renounced; but such pipe dreams are unlikely to be realized.

Likewise, if it is claimed that our instincts may be directed to other ends, then an implicit acknowledgement of the primacy of ideas — of beliefs and theoretical possibilities constructed by the mind — is made. How could aggression or instinctual reactions be *displaced* if we did not consider and reflect on how and where they should be displaced? In demanding an alternative to violence and war, instinctivists admit the possibility that ideas may be efficacious and hence undermine their own theory. To sustain instinctivism, other factors, especially cultural and rationalist aspects, have to be acknowledged. That logically dissolves instinctivism or reduces it to explaining certain human reactions under specific circumstances.[35]

Biological determinism does not terminate with instinctivism, though. More complex causal arrangements that invoke predispositions rather than single instincts are often espoused as reasons for man's waging war — the leading contender is aggression.

AGGRESSIONISM

The theory that the source of all forms of war is man's aggression can be termed aggressionism.[36] Aggression may be defined in this case as "the general tendency to attack members of one's own species."[37] Evidentially, some species are predominantly aggressive, others more peaceful; but most creatures become aggressive if sufficiently provoked or threatened.[38] Aggression, proponents of this theory argue, is a natural response to defend vital interests such as territory, family, or personal identity that may be under threat. They conclude that since all wars involve violence and vital interests, man's aggression is the root cause of war. However, it does not follow that a predisposition to aggression causes war.

Aggression can be either indiscriminate, as in the case of socio-pathic individuals, or it can be discriminate. Individuals above the socio-pathic level discriminate between those they care for and those they do not. Discrimination entails *choosing*, which in turn implies that objects of aggression are formed from ideas conceived through either reflection or cultural conditioning (in which the individual learns *and accepts* ideas promulgated by the group). Explicit or implicit justifications are necessary for a normal person to say that he or she "hates" other individuals or a group and wishes violence against them. These justifications can emerge through cultural structures, in the form of expectations held of other peoples — that they are untrustworthy, violent, inhumane, dogmatic, and so on. Such stereotypes are readily recognized in any culture's descriptions of other groups, and such descriptions usually last over many generations.[39] In any conflict, the treatment of the enemy reflects deep-seated beliefs regarding the moral status of the other.

To inspire a desire for violence against another group requires a stirring up of such stereotypes through the use of propaganda, which has been so effective in political wars. D.H. Lawrence rightly notes that: "Loud peace propaganda makes war seem imminent."[40] Probably propaganda becomes a necessary causal condition of at least aggressive wars above the military horizon, for the existence of an open society is characterized by a dispersal of allegiances. To form a common ideal and rationalization by which to fight is the object of propaganda, for without that common purpose wars can only be haphazardly organized. Illusions and stereotypes shatter once people realize or learn to reason that the enemy are persons.[41]

(A valuable counter to propaganda's dehumanization of others is a humanist emphasis on the similarities between people, the dignity of humanity, the freedom of the soul, the pursuit of secular goals, and toleration.[42] Politically, such a pro-human culture can only develop and evolve when the individual and his choices are deemed morally and legally sacrosanct and when the state's powers are accordingly limited. Insofar as states intervene in cultures for martial purposes, or insofar as cultures have had to sustain their existence through fighting, the importance of the individual over that of the survival of the group is diminished; humanism can hardly flourish where war is incessant.)

That we possess a capacity for aggression is undeniable, but against whom or what it is exercised is a matter of choice. Cultural-political warfare is different from biological reactions prompting aggressive responses; they are concerted efforts employing time and resources beyond what could be available in a quick reaction to forms of frustration. Whereas theories of aggressionism may explain domestic and criminal violence, and even be stretched to encompass the primitive warfare of hand-to-hand combat, the invention of long range weapons removes any advantage aggression may have: "Coolness, and the ability to keep aiming and firing steadfastly in the face of enemy fire, prevails."[43] Other species may fight amongst themselves over territory or sex and engage in animal warfare as a product of inherited instincts — as humans may react to threats with aggressive behavior — but humans also live by ideas. Ideas can promote or denigrate warfare, but no other species chooses to wage organized war on its own members for purposes beyond strict survival.

Eric Fromm claims that evidence supports the thesis that aggression is an innate defensive rather than aggressive response to threats and violence.[44] Accordingly, aggression may be viewed as a response to a violation but not the cause of the violation itself — what causes the violation remains to be established. Secondly, an individual's response mechanism causing him to react violently in a specific situation is very different from the possibility of a collective response mechanism — the so-called herd instinct, which turns peaceful men into warriors. A group may react as one in riotous conditions, yet wars above the animal level are planned and organized phenomena requiring a concerted effort (whether tacitly or explicitly organized). Group or national aggression in war is not the same as an instinctive reaction to extreme psychological or physical pressures that an individual may face and react aggressively towards. Thirdly, care must also be taken not to claim that aggression is the sole motive for human action; to define humans as "psychological belligerents" (i.e., necessarily aggressive) should be avoided. Logically such a claim implies a closed argument, which is unassailable by conflicting evidence: i.e., when wars exhibit forms of aggression, aggression is assumed to be the cause, but when they do not, aggressionism is not rejected, for proponents may claim that it takes alternative forms, or is latent, or implied.

Finally, as Fromm argues, the concept of aggression should be divisible into benign defensive aggression and malign offensive aggression. Defensive aggression assists in the maintenance of life, whereas offensive aggression is a peculiarly human trait and is innately destructive.[45] Offensive aggression may play a role in the initiation of conflict, but that may not imply it is the cause of conflict — it may be an effect.

Such criticisms permit a better understanding of aggression in human interaction and weakens aggressionism: the reasons behind malignity now have to be examined. Yet offensive aggression is the essence of all predatory animals, and it is not farfetched to ascribe such predatory behavior to man; but any theory proposing "man the predator" could not rely completely on a biological thesis for its explanation, for man's relations with other men are predominantly peaceful rather than predatory.

Robert Ardrey contends that aggression arises within the species once personal ties are formed. This differentiates an "us" from a "them".[46] The capacity to differentiate between members of the group is the first step to bond-forming and to the reduction of violence within the group, but, Ardrey asserts, it is also the first step to increased intragroup tensions and hence human war. As the social group forges its own identity and rules of conduct and of membership, it raises cultural and political barriers against other groups. Implicitly, the other is thereby morally relegated in the eyes of the close-knit group, and moral relegation lends itself to the easy use of violence against the other.[47]

Ardrey's theory is questionable on a number of levels. Cruelty and destructiveness in war are certainly geared towards enemies who have been dehumanized or objectified, but while the capacity to sympathize may plausibly involve only immediate kin, sympathy readily and naturally can extend beyond the family or "one's own group". In particular, isolated groups need to be receptive to outsiders to ensure a broad genetic base for reproduction.

The dehumanization of others is most likely not an instinctive but a cultural trait embedded in a group's language, customs, humor, and so on, that may be the product rather than the cause of war; it may be entwined in pre-rational structures in which people learn to dehumanize or to objectify other people, seeing them as animals or beasts, as *Untermenschen*. Instinctual sympathy often overrides parochial bigotry, and there is no evidence to suggest that bigotry is inherited biologically. Often basic instincts reject social divisions — children learn prejudices, they do not inherit them; and most importantly, the driving social instinct of sympathy may override mistrust and learned hatreds of others in all except the most intransigent of people (an intransigence I consider to be derived from persistent rationalizations that generate a dogmatic adherence to an articulated worldview). While the ability to sympathize diminishes, the further removed the object of sympathy is, sympathy has the power to transcend not only geographical borders but also historical — for instance, a man may weep at the betrayal of Caesar, as Adam Smith observes.

> When we read in history concerning actions of proper and beneficent greatness of mind, how eagerly do we enter into such designs? How much are we animated by that high-spirited generosity which directs them? How keen are we for their success? How grieved at their disappointment? In imagination we become the very person whose actions are represented to us: we transport ourselves in fancy to the scenes of those distant and forgotten adventures, and imagine ourselves acting the part of a Scipio or a Camillus, a Timoleon or an Aristides. So far our sentiments are founded upon the direct sympathy with the person who acts.[48]

The theory that group solidarity generates aggression does not describe an instinctual but a cultural cause of aggression, which is learned from inter-cultural solutions to resource and population dispersal or from conflict resolution. If we were to ignore wars for the moment and consider the reproductive aspects of human cultures, we may perceive cultural and ritual mechanisms for ensuring genetic diversity — the welcoming of new blood into the group.[49] If a culture or polity evolved or imposed on its members a more restrictive policy towards strangers, in the long run the group would genetically weaken through in-breeding. Instinctually humanity reacts against "purity of the blood" and is, on that account, more predisposed to a cosmopolitan cooperation than tribalism, in which blood ties are more crucial than commercial or romantic ties. In war, on the other hand, any mutually binding values may be completely destroyed in a cultural dehumanization of the enemy. In total warfare, in which no moral boundaries or sanctuaries exist, such a dehumanization is necessarily absolute, whereas in regulated warfare the rules of just war ensure a modicum of humanitarian considerations that sustain mutually recognizing cultural and political agreements.

AGGRESSIONISM AND NATURAL SELECTION

Aggressionism can be further developed to claim that aggression is a necessary condition for natural selection.[50] More aggressive creatures, it is implied, will be more likely to reproduce and hence to continue their genes compared to more passive creatures; aggressive virtues are therefore useful if not necessary for the survival of a group. Accordingly, war should be held as a form of natural selection in which more aggressive traits are successfully reproduced, which in turn leads to more aggression in human society promoting the reproduction of further aggressive individuals, and so on.

The initial problem with this theory is that aggression has to be sexually attractive or sufficiently dominant to ensure that reproduction occurs. Evidence may support this theory in some species,[51] but that does not mean it will be true of humans. The value of human aggression is much more complex than the securing of a mate,[52] and other values are even more vital for successful reproduction — such as cooperation in the rearing of children and securing of resources. Since the human infant cannot wean itself, it requires much investment on the part of a parental community to feed and stimulate it; an aggressive sexual act may secure conception, but it does not necessarily provide for the security of successful reproduction. Besides, the propagation of cultural values (what Dawkins calls "memes") is an important function of human propagation, since humans evolve more quickly on a cultural level than on a biological scale.

This is not to understate the aggressive reproductive instinct which may govern an element of male sexual violence against women victims in war,[53] but such atrocities are also tied up in an entire matrix of cultural beliefs and desires, desires to humiliate, bully, intimidate, violate, and annihilate self-worth, etc.

Culturally-generated aggression towards outsiders plausibly may play a crucial role in fostering communal values necessary for a social existence (for example, the emergence of the nation state of England in the face of external threats from others — the French, the Germans, the Spanish, the Scots, etc.), but any intensification of aggression to the point of biological autarky would generate an evolutionary precariousness which may overwhelm other requirements, and which can therefore make a species or culture vulnerable to extinction. Biologically, an overdeveloped capacity for aggression that is phylogenetically inherit-able may become useless or even inimical to the survival of the group.[54]

A stinging critique of aggressionism is present by Richard Dawkins, who describes evolutionary stable systems that evolve spon-taneously through the interaction of life's elements, from basic molecu-lar structures to DNA strands to social systems. The governing element in human life, he notes, is not the good of the species but the survival of an individual's genes, and the chances of survival are increased neither by pure aggressive strategies nor pure pacifistic strategies. By running models of various game theories, stable situations evolve, and if they are then disrupted a new stability may arise till that is itself disturbed — the centripetal force is the overarching "need" for stability, without which things would fly apart.[55] An aggressive individual could profit in a predominantly passive population, which would lead to a rise in the number of aggressive individuals, until endemic violence swayed the incentives back to pacifism — i.e., those who back down from fights would reap the rewards and hence their numbers would once again rise. Oscillations around evolutionary stable situations would be the normal state of affairs; the theory can be complicated by adding in dif-ferent strategies (such as retaliating or bullying), but the general find-ing remains that a purely aggressive instinct is not a permanently stable situation: its costs are high compared to alternative strategies (such as posturing, or aggressing only in retaliation). Individuals within the group pursue strategies that benefit themselves, not the group *per se*, although incidentally the group may benefit (or not) from their actions.

Philosophically, the theory of natural selection through aggression can also be read as a twist on Hegel's master-slave theory, in which a group can only be said to gain an identity through its activities in rela-tion to another entity that it seeks to dominate. Humans, according to Hegel, cannot help but become masters and slaves, either with one an-other or in themselves, as Copleston describes:

> The master is the one who succeeds in obtaining recognition from the other, in the sense that he imposes himself as the other's value. The slave is the one who sees his own true self in the other.[56]

The Hegelian concept is taken up by Marx and is even found in the existentialism of Sartre;[57] it infers that war or conflict necessarily results from the inexorable development of the master-slave relationship or, in anthropological circles, between the group and other groups. The relationship is not something that can be properly overcome; hence war remains a perpetual threat to humanity.

Although the formation of identity in the existence of the other may be necessary (for human identity is intimately wrapped up in a social existence), arguably, once self-identification is initiated, it does not require a continued reckoning and acknowledgement in the face of another. The self, or group identity, can be sustained through introspection, for example.

A mental extrapolation of the master-slave thesis also undermines its coherency, especially in the collectivist form usually proposed: if all national borders and group identification disappeared — the cosmopolitan dream — would humanity have no identity? Or, if a group possessed no external contacts with other groups, would it lose its identity? Does the anchorite lose a personality? Obviously, massive gains are to be enjoyed through social interaction, and autarky and isolationism are not conducive to social or personal growth, but it is very different to claim that personal (self or group) identification can *only* emerge through a constant friction between the self and the other.[58] Finally, although a people may gain a deeper understanding of what unites them at a deep cultural level in the face of common threats, this presupposes that unifying elements already exist.

AGGRESSIONISM AND FRUSTRATION

Finally, this theory explains aggression as a product of human frustration. Frustration in an individual, it is argued, leads to aggression; and theorists expand the causal sequence to groups: if a group is frustrated in its endeavors to secure sufficient resources for its survival, or if its attempts at economic or political progress are thwarted, the group as a whole may seek solutions in aggressive warfare with neighboring groups. Whenever war arises, this theory claims that it must be the product of a pent-up frustration of energies that do not find a more peaceful outlet. This reputed phenomenon in which the belligerent urge can be damned up is analogously referred to as the "hydraulic mechanism." An agent, or humanity as a whole, must periodically go through a catharsis, releasing frustrated, aggressive energies in warfare or in some other violent or active pursuit.[59]

Historically, scapegoats have been used by societies as the symbol for a frustrated group. For example, ancient Jewish high priests would use two goats; they would sacrifice one to Yahweh, while with the other, the priest would lay his hand on the goat and recant Israel's sins, thereby transmitting them to the goat. The goat was then cast out into the desert and the supposed realm of the devil Azazel.[60]

Arguably, the institutional use of scapegoats can emerge spontaneously, for it certainly can be said to play an efficacious role in quelling a discontented society by producing a symbolic release. War therefore may be explained as the phenomenon of striking out at a scapegoat, in which neighbors and other cultures are accused of causing the ills befalling a people. The scapegoat theory may be used to explain some wars, but not all. Plausibly, Galtieri invaded the Falkland Islands (1982) to channel domestic discontent into a common cause, but other wars, such as the Crimean War (1854), cannot be said to emanate from a desire to blame a scapegoat, but from balance of power considerations.

There are several other problems with this theory. Firstly, a logical gap exists between an individual becoming frustrated and a whole community becoming so, the latter supposedly being a necessary condition for wars to take place. Secondly, being frustrated is a common experience to all creatures, who cannot have their preferences met all of the time. Living demands adaptation to environment, society, and an individual constitution, and the reality matrix is not always going to provide the preferred circumstances. And given that humans are not omniscient, it is inevitable that mistakes are made in acting; so the feeling of frustration is a natural reaction.

Thirdly, the "hydraulic mechanism" is empirically and logically dubious. It is not always the case that individuals or even whole groups must periodically find a release for energies which somehow charge up inside. The hypothesis is testable,[61] but simple counter factual evidence is sufficient to render the theory invalid: some individuals never strike out angrily, and likewise some cultures, such as the Amish, absolutely prohibit violence (i.e., they impose a strict rationalistic and cultural code against the use of violence).

The "hydraulic mechanism" thus permits absurd conclusions: the most placid man should be assumed to be most dangerous, for he should possess a greater level of pent up energies than one who obviously releases tension frequently. This is by no means the case, and we have more to fear from persistently aggressive individuals than from commonly passive folk. The retreat to the hydraulic mechanism analogy also creates the impression that instinctivists tender a closed argument, which is impossible to refute and which undermines criticism using its own premises. To avoid lapsing into dubious closed arguments, the counterfactual evidence of peaceful societies is sufficient to undermine the broad assertion that humans are biologically warriors.

Nonetheless, if we accept the possibility of pent-up frustration, this still does not imply that we must become aggressive, never mind organizing society for war. Such behavior can only emanate from a deliberate decision to take out frustration in a violent manner. Other decisions are available, such as to try again to achieve one's goals, or to come to terms with the facts impeding one's preference satisfaction.

Frustration results from not achieving or not being able to achieve goals. It is considerably ideational to the extent that people's conception of their goals and the means they seek to employ emanate from their ideas; and if those ideas do not relate well to the nature of the world, to the facticity of others' actions and decisions, or to the appropriate means, then frustration will occur. For example, frustration would not be likely to dissipate in war if the goal were an increased standard of living, for war is not conducive to economic prosperity.[62] Nor is it likely to be displaced through war if independence or self-sufficiency is the goal, for again, aggressive war fosters parasitism on others, or, if the lands desired are secured, further population growth would imply the demand for more *Lebensraum*. On the other hand, the achievement of goals is more practicable through cooperation, for cooperation permits an intensification of the division and specialization of labor, thereby generating greater returns than any form of non-cooperation.[63] Trade is conducive to peace, whereas isolationism and non-cooperation is more likely to increase prejudices and belligerent hostilities.

Wars cannot be explained by aggression alone, since other factors, namely cultural and rationalistic factors — ideas — are involved. The simplistic resolutions of aggressionism are useful for noting innate mechanisms that all creatures are endowed with, but the theorists do not differentiate adequately between offensive and defensive aggression, nor explain how an innate individual reaction becomes a collec-tive phenomenon of war, nor explain why the use of modern weapons requires cool thinking over aggression.

WAR AND INHIBITIONS

Students of war may ask whether man is naturally inhibited against killing his own. Theories may claim that man's natural pacifism is rendered redundant by civilization, as Rousseau argues, or by the advent of weapons, urban living, environmental devastation, and so on. Other theories may hold man to possess few if any inhibitions against intra-specific killing, hence the need for artificial, cultural, constraints on his behavior (as Hobbes argues) — states, laws, taboos, morals, etc.

An inhibition is the automatic stopping or retarding of an action or process — the "conscious or unconscious constraint or curtailment of a process or behavior, especially of impulses or desires."[64] If humans possess inhibitions against certain actions, specifically against killing each other, then war must be seen as a thoroughly unnatural practice. And if war is unnatural, then consequently a return to a more instinctive mode of living will be sufficient to abolish war (a theory in Rousseau's critique of modern society). Alternatively, those activities that aim to overwhelm biological inhibitions against killing or dehumanization ought to be abolished, which would free man from war.

Apparently, man possesses few inhibitions against killing his own kind. For instance, Lorenz reasonably conjectures that inhibitions were not required in a time when killing was a "difficult process" (i.e., by unarmed combat); hence controlling inhibitions did not evolve phylogenetically. But the use of tools made killing physically "easier", and any inhibitions against killing had to evolve through customary laws and rituals rather than from genetically inherited structures.[65] Accordingly, the pertinent media of adaptation to powers unleashed by human creativity are culture and reason rather than biology. Forms of responsibility and accountability are thus cultural and rational arrangements which become necessary for social peace, given the lack of innate biological inhibitions against killing.

Yet is humanity completely without inhibitions? Killing another person seems to be instinctually wrong when there are emotional attachments to the person — when the attacker can engage sympathetically with the life of the other.[66] Perhaps humans have developed a phylogenetically inherited inhibition to some extent,[67] for example, against killing known kin, but weaker inhibitions against killing those further from the sympathetic circle of the attacker. Beyond ties of friendship and kin, respect and sympathy for others diminishes.[68] Beyond the sympathetic circle, representations of others may become dehumanized through culturally evolved prejudices or fear of the unknown, hence the easy characterization made by most warring societies of the "enemy" as objects or subhuman.[69] Yet some people do kill their parents, children, spouses, and so on, which suggests that whatever inhibition exists against killing a blood relative, it is not strong.

Plausibly, man has few natural inhibitions against committing violent acts, and the inhibitions we do exhibit are derived from taboo-forming rituals, customs, and articulated reasons to protect the group against intra-group aggression.[70] But a lack of inherited inhibitions does not excuse the killing and dehumanizing of others. The extension of the group morality beyond the boundaries of territory and common culture requires more than exercise of reason, for reason is so vulnerable to the overwhelming momentum that is built up in cultural prejudices and the reaction to defend the herd against "outsiders".

The admonitions of the UN, or the negotiations between leaders or even third parties who attempt to broker peace agreements are likely to fail persistently in the face of deep-seated cultural dispositions for violence and for war. Only a cultural merging and a resulting blurring of distinctions can reduce the antipathy different religions, areas, tribes, clans, or nations hold of each other. Social engineering, with its host of educational measures will continually disappoint in the absence of a free and voluntary interaction between hostile peoples, that is, in the absence of trade and commercial arrangements which inherently expose the cost of prejudice and thus promote market processes that reduce hostilities.

Notes

1. "The trumpet's loud clangour/Excites us to Arms/With shrill notes of Anger/And mortal Alarms." John Dryden, "Song for St. Cecillia's Day", recently put to music by Karl Jenkins in *The Armed Man*, Virgin Records, 2001.

2. "Thales" in *Early Greek Philosophy*, trans. Jonathan Barnes.

3. Will and Ariel Durant, *The Lessons of History*, p.18

4. Which implies that if war does strengthen the species, as some commentators deploying social Darwinist thinking have claimed, then it should be accepted as part of man's life cycle. However, it is not war that has enriched man but trade and the expansion of the division and specialization of labor.

5. Mary Midgley, *Beast and Man*, p.31

6. Quoted in Keegan, *Soldiers*, p.39

7. G.F. Nicolai, *The Biology of War*, pp. 15 -21

8. Will and Ariel Durant, *The Lessons of History*, p.19

9. "On, on, you noblest English/Whose blood is fet from fathers of war-proof!" Shakespeare, *Henry V*, Act 3, scene 3.

10. The difference between instincts and predispositions is usefully described by Ardrey in *The Territorial Imperative*, p.24.

11. Cf. "Primacy of the Abstract", Hayek, *New Studies*.

12. The theory that there is a biological instinct to self-sacrifice is different from the ethical theory that self-sacrifice constitutes the good.

13. Urpo Harva, "War and Human Nature", p.49

14. Jaspers, *The Future of Mankind*, p.45.

15. Scruton, *Guide to Modern Culture*, Ch.2

16. This is not necessarily drawn out by the thinkers who argue this.

17. "Sacrifice." *Shorter Oxford English Dictionary*.

18. This certainly complements his ethical stance that a man who gives up his wealth to an undeserving beggar is committing a sacrifice that ought to be ethically condemned; if he gives up his wealth to someone more deserving of it (say, his beloved) then he is not sacrificing but trading a lower value for a higher and in doing so properly fulfils his self-interests. *Objectivism*, p.232. Cf. also Rand, *The Virtue of Selfishness*, p.44

19. "Sacrifice." *Shorter Oxford English Dictionary*.

20. Peikoff, *Objectivism*, p.235

21. Mises argues that such the science of examining human choice should reject all discussion of the ends people strive for and focus purely on the act of choice. *Human Action*, pp. 11-14, and pp. 47-48.

22. To lower one's expectations of one's self or one's goals is not in itself an irrational act but which nonetheless certainly could be described as living in bad-faith. Cf. Sartre, *Being and Nothingness*, pp. 47-48.

23. Darwin, *The Descent of Man*, Chapter V - On the Development of the Intellectual and Moral Faculties.

24. Glover elaborates on the collapse of moral responses under conditions of "entrapment". "War is often a trap and going to war is not often an aim of modern

political leaders." *Humanity*, p.155. This is a highly useful concept, for it captures the strains on self-preservation under extraordinary conditions — animals may turn vicious even against their own kin under such circumstances, while humanity may lose its morality. On the other hand, it can be argued that it is precisely in such situations that morality and ethical thinking is required.

25. Lorenz offers a plausible description of the options available as depending on a matrix of inherited instincts: "Man can behave very decently indeed in tight spots, provided they are of a kind that occurred often enough in the palaeolithic period to produce phylogenetically adapted social norms that deal with the situation. Loving your neighbour like yourself and risking your life to save his is a matter of course if he is your best friend and has saved yours a number of times; you do it without thinking. The situation is very different if the man for whose life you are expected to risk your own, or for whom you are supposed to make other sacrifices, is an anonymous contemporary on whom you have never set eyes. In this case it is not love for the fellow human being that activates self-denying behaviour -if indeed it is activated- but the love for some culturally evolved traditional norm of social behaviour." Lorenz, *On Aggression*, pp. 216-217 It can be readily agreed with Lorenz that human instincts have evolved over a long biological inheritance, and the extent that they will prompt seemingly moral acts is dependent on that inheritance, but Lorenz's argument contradicts his initial instinctivist thesis that war results from aggression.

26. Cf. Thucydides' *Pelopennesian War*.

27. On that note, Nietzsche sardonically writes that: "Our entire sociology simply does not know any other instinct than that of the herd, i.e., of the sum of zeroes — where every zero has "equal rights," where it is virtuous to be zero." Nietzsche, *Will to Power*, p.33

28. This philosophically also reflects an implied Kantian view of the mind, that it possesses specific structures by which to understand the world.

29. G.F. Nicolai, *The Biology of War*, pp. 15 -21

30. Raymond Aron, "Biological and Psychological Roots", in *War*, ed., Lawrence Freedman, p.77. Cf. Aron's *Peace and War*, pp. 340-344.

31. "The chain of causality which leads to emotions or acts of aggressiveness can always be traced back to an external phenomenon. There is no physiological evidence of a spontaneous impulse to fighting, the origin of which is in the body itself. The human animal happy enough to live in an environment offering no occasion, for motive for fighting, would suffer no damage, either physiological or nervous." Aron, in Freedman, *War*, p.80.

32. Aron in Freedman, *ibid.*, p.78

33. Aron, in Freedman, *ibid.*, pp. 80-81.

34. Cf. Konrad Lorenz, *On Aggression*, and William James, "The Moral Equivalent of War".

35. E.g., the phenomenon of shell-shock and post-traumatic disorders in which the mind and body react on a very pre-rational, instinctive level.

36. Cf. Lorenz, *On Aggression*. Aggressionism was particularly popular in the 1960s, following Lorenz's comparative work with animals, but the popularity or not of a theory is no guide to its veracity. Lorenz makes some useful insights into the bio-

logical aspects of human nature, especially with those that we share with the animal kingdom, however, the temptation with biologically based theories of war is to ignore the cultural and rational aspects of man.

37. Midgley, *Beast and Man*, p.54

38. In the vertebrate kingdom fighting is common, but what forms it takes differs. E.g., Howler monkeys' fighting is restricted to a shouting match, for the gibbons both sexes fight ferociously, and in gorillas only the males fight.

39. Cf. Granatstein's *Yankee Go Home: Canadians and Anti-Americanism* for the origins of anti-American sentiments in Canada, often provoked by American immigrants (United Empire Loyalists to draft dodgers) or by protectionist (i.e., anti free-market) lobbyists.

40. From *Peace and War*, in general quotations books.

41. Cf. for example, *The Long and The Short and The Tall*, by Willis Hall.

42. In the humanist tradition that emerged in the Italian Renaissance in the fourteenth and fifteenth centuries, Lorenzo Valla (1407-1457) and others asserted the goodness of pursuing pleasure: such secularism did much to morally level the various tribes of the world (in the humanist's eyes).

43. Barbara Ehrenreich, *Blood Rites*, p.9.

44. Cf. Fromm *The Anatomy of Destructiveness*, pp. 264-293.

45. Fromm, *ibid.*, chs.9-10

46. Ardrey, *Territorial Imperative*, Ch.8. Ardrey's argument begins with noting the distinctions between a herd and a community formed of social ties. Anonymity within the herd excludes intra-specific aggression, and this behavior has evolved for a reason, namely that the herd faces continually a predator presence. Aggressive behavior gains evolutionary support as soon as personal affections arise for certain members of the species, and bonds are formed that create distinctions between "us" and "them" within members of the group. Being a member of a well defined group, it is implied, reduces the level of intra-social conflict. Philosophically, this is an echo of the Hegelian idea that identity can only be formed through the master-slave process of continued attempts to dominate by one individual or group.

47. As Glover chronicles in *Humanity*.

48. Smith, *Theory of Moral Sentiments*, Part II, Ch 5.1

49. Examples are rife from the sharing of wives in Inuit cultures to Herodotus' description of Babylonian women having to offer themselves to a stranger once in their lifetime, *Histories*, Book 1.199, or the Massagetans who permit a more general promiscuity, Book 1.216.

50. McDougall, "The Instinct of Pugnacity", pp. 34-35

51. E.g., dogs.

52. There is evidence to suggest that echoes of this are still found in female sexual responses to more dominant or aggressive males (or men to women whose attributes suggest greater reproductivity), especially at a younger age, which may reflect the evolved instinctual reactions from our early history. However, the obvious broad range of human physical diversity emphasizes that such basic traits are no longer the overriding considerations in reproduction.

53. Again, this may be an echo of a very basic instinct from a distant past. The killing of the young and monopoly of the victors' genes occurs in a variety of species including cats.

54. Lorenz reports on the case of the North American Ute tribe; natural selection through continuous warfare with neighboring tribes led to a relatively intense phylogenetically inherited capacity for aggression. Within the tribe, culture and rituals evolved to ensure that aggression was not turned inward against members of the group, instead it was constantly directed outward against enemy tribes. However, in the new cultural environment of North America following its conquering by Europeans, such biologically inherited values are of little use. Lorenz, *op cit*, pp. 210-211. Similarly, a cultural overemphasis on martial values produces stagnation and inflexibility that are not conducive to adaptation to new situations or military strategies devised by an enemy. Such was the fate of Sparta.

55. Dawkins, *The Selfish Gene*. Ch.5

56. Copleston, "Hegel", in *A History of Philosophy*, Vol VII p.183.

57. "Beyond any knowledge of which I can have, I am this self which another knows." *Being and Nothingness*, p.261

58. Nietzsche characteristically disparages Aristotle's premise that man is a social animal: "To live alone one must be an animal or a god — says Aristotle. There is yet a third case: one must be both — a *philosopher*."

59. In the history of economic thinking, the French physiocrats of the eighteenth century explained wars on this analysis, by claiming that a leisure class having no decent, peaceful outlets for their abundant (youthful, masculine) energies seeks thrill and adventure in warfare, a theory also revisited by Ehrenreich in *Blood Rites*. "With the decline of the wild predatory and game populations, there would have been little to occupy the males who had specialized training in hunting and anti-predator defense, and no well-trodden route to the status of "hero" . . . Eventually, the presence of underemployed hunter-defenders in other human settlements guaranteed a new and "foreign" menace to defend against." Barbara Ehrenreich, *Blood Rites*, p.123.

60. "Scapegoat" in *Encyclopaedia of Religion and Ethics*, ed. James Hastings, pp.221-222.

61. "[T]he relevant data in the fields of neurophysiology, animal psychology, palaeontology, and anthropology do not support the hypothesis that man is innately endowed with a spontaneous and self-propelling aggressive drive." Erich Fromm, *The Anatomy of Human Destructiveness*, p.132.

62. Contrary to the claim of neo-Keynesianists such as J.K.Galbraith that war produces wealth — war destroys men and resources and increases the cost of present and future production by destroying the built-up capital stock of a nation. That American production increased during WWII is quite explicable without recourse to the absurdity of war generating wealth: firstly, Britain and its allies bought American goods using their own productive resources and credit facilities; secondly, the US government pursued an inflationary monetary policy which produced an artificial boom in the war goods industries.

63. The basic principles of the profitibility of the division of labour are famously described in Adam Smith's example of the pin factory in his *Wealth of Nations*.

64. "Inhibitions" *Encyclopaedia Britannia '98* CD-ROM

65. For Lorenz, the problem for humanity lies in its lack of natural weapons -having evolved no sharp teeth or claws proto-humans required no innate inhibitions against using force on their own kind. All fine and good for a defenceless creature, until tools were invented for hunting. Now humanity possessed the means for easy

killing but without the inhibitions other animals evolved to prevent intra-specific violence. *On Aggression*, p.207 Cf. also Ignatieff's *Virtual War*.

66. "Even the first compensatory function of moral responsibility, preventing the Australopithecines from destroying themselves with their first pebble tools, could not have been achieved without an instinctive appreciation of life and death." Lorenz, *ibid.*, p.215.

67. The extent may differ from people to people, as any genetic inheritance does — which would explain why some murder their own.

68. Adam Smith poignantly remarks, reflecting the ancient Stoic belief; "the loss or gain of a very small interest of our own, appears to be of vastly more importance, excites a much more passionate joy or sorrow, a much more ardent desire or aversion, than the greatest concern of another with whom we have no particular connexion." Smith, *The Moral Sentiments*, III.3.3, p.135.

69. Carlton's examination of war shows a variety of perceptions of the "enemy": non-people, political obstacles, economic rivals, uncouth barbarians, ritual outlaws, unbelievers, effete degenerates, ritual fodder, colonial intruders, opponents of democracy, class antagonists, and racial inferiors. *War and Ideology, passim.*

70. "Among the many phylogenetically adapted norms of human social behaviour," Lorenz notes, "there is hardly one that does not need to be controlled and kept in leash by moral responsibility." *Op cit.*, p.218.

CHAPTER SEVEN: Between Biology and Culture

From general determinist theories that claim man to be a pawn in universal laws from which he cannot escape to biological theories that claim man to be biologically constrained, we proceed to admit culture and reason into the picture we're devising to understand why man wages war. Thinkers from Plato to Freud have divided man into three parts which, in this work, are termed his biological, cultural, and rational aspects. Most theories that examine why man wages war fail by assuming that one of these aspects completely explains human action. The previous chapter dealt with those theories that assume biology explains man's belligerence and the next chapter will deal with culturalism — the theory that cultural analysis wholly explain war's origins; but war cannot be explained by one aspect of human nature alone.

While it is useful to divide man into these three general areas for ease of study, it is wrong to suggest that they are mutually exclusive. There are no clearly defined boundaries between them, although imagining there are has been the mistake made by many who distinguish between man's various elements. Between the (genetically) pre-determined and determining structures of man's body and the knowledge, rituals, rules, and tacit expectations he *learns* as a social animal lie those elements that emanate from his biology and impact on his ability to learn, or those cultural elements that similarly can affect his biological capacity to act.[1] Learning, beyond inherited predispositions to mimicry and emulation, is certainly a volitional act; hence as we move away from biology and into culture, thinking and belief systems become more important. But the ability to learn and to consider new information is constrained initially by biological factors (say, how much the individual's brain can process) and then by cultural factors (is the individual culturally free to question and to investigate in his community?).

Some elements of his behavior lie beyond the reach of reason or culture, but some fall in the middle — these include territorial and competitive predispositions and, as we ascend into the higher capacities of man to learn and act, into learned predispositions and complex motives. For example, morale — the spirit and sense of solidarity that can enthuse a group to concerted and powerful action ("Once more to the breach my dear friends! Once more to the breach!" *Henry V*) — is examined as lying between the forceful instincts of biology and pre-rational and cultural drives. Whereas territorialism and competition derive from the higher aspects of biologically determined behavior, motives — dispositions to act in a general direction — are infused by the realms of thought. Nonetheless, motives cannot be said to cause war in the absence of choices, or ideas concerning which choices are appropriate motivating dispositions.

TERRITORIALISM

Territorialism is the innate biological predisposition to posses and to defend territory. A predisposition means that the urge is not wholly instinctual but learned — perhaps, we could say, in the sense of being a necessary addition to man's skill base. War, it can be argued from this theory, results from man's innate drive to seek and defend territory.

The strong implication of territorialism is that without territory man could not evolve and develop as well or at all.[2] As a thesis, territorialism is attractive, but it does not provide an exhaustive account of man's drives and ambitions; it thus partakes in explanations of war but does not complete them by any means.

A territory certainly provides a spatial range for the privileges it bestows to its occupiers. Primarily that includes property rights over valuable resources, as well as filial ties, but in a more interdependent and urban economic system controlling land is not as crucial as it once was to the economic unit of the family, clan, or nation. This is because in complex societies, food production no longer is, or can be, self-sufficient. Trade is required to exchange values across peoples; exchange acts to diminish the isolation of territories, thereby reducing the political hegemony that land ownership can entail in favor of land ownership for economic benefits.

Nonetheless, the need to have one's own space as an individual, as a family, as a social group dominates much of man's biological and psychological aspects.[3] Man uses and needs space, and when personal space is denied or invaded, an instinctive reaction is to become frustrated and annoyed.[4] A dispossessed tribe, the implication goes, would be rootless and may turn to alternative activities to ensure a social cohesion and solidarity, such as visibly different clothes or manners from host groups; but there is no substitute for controlling territory. It is, for territorialists, a prerequisite for human existence. As such, utopian communities that are designed to supersede the need for personal property and personal ties quickly founder against what may be termed deep cultural structures that find a biological instinct to own things.[5]

The predisposition to occupy and control land also relates to fulfilling other needs, especially security, identity, and stimulation,[6] and this dear attachment, territorialists believe, explains why people fight.[7] The causes of war can, from their perspective, be explained by the need for and defense of territory as men fight over lands to secure not only access to resources but also to forge and maintain a sense of identity.

It can be agreed that wars certainly do not occur on a non-spatial plane in which freely floating Cartesian immaterial souls fight. Even virtual wars involving hacking into and destroying computer files or spreading a virus on a network still take place in the *physical* world of computers, hackers, and networks. War necessarily involves territory and the territorial environment has a great impact on the nature of wars fought;[8] but the deployment of resources and men on the land is a separate concern from a theory that claims man to be driven to own that land.

Categorically, without ownership of the land, economic productivity could not increase much, for ownership entails resource management for the market and permits an expanded division and specialization of labor, which is the ultimate source of wealth production.[9] Property rights are necessary for prosperity, but often war is motivated by rival land claims or by the desire of one group to reject the ownership titles of another.

For instance, as an ideology supporting warfare, territorialism complements the militarist doctrine of *Lebensraum* (i.e., the Nazi policy of land annexation). The policy of *Lebensraum* is, however, primarily an economic argument which asserts that a nation needs to be or must be economically self-sufficient. However, since complex societies cannot produce all their needs through the domestic markets, *Lebensraum* implies that the domestic realm ought to be expanded until all production falls within the jurisdiction of the state.[10] That is, lands must be annexed through conquest to gain sufficient resources.

But the goal of economic self-sufficiency is absurd for any group above that of a small population. To increase wealth it is better, indeed necessary, to trade and reap the economic benefits from the international division of labor and the unequal distribution of resources rather than to expand political jurisdiction over others' lands. From an economic perspective, Ricardo's theory of international trade explains how individuals or groups possessing comparative advantage in production may mutually benefit from exchange,[11] an argument exploited by later free-traders who emphasize the pacifist nature of trade in comparison to protectionism.[12]

Nonetheless, wars often possess an economic subtext in which land or the control of resources is the hidden agenda and this gives territorialism a good deal of credibility. The theory that war advances wealth is held by mercantilists, but it cannot be dismissed out of hand by pure free traders either.[13] Mercantilists assert a form of economic nationalism that claims a nation can only enrich itself at others' expense: they therefore propose various protectionist measures to impose costs on imports and curtail foreign access to markets – British mercantile doctrine supported the Eighteenth Century wars with France over control of the world's trade routes, thereby incidentally sparking the American War of Independence and forging the British Empire.[14] However, not all wars are about territory and property. Some wars are about honor, glory, creed, or power. Other ideologies can dominate the war motive. People may believe that they should fight for territory, but they are also capable of believing that they should fight for something else instead, such as liberty, religion (Crusades, jihad), ideology (Communism), race, or even the abolition of property, and so on.

Other philosophical problems remain for territorialism. Firstly, the concept does not apply to all animals or to all human cultures, which means that explaining human behavior in terms of other animals is open to severe empirical criticism[15] and that the account cannot be exhaustive. Secondly, the spatial jurisdiction of territoriality is often vague, permitting many overlapping areas in which others are permitted to travel or to reside without hindrance.[16] Thirdly, it is not obvious that the purpose of territory is not to avoid aggression:[17] wars can be geared to gain advantages rather than to defend territory,[18] and contrary to explaining war, territorialism can be used to explain the drive for peace. Territory and property provide claims and rights that can be readily acknowledged, thus dissolving possible conflicts.[19] In summary, territory and ownership confer useful benefits both on the individual owners as well as the groups in which they reside.

Some territorialists — certain pacifists, for example — argue that if man were to give up property, wars would cease. But if territory and ownership do not exhaust the possibility of man's social relations, then such arguments are likely to fail. Wars will not be abolished through the abolition of private property or of territory, as some socialists may contend. Attempts to abolish property (and trade, money, etc.) fail miserably for they ignore the importance of this function for mankind's prosperity and even peace. The desire to *own* may be culturally induced but the desire to possess a jurisdiction over which one or one's group holds sway apparently plausibly does have deeper biological roots, which are entwined in man's thoughts and are shared with many in the animal kingdom.

The benefits land confers are immense and the cultural pluralism of humanity's social development entails a need for several jurisdictions rather than one (or none). Heterogeneity, which is coming to be understood as a healthy sign of human progress, is more likely to flourish with the existence of separate cultural and territorial jurisdictions; and since man has to continue his adaptation to a complex world, experimentation and cultural evolution are more likely to arise where there is plurality rather than homogeneity and hence the potential for migration, change, and further cultural evolution.

In terms of military history, the expansion of productivity that often[20] results from property ownership indubitably attracts envious eyes. Archaeological records suggest that sedentary civilizations soon had to be build defenses to protect their harvests from neighbors and wandering warrior groups, but to blame the origins of war on the existence of property alone is to ignore the base reaction in those who do not envisage the benefits it accrues.[21] Whether that reaction is instinctually, culturally, or rationally derived is a matter for further consideration;[22] often the reaction against property is a misplaced reaction to facets of modern civilization. But asserting that property ownership is "theft" and calling for its abolition entail calling for the destruction not just of the accumulated capital of thousands of generations but also the death of much of the population that the present wealth of the world supports.[23] Property's abolition would not abolish war, for, as we are seeing, war's origins cannot be explained by a single overriding factor or motive.

Property rights — the economic vestige of territorialism — are required, both as representations of the actions of specific individuals in creating products and as vestiges of the deep cultural and biological need for territory. Yet few pacifists accept either the benefits or the moral validity of private ownership. In modern political philosophy, Jean-Jacques Rousseau stands as the most influential denouncer of private property.

> The first man who, having enclosed a piece of ground, bethought himself of saying, "This is mine", and found people simple enough to believe him, was the real founder of civil society. From how many crimes, wars, and murders, from how many horrors and misfortunes might not any one have saved mankind, by pulling up stakes, or filling up the ditch, and crying to his fellows: "Beware of listening to this imposter; you are undone if you once forget that the fruits of the earth belong to us all, and the earth itself to nobody."[24]

The advance of the division and specialization of labor goes hand in hand with the advance of property rights:[25] the two are inseparable; and property rights (and their defense and maintenance) constitute the foremost guardians against aggression, fraud, violence, and war. Most would agree that private property rights originally emanated from acts of violence and conquest;[26] but their consequent appropriation, production, and/or exchange from previous owners, exhibit their function as defining domains of exclusive jurisdiction and the avoidance of conflicts.[27] The utility of property rights is evinced in the commercial expansion they tend to promote, so it is not surprising that aggressive war seeks to secure valuable propertyand its income flows through violence or that martial and belligerent nations infringe or expropriate property rights for war purposes.

COMPETITION

Competition has similarly been judged and blamed for war.[28] Competition for resources, it has often been assumed, leads inevitably to conflict and hence to war.[29] However, it is worth making a conceptual distinction between "competition" and "conflict", for the two are often conflated, thereby causing unnecessary problems and besetting potential solutions.

Various theories denounce competition as socially divisive and destructive, or consider its alleged destructive capacity as beneficial. Social-Darwinists, for instance, argue that conflict is a necessary means for a society to survive and progress, while Hegelians consider conflict to be metaphysically necessary for self and group identity. Another move is made by those who argue that man is subject to a plurality of instinctual or motivational drives that are necessarily in conflict with one another — with man divided in himself, they reason, it follows that his life and interactions will also be rent with conflict and war, as Plato argues:

> Wars and revolutions and battles are due simply and solely to the body and its desires. All wars are undertaken for the acquisition of wealth; and the reason why we have to acquire wealth is the body, because we are slaves in its service.[30]

In Plato's model, man's various elements compete for ascendancy, a view of human nature that echoes in social-Darwinism and Hegelian notions in which *social groups* seek ascendancy through conflict. Conflict, however, does not enable man to progress: in a society characterized by an extended division of labor, only cooperation within a system of private property and freedom of exchange can offer that.

Nonetheless, organisms do *compete* for resources, and those who

best adapt survive over those that do not. But competition is not always the same as conflict and, conceptually, for understanding action,
the two should remain separate. Competition for resources, food, reproduction and so on can lead to physical conflict if the resources com-
peted for become scarce and threaten survival; but conflict is not necessary. Indeed, one of the purposes of private property is to create visible
limits to the ownership of values, which in turn ensures that each individual possesses control over his resources (e.g., harvested food to ra-
tion, or labor to trade for food). Where property is lacking however,
there can be no competition for resources, only conflict.

For animals, fighting is an instinctual form of self-preservation,
and likewise man, if his vital interests are threatened, will react
instinctively, i.e., on a neuro-physiological level.[31] But conflict *as a way of
life* for biological organisms is not logical in evolutionary terms, nor is it
for humanity;[32] on the other hand, competition is natural: individuals
compete for mates and for territory and often the losers — or one could
follow Dawkins and focus on the losers' *genes*[33] — fade from the
biological record.

However, the fact that endemic conflict is not sound on
evolutionary principles does not stop other humans from *believing*
conflict to be conducive to survival. This is an erroneous as well as a
highly dangerous belief, and arguably its ideological acceptance is the
source of much warfare: if I believe that *only* by robbing you can I enrich
myself, then I will seek to defraud and steal from you as often as I can.
But such conflict is highly costly and ultimately self-destructive,[34] but
it is not always the zero-sum game which sustains its ideological
attractiveness. Pacifists often contend that war does not pay, but
sometimes it does: either in the material values gained[35] or, most
importantly, in the moral values gained — glory, honor, power, respect,
and so on.

COMPETING MOTIVES AND COOPERATION

Although competition for resources may lead to conflict,
competing for glory or honor does not have to entail violence.[36]
Competition for such higher order values (i.e., values that require
complex instantiations or contexts to be comprehensible) involves

prioritizing and *choosing* between values, and to possess a choice is not in itself to be in conflict with anyone or anything. The chosen course of action may of course lead to conflict with others, their values, or the world, but possessing the capacity of choice in itself is not the same as being in conflict.

If the individual necessarily lives a life of competing motives (should I strive for honor or for wealth?), it does not necessarily follow that society will be in a constant state of conflict. Institutions can be formed to ensure that conflicting interests are dealt with peacefully by recognizing rightful claims. This is implied in the Hobbesian view of human nature, for Hobbes believes that without a state, humanity would be perpetually in a state of war. In the state of nature, Hobbes conjectures, men would seek the same resources and without an overarching authority, would fight for them. Self-preservation leads men to war, but fear of others — "the passion to be reckoned on, is Fear" — leads men to form a government to secure the peace.[37]

On the other hand, mutually benefiting cooperative arrangements[38] imply that people recognize and can act from a plurality of motives but that tacit or explicit cooperation can dissolve most conflicts of interest. Cooperation and exchange thus lead to peace and not to a "war of all against all." However, that does presume individuals are concerned to seek some benefit, whereas it is entirely possible for the nihilist to see no value in anything whatsoever. Logically such an anchorite poses a grave danger to the peaceful society of mutual cooperation.[39] Arguably, in the anchorite mentality and persona we find some of the ultimate causes of war and barbarism: of cruelty resulting from moral isolationism and distance, of cynicism and destructionism from a hatred of others and ultimately of life — literally in the non-cooperative anchorite, we find the Aristotelian outlaw who stands as a threat to peaceful society.[40]

Cooperation needs to co-exist with competition for man to thrive. In the market world, businesses have to cooperate within themselves (to foster an extended division and specialization of labor) as well as compete on price and quality with other businesses offering similar products *to attract customers*. Trade is thus neither predatory nor belligerent, inherently — it is a social process of non-violent resource distribution, one that requires no authority or central planner and hence no violence or threat of violence to coordinate. It is voluntaristic and hence is removed from conflict in which some seek to gain resources and values from others by deploying force and threats of violence. In seeking to maximize their profits, producers must serve the customer well — in other words, they must combine factors of production efficiently and cost effectively to offer a product at a price that will attract custom. Failure to do so entails a loss of custom to competing producers; only when there is a government supported monopoly can it be said that customers are *forced* to trade with that producer. Otherwise, so long as entry to an industry is legally free competition will flourish.[41]

Biologically, man is evidentially a competitive animal. All forms of life are, since they have to compete for resource use and dispersal. However, the benefits of competition in trade and property ownership are not readily understood, or may be rendered incomprehensible by conflicting systems of thought. Often cultures evolve rituals and taboos that foster a sanctity on such beneficial arrangements (which may be misread or misunderstood as conferring benefits on powerful authorities rather than the sanctity of property and exchange for the common weal[42]), before they are codified into abstract rules and laws and comprehended on a rational (articulated) level; such rules foster cooperative practices between members of the group and with those who reside outside of it.

Yet any instinct to cooperate may be overwhelmed by various forms of erroneous reasoning that suggest man may benefit more from conflict and war. Most economic policies, for example, till the 17th and 18th centuries, were founded on the premise that war, piracy, the annexation of land, and the formation of colonies could bring material benefits. Accordingly, policy reflected economic theory and the great Renaissance powers Spain, Portugal, France, England, and Holland vied for territory and for markets and engaged in much costly warfare. The global wars of the 18th century in particular were motivated by false economic reasoning. Adam Smith's and David Ricardo's lessons on the mutual profitability of trade and cooperation only began to influence policy in the 19th century, which partly explains the existence of free trade and liberal aspects to the imperialist British Empire as well as the western expansion of the United States: both employed the sanctity of private property ownership and the doctrine of free trade. However, popular political theory has not been able to shed its earlier militaristic and mercantilist skins, so trade is still viewed with a great deal of skepticism or at least as a necessary evil.

PREDISPOSITIONS AND MOTIVES

As we move upward in human complexity, we leave the biologically generated drives and instincts and enter the realm of pre-rational motives and general predispositions that are fostered and cultivated through learning and cooperation in a social setting. Behavioral predispositions often lie below articulated thought,[43] and they differ from instincts in that while instincts are pre-programmed reactions to events, such motives form more general rather than particular predispositions to action. For example, a baby's seeking of the mother's nipple is instinctual, but a child stealing a friend's toy is motivated by jealousy or attention-seeking; alternatively, a jealous child is predisposed to draw attention from others to himself.

To possess a motive is to have a propensity to act towards a goal. But while desiring a goal is biological, motives cannot be the same as biological instincts, for they overlap into what become *mental attitudes* to the world. For instance, that I am motivated to act honorably means that my actions in day to day life will be such that I believe (tacitly or explicitly) they will be viewed as honorable in the minds of my peers. Motivational beliefs may be reducible to reasoned arguments or to cultural conventions (e.g., that one should be brave in battle is based on the belief that, say, bravery is rewarded in heaven, or that it is the "done thing"). Possessing a motive is to possess intentionality, and intentionality is reducible to ideas and beliefs; or, generally speaking, motives are reducible to a mental attitude held *towards* something. All mental attitudes are explicitly or tacitly held.

Man is naturally motivated to wage war, it may be claimed; but it has to be asked what that means. Honor, revenge, and glory are commonly held motives that lead to war, but so too are justice, envy, jealousy, shame, self-preservation, group solidarity, and fear; and all of these may lead to other kinds of action — sporting, artistic, or commercial achievements. A single motive may be traced by the historian as the source of a particular war, or a plethora of motives may have contributed. But to blame all war on single motives entails abandoning man's ability to possess a host of motives and goals, which is effectively the same as reducing his motives to the status of reactive instincts. That the same motives may explain the pursuit of alternative goals — glory and honor can be earned on the sports field, and jealousy may motivate nothing more than acerbic gossip — suggests that man is not tied to motivational predispositions over which he has no control.

Those who consider motives to be biological or emotional impulses that act to overwhelm the capacity for choice and rational action believe man to be dominated by his instincts as they disclose themselves in feelings.[44] This counterclaim, which derives from a more complex instinctivist theory, is absurd, though: it implies that man is mindless — or delusional about his thinking. In claiming that the emotions or instincts are epistemologically or psychologically dominant, man's ability to order, prioritize, and to alter emotional reactions is denied: he must obey all impulses and hence possesses no ability or freedom of will to prioritize emotional reactions of attraction, repulsion, fear, animosity, emulation, or sympathy and love. Yet motives cannot be thus reduced to reactions, or to the overwhelming primacy of emotion, but to chosen actions.[45]

Man obviously orders and prioritizes claims on his time. He is not solely an instinctual or emotional beast, for firstly he possesses learned rules and traditions that guide and govern his behavior in the culture in which he resides, and secondly he possesses a mind to reflect on his self, others, customs, and the world.

Motivational action also resides in the sphere of moral decision-making, and hence is quite within the bounds of critique: we are capable of judging the morality of jealousy, sacrifice, fear, and glory.

The very plurality of motives determines that choices must be made,[46] and choices are complex philosophical beasts betokening both intention, result, bluff, counter-bluff, ignorance, deception, and so on. Clausewitz notes, for instance, that a hostile intention can exist without feeling hostile, as a calculated intention against an enemy,[47] Whenever motives compete, it is necessary to prioritize them; and prioritizing is the voluntaristic action of choice, a choice requiring reflection and reason, conjecture and imagination or recourse to cultural guides, rules, and conventions (to "what is done").

Motives acted on are chosen through the volitional act of value prioritization. Why an individual chooses a particular value over another is philosophically an irreducible phenomenon: the individual's mind is essentially private (although factors involved in making a choice can feasibly be isolated) and what can be claimed is only that the individual acts. For example, why Alfred sought to wage war against the Vikings who had almost taken his kingdom of Wessex in AD 878 ultimately can only be explained by the fact that he was the man he was.

IRRATIONAL MOTIVES

Some may argue that since the very nature of war is irrational, its origins must lie in some irrational choice or drive that spills over into man's thinking and acting. Predispositions and motives are not necessarily beneficial in themselves, for man, they argue, may pursue irrational or unreasonable ends or employ inefficacious means in the pursuit of his goals. According to such theories, man's irrational elements (e.g., Plato's appetite, or Freud's "id") may periodically overwhelm individuals, causing them to lose their rationality and hence to desire destruction and war.[48] Proponents emphasize the power of irrational elements in man's nature, saying that despite attempts to live and act rationally and reasonably, humans are beset by strong urges to do things which reason cannot at times stop (e.g., Freud's "death instinct"[49]).

Such irrational motives may have the strength to override all cultural or rational codes that inhibit men from fighting one another.[50] In its strongest version, reason cannot control the lower drives at all; hence no one can be blamed for causing a war, or for any event that can be described as the result of irrational motives such as fear or envy. Thus, if primeval forces may control man and even entire groups, warfare is unavoidable.

However, optimists within this camp, such as Freud and James, allow that the released energies can be channeled into other activities that occupy the destructive irrational nature of humanity.[51] Others suggest that, armed with reason, man ought to be able to master himself and stoically keep his lower orders in strict control.[52]

Philosophically we have to be careful about appropriate language, here. By "irrational" is meant going against the interests of either the self or the species as a whole.[53] The two do not have to be complementary, of course, for I may be asked to do something that is irrational to me yet rational for the group as a whole, e.g., sacrifice myself by running at an enemy position to test its fire power before the brigade advances. Irrationality, in the broad sense, is not necessarily contrary to reason, and it may be the product of a complex articulated argument (a rationalization). Irrationalism, however, also stands for an epistemological position, which holds that reason is either not conducive at all for understanding the world, or that it is superseded by other forms of knowledge such as intuition, emotions, higher ideals such as World Spirit, God, and so on. Irrationalist belief systems and how they relate to war are taken up below. Here we examine whether irrational drives prompt men to wage war.

However, the thesis that human irrationality causes wars may be refuted on five points. Firstly it is based on a reductionist fallacy that wars can be explained by a single element of human nature such as the "death instinct" or "fear". Attempting to explain human events by a single hypothesis (appetite, emotion, id, etc.) is erroneous, for human motivation is intricately pluralistic. This is especially so and intensified in such a complex phenomenon as war.[54]

Secondly, a false conclusion is drawn when it is claimed that irrational motivations necessarily entail war. Even if irrationality exists as a predisposition (and there are good evolutionary arguments to counter that general irrationalism in a species is illogical[55]), it can lead to other events, such as suicide or to standing on one's head. Given the strongest emotional or appetitive desires, choices still have to be made and war is only one such choice; hence it remains a volitional event.

Thirdly, "war" may be characterized as being synonymous with a "herd instinct", in which entire nations are overwhelmed by irrationality and hence plunge themselves into war, just as buffalo periodically stampede collectively. But this ignores counter-factual evidence that not all humans get caught up in hysterical mass movements, and that even mass movements assume a direction of sorts — i.e., the object of the collective movement may be tacitly assumed or explicitly verbalized by individuals.[56] A rioting, poor community avoids damaging the pawnbrokers but will attack those shops people can pillage without obvious harm to their own interests.

Fourthly, it can be countered that instinctive actions properly belong to individuals and not to groups. An explanation is required for how individual motives and beliefs spill over into forms of collective behavior in which individuals renounce part of their own agency in favor of that of the group. Unless the group is acting like a herd in which no one individual leads but all take cues from any individual, leadership of sorts must arise to command and organize the group. This is a rather simplistic explanation, but it can be given greater credence by acknowledging that individuals may see themselves as being part of a group and identify their own interests with those of the group. The act of identification remains a voluntary choice.

Finally, the presupposition of an irrational side to human nature is disputable.[57] Irrationalism offers superficial explanations of behavior and problems that can be adequately and accurately described by the workings of the mind in conjunction with ideas.[58] People can be mistaken about what their proper goals or methods ought to be, but mistakes are rarely repeated, for man is capable of learning from his errors (if he wishes to, of course).

Irrationalism cannot explain war, although in the particular it may explain actions in war, or even in the decision to go to war. For example, a leader may be irrationally obsessed with a specific goal or target.[59] Military incompetence, so well described by Norman Dixon,[60] is rooted in forms of irrationality — the refusal to reconsider strategies, tactics, or goals in the face of mounting counter-evidence, the refusal to innovate or adapt generally, and so on. The very nature of irrationality is not conducive to achieving goals (whether because the goals themselves are irrational or the ends are counter-productive); whereas rationality — the explicit use of reason to determine ends and means — is subject to unforeseen events, lack of knowledge and a variety of imprecise and rough estimates. But the application of reason does attempt to integrate and use knowledge rather than either ignore it or leave it unintegrated. As a doctrine of anti-reason, irrationalism is wholly dangerous for the mind and for life. The universe is not of our making, nor are its laws;[61] we are subject to them and it is in our interests, to say the least, to try to comprehend them.

Biological drives do not end at some conveniently placed point where reason or learning can begin, and this has to be born in mind when we look at war, or any human phenomena. The biological seeps into our thinking (framing it, delimiting it) but our thinking also seeps into our biology (channeling energies and thoughts and thereby working out the body and mind); a man engrossed with maths will develop those patterns of thought that flicker through the brain and become more proficient in his skills — his ultimate capacities perhaps being limited by the "hardware" he inherits. A warrior tribe or group is likely to reproduce those biological aspects more suited to war — strength, agility, hand-eye coordination competencies, etc., which in turn generate energized and active children; but so too can an unfit person train himself to be a soldier.

More importantly, the forms overlap and are not shed as we complicate human nature in admitting thought. The final section of this chapter considers the position of the private as a metaphor and analogy of the philosophy of war argued for in this book.

MORALE: THE PRIVATE AND THE WARRIOR SPIRIT

The archetypal Private in the army embodies instinct — the pure reaction and obedience to orders. He is not an independent entity, standing free of philosophy or method, but is an element or aspect of human nature in war, especially modern war. He is the trained and drilled automaton that obeys orders and reacts without thought. His decisions have been made for him by his training and his orders; his is not to reason why, but to do, to act, to obey. The private is the *ideal* that the newly trained recruit should embody, but he is also a persistent element in all members of rank and status.

Importantly, the Private is not shrugged off by the Captain or General; he cannot be ignored by the Colonel — he remains the common denominator between soldiers of all ranks; for the General may have to follow orders, and may be called upon to react as his training and instinct have taught him to act, and he may withdraw or collapse into the Private, into a thoughtless beast of battle, and thus fail in his duty to envisage the war. The Private embodies the instinctual obedient automaton required on Western battlefields since the organized legions of the Romans.

Obedience in battle is however, not sufficient to produce a good warrior; from memoirs and accounts of battle, it appears that what is crucial is a sense of the warrior spirit, at its simplest a sense of morale, which can infuse the most beleaguered regiment with an intransigence and bravado that otherwise would be lacking. Holman S. Melcher rescued the 20th Maine from defeat in the US Civil War. The regiment was almost out of ammunition and was facing an imminent attack when Mechler rose, waving his sword. "Come on! Come on boys!", he shouted, charging down into the surprised Confederates.[62] The 20th took four hundred prisoners for the North and the engagement was a key turning point in the Battle of Gettysburg (1863).

Morale is both an individual and a group emotion; it reflects the self respect of the person or the regiment, and for Napoleon, while "an army's effectiveness depends on its size, training, experience and morale . . . morale is worth more than all the other factors combined." Morale can turn a victory into defeat, as Marshal Soult found out on May 16, 1811, when his French soldiers attacked an allied regiment of the 3rd Foot, nicknamed the Bluffs and the 57th, nicknamed the "Diehards" after the battle. Soult commented, "There was no beating these troops. They were completely beaten, the day was mine, but they did not know it and would not run." What held them together was the action of 16-year-old Ensign Thomas, who refused to surrender the regiment's colors to an attacking cavalry officer. "Only with my life!" he shouted, as he was cut down. The colors were grabbed by Lieutenant Latham, who managed to rip the colors off their pole and stuff them into his jacket as he too was cut down. Colonel Inglis of the 57th was shot through the lung but managed to utter, "Die hard, 57th. Die hard." These acts inspired a solidarity against the odds to turn the battle around.[63]

Morale is boosted by such acts of bravery, as when Julius Caesar moored his invasion fleet off the coast of Britannia, and the *aquilifer*, who carries the Legion's eagle, jumped from his ship into the sea to wade towards the shore full of defending Britons, thereby urging his reluctant comrades into battle: "Jump down, soldiers, unless you wish to betray your eagle to the enemy!"

Morale encompasses the solidarity of the tribe; the momentum can be sustained or generated by a single individual's own bravery, or by the recollection of the tribe's previous deeds or greatness. At the battle of Waterloo, an officer reminded his men of the regiment's actions at Alexandria in 1801. "Twenty Eight, remember Egypt!", and despite most of them having been absent from that battle, the reminder of the tribe's history was sufficient to instill in them bravery against an onslaught of cavalry.[64]

Morale enables the troop to keep together under fire; it is part of the battlefield rather than a cause of war.

The morale boosting of the soldier's rhetoric is a useful element of war, and its stirring tones can certainly invoke martial solidarity with citizens, as Churchill proved in his rousing war time speeches. Shakespeare, too, was all too aware of the phenomenon:

> We few, we happy few, we band of brothers;
> For he to-day that sheds his blood with me
> Shall be my brother; be he ne'er so vile,
> This day shall gentle his condition:
> And gentlemen in England now a-bed
> Shall think themselves accursed they were not here,
> And hold their manhoods cheap whiles any speaks
> That fought with us upon Saint Crispin's day.[65]

Yet the hard morality of fight or die is not one that is conducive to human happiness. It is the morality of the extreme situation, when the defensive instincts required to save a community, a regiment, or a platoon, must act. They may be instilled as automatic reactions amongst the drilled Privates, but more often, judging from battle accounts, they have to be reminded: hence the courage that is stimulated by the actions of one or the rhetoric of an officer or the strong-willed courageous man whose charisma and tenacity drives others to action.

The martial values embedded in the warrior's morale are an element of human life, but that element should remain separated from the cooperation required for a peaceful existence. When the same *esprit de corps* is directed back into the complex society to order and control its institutions and cultural processes, its effect is disastrous. Morale, or in general, self-esteem, is a vital factor of all aspects of life, but it can emanate from successful cooperation in peaceful enterprises or from success in individual work or production.

The *Red Badge of Courage*, chapter 23, possesses wonderful descriptions of the power of men's courage and the expected duplicity (as would occur in peace) of the privates falling behind their officers as they thrust themselves upon the enemy:

The colonel came running along back of the line. There were other officers following him. "We must charge'm!" they shouted. "We must charge'm!" they cried with resentful voices, as if anticipating a rebellion
against this plan by the men.
The youth . . . expected that his companions, weary and stiffened, would
have to be driven to this assault, but as he turned toward them he perceived with a certain surprise that they were giving quick and unquali-
fied expressions of assent . . . the soldiers sprang forward in eager leaps.
There was new and unexpected force in the movement of the regiment.[66]

The story unfolds in any group action; but culturally some groups
are more adept at concerted cooperation on the battlefield than others.
Militarily, cooperation typically wins out over groups that dissolve or
panic: such were the famous victories of the Greeks over the Persians,
and the Romans over the Celts.[67] Tightly organized groups of soldiers,
cooperating, whatever the nature of their tactics, more often than not
overwhelm the loosely organized, unless the latter are loosely organized
in order to permit greater individual initiative and effort: such becomes
the menace of the guerrilla or the terrorist (the more advanced guerrilla,
who employs civilian cover for his tactics and who deploys total or
unrestrained war against civilians).

The levels of coordination are much more fluid in such organizations permitting the decentralized cells to work effectively and self-
sufficiently. Waging war against terrorist and guerrilla groups invali-
dates tactics that are useful in the classic pitched battles of the modern
era, yet, as with all armies, such cells need supply bases and directing
leaders to sustain them. These become the targets for those having to
wage war on an apparently amorphous enemy. Limiting or shutting
down the communication between the small networks and their centers of control, honing in on the essential personnel and supplies, and
constraining their possible movements reduces the possible fluency of
co-operation between and within cells. Unless that is achieved, the
smaller, more fluid coordinated group is likely to survive against a
highly coordinated but massive war machine — individuals can escape
easier than regiments.

More importantly though is the war for ideas that has to be
waged to undermine the belief systems that support or sympathize
with the use of force and violence. As the following chapters argue,
ideas underpin man's actions — and when ideas are supportive of war

and collective aggression, wars are likely to be sustained or re-invoked, even when a culture has apparently settled upon a peaceful life.

CONCLUSION

Moving from the instinctual claims on man to biological and motivational predispositions takes us to the ideological aspect of man's nature. Here we find the most dominant and indeed most interesting causal conditions. Motives are resoluble into learned beliefs about their management and propriety, and war and any part of man's actions that are above the animal instinctual level are a product of man's beliefs. Instincts remain active residents, for we are biological creatures; but since we are also cultural and rational beings, the categories of thought and choice are more vital to an understanding of the motivation and hence the cause of war.

Notes

1. Man's various aspects tend towards or converge on indivisibility, but not fully so: I retain biological functions that progress independently of my mental abilities and will.

2. Robert Ardrey contends that territorialism is a predisposition rather than an instinct, for territorial boundaries have to be learned, and if the land is shared one learns likewise whom to tolerate, whom to expel. Ardrey, *The Territorial Imperative*, p. 24.

3. Fromm remarks that possessing a certain amount of space is a fundamental requirement of a healthy life for all animals. *Anatomy of Destructiveness.*, pp. 153-157.

4. Cf. Fromm, Anatomy, pp.153-157.

5. For example, Midgley notes the necessary redevelopment of family life in the Israeli kibbutzim, *Beast and Man*, p.329.

6. Ardrey, *ibid.*, p. 170.

7. This is the general thrust of Ardrey's thesis in his *The Territorial Imperative*.

8. Cf. Keegan, *History of Warfare*.

9. Classical liberals and free marketeers extol the benefits that private property and the market system entail. The market order, they argue, promotes increasing levels of production and standards of living and thereby generates pacifistic cultures. The Durants note a distinction between trade and warfare: "Normally and generally men are judged by their ability to produce — except in war, when they are ranked according to their ability to destroy." Will and Ariel Durant, *The Lessons of History*, pp. 54-55.

10. It remains a perennial policy to nationalists and economic isolationists who view trade with foreigners as somehow demeaning or as weakening a nation's economic or military might.

11. David Ricardo, *The Principles of Political Economy and Taxation*, pp. 77-93.

12. E.g., Jeremy Bentham, Richard Cobden, John Bright and others of the Quaker movement, who conjoined their pacifism with the free trade doctrine of Ricardo and Frédéric Bastiat.

13. Free traders underline the old humanist line that war can benefit neither defeated nor victor, but Mises rightly points out that wars can benefit individual aggressors even though the effect on the world as a whole may be negative. Mises, *Nation, State, and Economy*, p.152.

14. Mercantilism complements imperialist policies in the sense that as mercantilism views the world's wealth as fixed and trade's benefits as asymmetric, the state has a pressing duty to secure cheap resources wherever they are found as well as cornered or controlled markets to sell its products to. The Boston Tea Party reflected locals' frustrations with the British government's trade policy of monopolization backed by armed force. Cf. 1773 Tea Act and ensuing Intolerable Acts 1774.

15. Caribou, elephants, and sea otters seemingly possess no territory, for example. Cf. Carrighar, "Aggression".

16. Fromm, *op cit.*, p.164.

17. Part of the popularity of territorialism as an explanation for war in the 1960s complemented radical Marxist voices in vogue at the time that saw property, following

Proudhon, as theft and the source of all ills.

18. Fromm, *op cit.*, p.164

19. In experiments with territorial male sticklebacks, Niko Tinbergen, witnessed predictable diminution of aggressive behavior by attackers as they approached the defending fish's territory, and concomitantly, the defender became more aggressive the closer he was to his own territory. Dawkins, *The Selfish Gene*, pp. 79-80

20. Expansion is not necessary for any economic activity or increase in production requires a concerted effort on the part of the owner. The Soviet Union controlled some of the richest agricultural lands in the world, but since it removed the incentive to work them well (and in the process killed millions of Ukrainians), productivity fell and the Soviet Union had to import its grains.

21. Property ownership can increase productivity and hence support a higher living standard and a larger population.

22. Cf. Helmut Schoek's *Envy*.

23. Cf. Reisman, *Capitalism*.

24. Rousseau, *Discourse on the Origin of Inequality*, p.84

25. Mises, *Human Action*, pp. 160-61

26. E.g., Locke, *Second Treatise*, Ch. 16, §175.

27. Hoppe, *Democracy*, p.226

28. "[War] promotes competition because it is the ultimate form of competition." Will and Ariel Durant, *The Lessons of History*, p.19.

29. The notion that competition and conflict are two sides of the same coin (politics) is the political philosophy of mercantilism.

30. *Phaedo*, trans. Hugh Tredennick, Penguin Books: Harmondsworth, 1969 [1954], 65c-66e, p.111. Cf. also William Charlton, "Trisecting the Psyche".

31. As Fromm comments: "the conclusion seems unavoidable that aggressive behavior of animals is a response to any kind of threat to the survival or...to the vital interests of the animal." Fromm, *op cit.*, p.139

32. In an interesting passage, Wright notes that: "It is to be anticipated that man, having organized his societies toward intellect and progress, will not converge toward the ant's "societies" emphasizing instinct and stability, though despotic totalitarianism would lead in that direction. The mechanism of formic social solidarity throws light, however, upon the irrational foundations of human societies. The history of both types of society indicates that there is survival value in minimizing predation, parasitism, and other forms of violent behavior. In this respect convergent evolution of the human and insect types of society may be expected." *A Study of War*, p.52

33. Richard Dawkins, *The Selfish Gene*.

34. Individual aggressors obviously face potential costs in initiating a fight, even if they are likely to win — persistent aggression amongst the individuals of the group is not sustainable over the long run, Dawkins relates, for pacifism in the face of aggression would soon begin to pay for an increasing number of individuals. Cf. Chapter 5, *The Selfish Gene*. However, the link between cost and benefit is severed in complex warfare — for often the generals or authorities are aggressive, but the soldiers and civilians bear the brunt of the destruction and death. The extent to which war diminishes the wealth of the belligerents and of the entire world depends on the

nature and extent of the division of labor: the more intricate the commercial ties between belligerents, the greater the economic cost of fighting. Cf. Adam Smith, *Wealth of Nations*, V.i.a. for a classical exposition on the increased opportunity cost of war for advanced societies.

35. Especially if a target nation restricts trade. The British Opium Wars with China (1839-42 and 1856-60) sought to open up China to the opium trade as well as to secure other trading privileges for itself and France – they provide a fascinating study in mixed motives: on the one hand, the securing of privileges by force being thoroughly mercantilist, while the removal of trade barriers complementing the free trade doctrine of the mid-Victorian era. However, most free-traders of the Manchester school decried the use of force as well as the founding of colonies abroad, for which they received the epithet, 'Little Englanders', a term that implied an insult in a growing imperialist era.

36. The diversion of such motives into more pacifistic endeavors is the central thesis of William James's "The Moral Equivalent of War."

37. Hobbes, *Leviathan*, p.200

38. Expressed very well in economic theory.

39. As Locke in the *Second Treatise* is wont to warn.

40. "[M]an is by nature a political animal. Anyone who . . . has no state is either too bad or too good, either subhuman or superhuman — he is like the war-mad man condemned in Homer's words as 'having no family, no law, no home'; for he who is such by nature is mad on war: he is a non-cooperator like an isolated piece in a game of draughts." *Politics*. trans. Sinclair. 1253a.

41. Possible exceptions include producers that own the only source of a particular product, e.g., mines. It is also true, however, that talented entertainers are pure 'market monopolies' (in contrast to legislated monopolies such as the Post Office): there is only one Pavarotti, and he can charge extraordinary rates for his appearances limited only by the available substitutes (Domingo, Carreras, etc.) who may offer cheaper shows.

42. Cf. Hayek, *The Fatal Conceit*, "Superstition and the Preservation of Tradition", p.157

43. "All moral duties may be divided into two kinds. The first are those, to which men are impelled by a natural instinct or immediate propensity, which operates on them, independent of all ideas of obligation, and of all views, either to public or private utility. Of this nature are, love of children, gratitude to benefactors, pity to the unfortunate...the person, actuated by them, feels their power and influence, antecedent to any such reflection." David Hume, "Of the Original Contract', p.479.

44. William James for example asserts the moral primacy of instincts: "[Man's] instinctive impulses . . . get overlaid by the secondary reactions due to his superior reasoning power; but thus man loses the *simply* instinctive demeanour." James, *Talks to Teachers*, p.43; and "our judgments concerning the worth of things, big or little, depend on the *feelings* the things arouse in us. When we judge a thing to be precious of consequence of the idea we frame of it, this can only because the idea itself is itself associated already with a feeling." James, *ibid.*, p.229. Man's actions and judgments are therefore dominated by his more primal instincts and emotions.

45. Cf. Mises: "Man is not a being who cannot help yielding to the impulse that most urgently asks for satisfaction. Man is a being capable of subduing his instincts, emotions, and impulses; he can rationalize his behavior. He renounces the satisfaction of

a burning impulse in order to satisfy other desires. He is not a puppet of his appetites. A man does not ravish every female that stirs his senses; he does not devour every piece of food that entices him; he does not knock down every fellow he would like to kill. He arranges his wishes and desires into a scale, he chooses; in short, he acts...It may happen that an impulse emerges with such vehemence that no disadvantage which its satisfaction may cause appears great enough to prevent the individual from satisfying it. In this case too there is choosing. Man decides in favor of yielding to the desire concerned." Mises, *Human Action*, p. 16.

46.   "Mankind has various instincts and principles of action, as brute creatures have... [and] several which brutes do not; particularly reflection or conscience, an approbation of some principles or actions, and disapprobation of others.

"Brutes obey their instincts or principles of action, according to several rules; suppose the constitution of their body, and the objects around them.

"The generality of mankind also obey their instincts and principles, all of them; those propensions we call good, as well as bad, according to the same rules; namely, the constitution of their body, and the external circumstances in which they are in. Therefore it is not a true representation of mankind to affirm, that they are wholly governed by self-love, the love of power and sensual appetites: since, as on the one hand they are often actuated by these, without any regard to right or wrong: so on the other it is manifest fact, that the same person, the generality, are frequently influenced by friendship, compassion, gratitude; and even a general abhorrence of what is base, and the liking of what is fair and just, takes its turn amongst the other motives of action." Bishop Butler, *The Works of Butler: Volume 1*, "Preface", p. 9.

47.   Clausewitz, *On War*, Book 1, Ch.1.3, p. 102.

48.   Some historians consider the First World War to be the result of such neuroses, e.g., Howard, *The Causes of War*, p. 9.

49.   "[W]e are led to conclude that this [destructive] instinct functions in every living being, striving to work its ruin and reduce life to its primal state of inert matter. Indeed it might well be called the "we are led to conclude that this [destructive] instinct functions in every living being, striving to work its ruin and reduce life to its primal state of inert matter. Indeed it might well be called the "death instinct", Freud, "Why War", p. 77.

50.   Strachey argues: "It must be remembered that the destructive instincts which, when all is said and done, are the greatest cause of war, *are* instincts and that they are impossible to eradicate altogether, greatly though they may be modified." p. 266

51.   Freud, "Why War" and James, "The Moral Equivalent of War".

52.   E.g., Ginsbery, "Philosophy versus war", p.xvi.

53.   Perhaps 'unreasonable' may be of better use.

54.   Fear for example may be a response to a sudden unexpected noise in the dark, causing an impromptu increase in adrenaline, but the growth of a neighbour's power which causes fear, may also prompt a line of consequentialist and balance of power reasoning. Humans may react with surprise to a single event, but political events are of much greater complexity than a sudden "boo!" from a hidden corner.

55.   Perhaps it could be argued that 'irrational' reactions are presently irrational but were once not — e.g., the sudden shock re-awakening of the body on the verge of sleep may have had its reasons in humanity's prehistory (fear and vulnerability of predators for example). The complexity of modern life is a very recent phenomenon

in human evolutionary terms, which implies that biologically and even emotionally, humanity may not yet have adapted to this new mode of life.

56. In the flight of refugees, for example, their path may be to the closest sanctuary they can know or have word of. But with regards to war the necessary prerequisite of having to plan and divert resources entails the passing of a period of time during which it cannot be maintained that those engaged remain under some form of hysteria.

57. Cf. John McCrone, *The Myth of Irrationality.*

58. Cf. McCrone, *ibid.*

59. E.g., As Sir Anthony Eden apparently was with the Egyptian President, Nasser in the Suez Crisis, 1956.

60. *The Psychology of Military Incompetence.*

61. Despite the varieties of natural law objectives they all "contained a sound idea which neither be compromised by connections with untenable vagaries nor discredited by any criticisms...first the idea that a nature-given order of things to which man must adjust his actions if he wants to succeed. Second: the only means available to man for the cognizance of this order is thinking and reasoning, and no existing social institution is exempt from being examined and appraised by discursive reasoning. Third: there is no standard available for appraising any mode of acting either of individuals or of groups of individuals but that of the effects produced by such action." Mises, *Theory and History* pp.44-45

62. From Keegan et al, *Soldiers,* p.40.

63. Keegan et al, *Soldiers,* p.47

64. Keegan, *et al,* p.46.

65. Shakespeare, *Henry V,* Act 4 , Scene 3.

66. Stephen Crane, *Red Badge of Courage,* p.147

67. Ably recounted in the old classic, Sir Edward Creasy's *The Fifteen Decisive Battles of the World.*

CHAPTER EIGHT: Culture and War

> "Even at the earliest dawn of culture, when the invention of tools was just beginning to upset the equilibrium of phylogenetically evolved patterns of social behavior, man's new born responsibility must have found a strong aid in cultural ritualization."
> — Konrad Lorenz[1]

> "War may well be more resistant to the human will than our everyday thinking would suggest . . . Human beings stumbled into war and we can see no guarantee that they will not just as inexplicably stumble out of it again."
> — Paskins and Dockrill[2]

In developing motives and learned predispositions towards certain kinds of behavior, man becomes a cultural being and hence infinitely more complex, as Shakespeare's Hamlet comments, albeit ironically:

> What a piece of work is a man! how noble in reason! how infinite in faculty! in form and moving how express and admirable! in action how like an angel! in apprehension how like a god! the beauty of the world! the paragon of animals!

The majority of a man's behavior is learned from the manner in which his parents and peers act; much is taken on-board implicitly, although often with some conscious nod in agreement even at the earliest development of the child's mind. War's origins certainly take on culturally relative characteristics that suggest war is of a cultural origin, yet cultures are made up of individuals who make decisions to act individually and cooperatively, or to act in concert, or not to assist at all. Too often the debate between nature and nurture assumes that only one side can be correct, and similarly with community and individuality. A sound philosophy of war should bridge the divides between the polarities to provide a stronger and more consistent explanation of war and warfare. In this chapter we deal with the proposition that war is wholly a cultural phenomenon.

The culturalist thesis — as those theories that explain war's origins exclusively in terms of culture can be called — is rejected, but not without accepting the merits it offers; for human interaction produces intricate formulas of understandings and behavior that individuals soak up in order to become (on an evolutionary mechanism) more adapted to the complex of social arrangements in all of its nuances and complexities. The mind is capable of discerning the nature and pattern of cultural phenomena; however, it is wholly incapable of re-inventing them or beginning afresh with all that humanity has learned over the millennia, a thesis — the rationalist program — that is dealt with in the following chapters.

If war is a cultural phenomenon, we must ask: what is a culture? A culture comprises the matrices of learned rules, customs, norms, rituals, and etiquette that are generated by social interaction and that a group generally holds in common; such structures are also subsumed in the group's language and behavior.[3]

Individuals are born into a culture, and in biological terms maturation within a culture is a necessary condition for psychological and sociological development. Without social interaction, an individual does not mentally (nor even physically, in terms of the brain's development) mature.[4] Cultural institutions — such as rules of conduct and of language — evolve as an outgrowth of human biological development. Learned rules of conduct for the most part evolve with social interaction,[5] and therefore, as Hayek argues,

> Just as instinct is older than custom and tradition, so then are the latter older than reason: custom and tradition stand between instinct and reason — logically, psychologically, temporally.[6]

Plausibly this implies that the formation of social rules in any species begins with phylogenetically inherited limitations to general or to specific forms of behavior.[7] But then instinctual rules evolve, in the more intricately wired creatures, into *learned* forms of behavior. Broadly speaking, if a rule is learned then it is part of culture; if it is inherited, it is part of biology (although there is necessarily an overlap between abilities to learn and capacities that may be subsequently developed to learn).[8]

The rules and conventions that societies generate are crucial to assist social life and recognition of this deepens the Aristotelian insight that man is a social animal subject to natural laws, for it provides an etiology of those rules man produces through interaction.

Behavioral limitations may be placed by our genetic heritage, but most rules evolve through social play and intercourse. However, many rules cannot be explicated verbally *prior to action*. We cannot consciously *know* beforehand everything that is "in our nature" or "against our nature", since we lack omniscience; we may consciously choose a mode of action, but that does not mean that we have to understand its nature or implications. Accordingly, specific *a priori* and explicit commandments are generally useless for human action. The conventional laws — the rules and norms of behavior that form from *social interaction* — that evolve do so through processes of trial and error and through spontaneous mutually beneficial arrangements. These form matrices of social experience and knowledge: i.e., broad bases of "know-how" and social principles, which in turn may assist personal reflection on what ought to be done in particular predicaments. Sometimes newly emerging rules may be inconsistent with other more important values, and people err in forming rule judgments. Hence, evolving rules may in the first instance be corrected[9] through simple trial and error, but they may also be corrected through a rational examination of their content and implications, as far as man is able to consider those consequences.

Since arrangements of moral laws, codes of conduct, and etiquette evolve for the most part on a tacit level, social rules may be said to emerge spontaneously and hence independently of the intention of particular agents' or authorities' attempts to construct explicit rules.[10] Humanity converges onto norms that are *useful*, even though the origins and the historical adaptations have been lost. Some things are "just done" and if jettisoned (by edict or state decree) by a society they can cause subtle disruptions that have chaotic ramifications. Cultures are constantly changing and adapting to the evolving modes of human life — not because they are organic wholes that possess a singular existence ("America will adapt") but because hundreds, thousands, and in the larger nations, millions are subtly and individually, infinitesimally changing their behavior over time, adjusting to changes wrought by other individuals, by legislation, states, music, literature, art, and war.

Functionally, cultures provide the general conditions for human learning. They are very flexible and efficacious media of and for adaptation. They allow new ideas[11] and behavior to spread quickly (that is, so long as humans are free to conjecture and to pursue new ideas), and thereby permit new ideas to gain popular ascendancy over no-longer-useful or generally ineffective ideas. For example, in relation to war, innovations in the treatment of prisoners of war — enslaving rather than killing them — may have quickly been taken up in a variety of interrelated cultures, given the benefits accruing from the possession of productive humans over dead humans. Much cultural adaptation may proceed on tacit levels, or in emulation of innovating individuals who attempt to react against traditional norms.

Much of our everyday knowledge is subsumed into culturally specific structures — language and moral conventions that have been learned through maturation to adulthood, tampered gently by individual and group innovation and reaction. (Arguably, an element of civilization is the expansion of recognizing mutually beneficial arrangements from the simple transfers of trade to the most complex legalities of market systems.)

However, the mistake should not be made that we are *purely* cultural creatures, that we are *solely the product of the social group* we mature and reside in (a mistake that many writers do make). For want of a better term, "culturalism" is the theory that claims the logical, political and ethical primacy of cultures over individuals. That is, an individual's actions and thoughts cannot be explained without an exegesis of his cultural milieu and cannot be explained by anything else, such as his genetic heritage or his own thoughts on matters.

As a reductionist explanation of war, culturalism primarily neglects man's biological as well as his rational nature. Yet the cultural aspects of war need to be emphasized without promoting them to an epistemological hegemony that negates reason and biology. Culturalism should be rejected without renouncing all of its explanatory elements.

CULTURALISM

Culturalism is the theory that all human action is a product of cultural forces — specifically the language, mannerisms, etiquette, rites and rituals that have evolved within a group in its specific locality.[12] Culturalism denies any biological or rational influences on human behavior, committing the grave fallacy of assuming that human behavior or action is devoid of biological cause,[13] or effect, even; and then it closes the possibility of impartial reasoning and choice by denying the mind the tools of reflection, imagination, conjecture, and universal logic. The mind's contents, it assumes, are wholly relative to the time and place in which it develops; hence truths are relative to community.[14] To understand the ancient Romans and their wars it would be necessary to first comprehend the Roman culture — what was expected of its commanders and citizens, how other groups were to be treated, and so on.

While this is attractive and indeed is a sound proposition for the most part, it should not entail that intercultural principles cannot be garnered and learned, or that common principles of conduct do or should rule men's lives. That is, although culturalism's description of war is valid enough, it does not follow that what is ought to be the case. For example, culturalism entails that aggressive and defensive wars can only be judged relatively — i.e., no absolute condemnation of aggressive war is possible: if war is deemed a particular and appropriate cultural response that has evolved for that group, no universal definition of war (or, therefore, ethical analysis) can be proposed, since one group's definition is unique and epistemologically sacred.

Perhaps the most serious implication of culturalism and its corollary of cultural relativism is that social laws are as relative as the laws of etiquette appear to be between cultures. While a relativist theory concerning the laws of physics is risible,[15] many have denied the universality of economic laws, for example, or in war have rejected strategic principles of falling into dangerous errors of underestimating the enemies' mental or fighting capacities.[16] That is, the relativist looks upon a society and believes that the laws of economics, the lessons from past mistakes, the demographic or sociological issues that have affected the culture in the past, or which have affected other cultures, will now not affect this society in the same manner.

Objective values and the possibility of universal laws are rejected by culturalists as being essentially relative to the community propounding them. Culturalism relates well therefore to theories of moral relativism, namely, the theory that one cannot judge other communities except from one's own cultural (ethno-centric) background. Now, the gravest concern leveled against such relativism is, what ought to be done with a culture that deems war against other cultures as somehow heroic, natural, or necessary? The relativist has no solid answer, whereas from the moral objectivist standpoint, peace and cooperation are values that ought to be upheld universally, for they are objectively conducive to human survival. Cultural relativism may be developed into two possible theories.

Firstly, it can be held that cultural differences are irreconcilable, in which case either man is necessarily subject to constant warfare, or that one culture should (has a "duty" or a "manifest destiny") police the world to minimize conflict. Or, secondly, cultural differences can be held to be reconcilable, in which case the prescription might be either to foster educational ties and cultural exchanges and to form cultural federations, or, again, that it behooves one group to impose its culture on the rest of humanity: that is, that imperialism offers the method by which to resolve cultural differences.

Although it can admit that cultures change through migration, and especially technological change and intellectual developments, and so on, culturalism offers no prescription for abandoning warfare through reasoned arguments. It raises the question of why people migrate, invent technologies, conceive new theories, and so on, and offers no adequate explanation for an alteration to customs and rules from applied reasoning, since it alleges that culture is considered to be of greater epistemological status than biology or reason. That is, man is tied to his cultural base.

But both biology and reason can affect culture, and in turn can both be affected by culture. Certainly, the mind's conscious reasoning can affect the development of a culture more quickly than that of biological evolution. Nonetheless, using the premise that cultures belong as much to the pre-rational mind as well as the rational mind, cultures may manufacture a general disposition to war in agents' minds that is logically prior to or distinct from rational discussion — that is, *liminal* expressions of beliefs manifested in action. War can hence be a cultural construction;[17] indeed, this is a powerful explanation and one that goes a long way in explaining wars, but philosophically it cannot be held to be the *only* explanation.

The arguments that follow assert a more flexible thesis to acknowledge the power of cultures to define and to generate human actions by virtue of their tacit as well as explicit sanctions, rules, and language, while allowing reason to supplement, deny, and to influence cultural structures. The explanation of why this should be so is intricate but points generally to areas that ought to be explored more — namely the complex interactive overlapping of biology, culture, and reason, and between the corresponding ontology or categories of events, behavior, action, and will as products not just of reason or of culture or of biology, but a complex mixture of the three.

To return to the causal fulcrum being advanced, it is in the realm of general predispositions or *motives* that we find the beginnings of a plausible account for why wars occur. The very reason for the efficacy of motives is that they are essentially mental attitudes — derived from, created by, and maintained by human thinking. Therefore, the appropriate mental attitudes, whether initially culturally imbibed or rationally cultivated, form the proximate causal conditions for war — as they do for any human behavior or action above the instinctual and physiological events of digestion, blinking, breathing, etc, and conditioned cultural responses.[18] The crux is that such motives are not always amenable or even accessible to reason, but they are products of human endeavor, sometimes unintentionally, sometimes evolutionary. They exist and as far as they can be "owned" or acknowledged, they can be understood and countered, dissembled, or ignored.

WAR AND CULTURE

When conflicts arise in or between societies, how they are dealt with depends initially on the presiding cultural mechanisms for conflict resolution.[19] Previously encountered problems can be dealt with by individuals acting within and from their cultural framework, drawing on the intellectual capital base of the group and its precedents and rules. To the extent that new problems can be dealt with, they can be dealt with by relating them back to the framework provided by the older methods of resolution. In generating solutions to new problems, a culture necessarily evolves; in repeating the measures of the past, they repeat their mistakes or successes but they cannot be said to evolve.

If a culture does successfully adopt new solutions or conventions, they may then be passed on via the relevant behavioral and linguistic alterations, for example in the myths and visions of the group, which are then assimilated or rejected (tacitly or explicitly) by the members of the group over time. Hence a culture — the tacit and explicit knowledge held by a group in its behavior, rituals, language, and so on — is a useful medium for communicating aims, solutions, ideas, codes of behavior — in short, the self-conception of the group.

All change in the group emanates from individuals, and permitting adaptation at the individual level to new issues fosters a speedy dissemination of new ideas and behavior throughout the group.[20] The difference between open and closed societies is that open societies foster a "bottom-up" adaptation, permitting individuals to freely adapt as they see fit, learning from their mistakes as and when they occur. A closed society on the other hand imposes change or adaptation from above, and hence lends itself either to arbitrary tyranny in which a leader imposes his will on the people, or to rationalist, social engineering, when blue-prints outlining society are imposed. While the political differences between the willful tyrant and the social engineer are evident, the results are very similar: both constrain individual responsibility and freedom to adapt at the local level in favor of centralized enforced change.

Nonetheless, even if we have a thoroughly open society, not all that develops or evolves culturally is necessarily conducive to survival and adaptation. Man makes mistakes; indeed, we can only learn if we make mistakes. The existence of culture is thus no guarantee of the validity or the appropriateness of produced values. Lorenz warns: "With humanity in its present cultural and technological situation, we have good reason to consider intra-specific aggression the greatest of all dangers."[21] His fear is that the broad base of cultural knowledge and experience has yet to catch up with the technology at man's disposal: analogously, this is like giving a young child an armed gun to play with.[22] Children do not possess the requisite comprehension of time and consequences that underpins morality, and man's ability to deal with virtual and nuclear wars may be analogously judged as lacking a full comprehension of the effects unleashed. In this respect war can be said to unleash a barbarism and vehemence that overwhelms people's ability to conceive of distant temporal horizons. That is, they will discount the future heavily in favor of living for today, which implies a reduction in the willingness to consider temporally remote effects of present actions. Understanding the disseminating role of culture provides a useful basis from which to understand some of the causal conditions for war: cultures, in respect of the inter-generational transmission of beliefs, sustain tacit and explicit beliefs through time.

However, knowledge of a culture does not imply infallible predictability of how members will act and or desire their government to act when encountering a different culture. Assuming that past behavior is a reliable indicator of future behavior is methodologically problematic.[23] Past behavior may provide useful data on which to form a qualitative prediction — i.e., at least offer a broad indication of how a people may react or in which direction they may react; but it cannot provide a scientific, quantifiable indicator.[24] That a general has up till now reacted to the enemy's advance by an alluring but trapping retreat provides no certainty for what he will do next time.

This is an important point for when cultures clash. The fusion of two cultures generates change on a variety of levels, and inevitably, both cultures will change regardless of any conservatism or unwillingness to change on the part of one or both. The fact that a new set of customs and conventions is encountered necessarily produces an impact and a need for change, even if, at the minimum, that change is a reaction. Arguably, what happens depends on the extent to which the individuals of a culture deem theirs worthy of saving in the face of alternatives.[25] Cultural change is inevitable when two cultures meet, but the ethical and political aspect is whether such change is forced or voluntary.

War imposes change upon a society. Even if a people do not adapt to the encounter, they will still lose lives and lands, which ineradicably alter culture. War is a particularly vicious method of cultural change bringing hardship and death on both sides. Yet many philosophers have considered war to be the best or most invigorating and even most healthy mechanism of change. War certainly is a highly visible means to bring about change, yet the most important and beneficial intercultural transaction is through commerce, the effects of which are subtle — often hidden in the archeological record — and for the most part peaceful, involving mutually beneficial agreements and trades.[26] The low visibility of the proliferation of trade's benefits often diminishes its importance relative to the most devastating and brutal events of war. Wars, conquests, and invasions leave obvious imprints in the historical and archeological record, which often give them greater weighting in popular historical interpretation. The annals of ancient civilizations, their myths and legends of wars and battles, the heroes and villains, the struggles, losses and victories, enliven a national identity and provide the basis for further stories, songs, operas, symphonies, festivities, and days of remembrance. Trade rarely captures the imagination in such a manner; despite its inherent peacefulness, the culture of war can easily overwhelm the culture of trade if it is of a recent development.

Paradoxically, both war and commerce have tendencies to spread from culture to culture.[27] This is readily understandable in the case of commerce, which presents mutually beneficial arrangements to both groups.[28] Whereas war involves a policy, ritual, or response of blatant destructionism — people die and capital is destroyed. Its effects are obviously destructive and hence costly to both sides — except where the instigators of aggression are removed from the costs of battle.[29] However, war presents the possibility of gaining values swiftly, and perhaps permanently — taking slaves, land, and property without trading values; this means it can remain of a perennial attraction to societies that have a history of success in warfare. And war can be deemed beneficial if non-material values or beliefs are added to the equation, which requires us to rise above the purely mechanistic, biological explanations of war, whose modular paradigms are too quantitative to be of use in assessing cultural and ideological causes. For example, the incentives of Kamikaze suicide pilots that harassed US ships in the last two years of the Second World War can hardly be modeled by game theory.[30]

Economics may elaborate on the mutual benefits to be drawn from peaceful commerce,[31] but the subject and its results are historically very new and despite the iron-clad nature of its laws, most people throughout history and today are not economically literate. For a while in the 19th century, the free trade doctrines of Adam Smith and David Ricardo liberalized foreign and domestic policy from protectionist measures. Nonetheless, atavistic beliefs about how wealth is generated and distributed remain solidly popular and generate confused theories of war's origins and justifications; some thinkers such as John Ruskin and Thomas Carlyle played down the economic costs of war in favor of the moral enrichment war brings. In this, they followed Hegel's philosophy of war that it is necessary for the development of a state's national identity.[32] If there is no understanding of commercial benefits, of permitting traders to seek profits within each community, a general population and its leaders will remain attracted — both on a cultural and rational level — to the benefits aggressive war may bring, and it behooves a group, if attacked, to take up the same method in response.[33] If there were passive societies that encountered war and did not adapt, they have either fallen, been assimilated or enslaved, or taken up belligerence to survive in some form.

The internal logic of war, if no voluntary brakes are applied in the form of a treaty or codes of conduct and justice, entails a spiraling destructionism into total war.[34] Only for very few societies, notably the Inuit, the Australian aboriginals, and the Lepchas of Sikkim, is war an alien concept.[35] For these groups it never evolved as a solution to their inter-social problems, for they were sufficiently isolated from the contagious impacts of war or had turned away from war as a useful solution. Instead, they evolved other solutions to domestic problems. At this point it is futile to note which societies made the better choice, for what is important are the rules and institutions that were successful in achieving what the people expected from life and from one another.[36]

The ultimate and verifiable standard to which the good can refer is the maintenance and progression of the species: does the species propagate and flourish, or does it fail to adapt and hence does it decline? This is a rather primordial notion of the moral good, but what other candidate exists? If a species dies out, then its members have failed in adapting to changing conditions. If, on the other hand, its population expands healthily, then it is, at this very basic level of reasoning, succeeding in living. For the more complex creatures, reason elucidates that the activity most conducive to survival and progression is cooperation, as well as a host of other acts such as productive and entrepreneurial endeavors. Paul Johnson observes that whereas the ability to unite increases with civilization, the characterization of aggressors is:

A society . . . led by men whose status rests solely on force, possesses great initial advantages. But its strength is more apparent than real; it has no self-sustaining moral authority, no internal discipline other than violence; it can satisfy only a limited spectrum of human desires; it is inherently corrupt; it possesses no collective wisdom except in the narrow field of military expediency; it can tolerate no freedom of discussion, and therefore has no capacity to respond to changed conditions; its victories generate anarchy, and its defeats despair, for it has nothing worthwhile to defend.[37]

It is reason and not biological instinct that explains the importance of increasingly universal cooperation. While cultural evolution may or may not stumble on the efficacy of extended cooperation, some cultures may foster an ethic of internal cooperation (without which it would be difficult for a group to last very long) but maintain a ethic of non-cooperation with other groups. With biological triggers instigating a defense of security and identity, attempting cooperation beyond the close group or the common culture seems an intrinsically difficult issue for political philosophy. It apparently requires a great deal of articulated education and reasoned prodding to overcome xenophobic cultural inhibitions that have evolved in most societies. Yet the inherent possibility of mutation can never sustain such isolationism indefinitely; the drive to interact with the unknown, to explore the forbidden, and breach the taboos attracts maverick individualists who in turn generate a host of cultural effects from their exploratory quests into foreign or alien territory.

Shakespeare's *Romeo and Juliet* presents a pair divided by the strongest of clan hatreds, yet love triumphs; and such friendships that arise between peoples of different cultures, classes, and races act to ensure a constant interchange and dispersion of both genes and more importantly *ideas*. Tools traded afar across Neolithic communities, as genes would have done; but the dissemination of tools and techniques is accompanied by ideas, some flourishing better in their new environments, others being echoed but not worked upon.

Despite the beneficial interaction that arises from the meetings of cultures, deeply embedded cultural suspicions against the foreigner are easily roused. This is because most cultures consider outsiders as potential threats, especially where property rights are ill-defined or are subject to arbitrary violation by foreigners or outlaws. No doubt, as Hayek notes, thousands of years of living in small groups needing to defend hunting and foraging grounds has aroused deep cultural biases, although it is doubtful that a phylogenetic adaptation to distrust those outside of one's group has occurred.[38] The mutual hatred of German and Slav contributed to centuries of warfare, a tension that has presently eased with Germany's incorporation into the European Union and its demilitarization following the Second World War. But the absence of war does not entail that such animosities have vanished forever: culturally transmitted beliefs die hard and the benefits of cooperation and free trade are easily renounced.

Cooperation, as John Stuart Mill recognized, can only be learned and practiced.[39] The virtue of cooperation (i.e., the habits and teaching the values required for cooperation) is a requirement of peaceful society that has to be learned, for it is not absolutely innate in human biology, although it is plausible that some people are may be genetically more or less adapted to cooperative behavior than others, as some wild species are more or less so disposed. Cooperation is certainly a delicate value that can be rejected for short term gains, for to stir men to war on a cultural level is easier than to rouse their interests in global cooperation, despite the long term consequences of internecine warfare and the long term benefits of increasingly expanding spheres of cooperation. Cooperation teaches man increasingly to be aware of the more distant repercussions of his actions; in effect the time preference for civil societies falls in terms of the opportunity cost foregone of present for future consumption; cooperation and civilization create a culture in which increasingly round-about methods of production (more capital intensive) are taken up as people save present income in favor of later dividends, permitting an overall increase in wealth production.[40] Warrior cultures, like children, often do not perceive the longer term gains to be enjoyed from foregoing present consumption — or destruction — and hence remain wedded to a myopic vision of their future (if the future comes into their thinking).

Cultural rules and ideas remain efficacious in promoting and causing war against the advice of reason and against the often fragile culture of trade and production. This is because cultural rules are resolvable into tacit and explicit forms.[41] Explicit ideas are the result of articulated thinking, of enunciated reason and of explicit deliberation, whereas tacit ideas are those learned structures that are generally not enunciated — if they can be enunciated at the deep levels of basic cultural rules — but which nonetheless are causal and learned forms of behavior. [42]

Tacit ideas, the liminal and subliminal expectations held by a group of its own worth, its own position in its locality and with regard to neighbors, of its military potential or greatness are often sustained over generations. They leave recurring footprints in history when they rise to the surface of articulated thought and policy, sometimes stretching over great periods of time.

The next chapter deals with some of the ramifications of culturally imbibed ideas in the form of unintentional war, but to assess the latent proclivity of some cultures for war it is worth taking a random issue in military history to examine the power of cultural momentum. I chose a random page from the Dupuy and Dupuy *Encyclopaedia of Military History* and checked the previous and ensuing history of the peoples who had inhabited the area. The war happened upon was the Thirty Years War and the culture was that of Bohemia.

THE PERSISTENCE OF CULTURE: BOHEMIA

Cultures pervade over and through generations and in so doing they may sustain the belligerence and martial dispositions of past beliefs. The ideas of previous generations are sustained in the language and expectations of the present generation; each generation owes much to the thinkers and movers of the past and focusing on any cultural group we see a continuity that is often surprising — a source of stereotypes, on the level of base humor, but also a source of understanding for policy makers and for those interested in peace and war on higher levels of analysis. The individual leader is always free to break from the expected trend and force a new cultural path, but his power often emanates from the enduring flow of ideas submerged in folk history, song, poems, the whisperings of parents to children, architectural reminders and art.

The overarching culture of Bohemia stretches back at least a millennium, with some elements of its "foreign policy" going back to the Romans. There is indeed a long-lasting unity amongst the military and foreign policy history of the people, but that does not mean that there is no change, as the historian Barzun notes regarding culture; "Unity does not mean uniformity, and identity is compatible with change. Nobody doubts the unity of the person from babyhood to old age."[43] And by implication, no one should doubt the unity of a culture through the ages. Bohemia certainly develops: notably it becomes an independent *intellectual* center that draws it into the center of the Reformation in the 15th century and which is also sustained down to the present day;[44] it also produces a highly skilled workforce from Germanic immigration in the Middle Ages, a legacy that still separates it from its poorer eastern neighbor, the now independent Slovakia.

The date alighted upon in the Encyclopedia was 1608, when the Thirty Years War started as a religious war between Protestants and Catholics. Its origins can be found in a Bohemian revolt against Austrian rule. The Bohemians, we find, regularly fought for their independence in a history that reaches back to pre-Roman times and comes right up to the present day. In 1609 King Rudolph claimed religious freedom for his Protestant subjects, but he was deposed by his brother, Matthias, which led to a civil war in which a revolutionary army attempted to secure Bohemian independence. As often in its history, the larger powers surrounding it allied together in a Catholic league to defeat the Bohemians; what is fascinating to see is that in the Spring of 1968, the Bohemian people, tapping into their cultural heritage, asserted their cultural and political independence (soon squashed by a Russian invasion) and in 1989 they finally secured that independence they had long fought for, thus fulfilling a movement of beliefs and expectations that had been forced underground by the Habsburg hegemony that dated from Bohemia's defeat in the Thirty Years War.

But if we go back to Roman times, we see a culture develop that retains some marked characteristics throughout the next two millennia. The Celtic Boii tribes moved into the area that is now the major part of the Czech Republic by the fifth century; the land is bounded by Austria to the south, Bavaria to the West, Saxony and Lusatia to the north, Silesia to the north east and Moravia to the east. In 58 BC the Boii attempted an invasion of Gaul but were defeated by Julius Caesar. The wandering Marcomanni tribe supplanted the original Boii in AD 5 but maintained a similar foreign policy of forging alliances with larger powers while securing some independence back home; a growing confidence and assertiveness prompted them to invade northern Italy in AD 167, but they faced another capable leader, Marcus Aurelius, who fought and contained them until his death in 180. The pattern of local independence with external links to greater powers, followed by quix-otic attempts to annex surrounding territories or even take on the great powers, was formed.

Following a brief subordination to neighboring Moravia in the late ninth century, Bohemia grew to become a central political entity that held influence and power with, and sometimes over, its neighbors. In the tenth century, Bohemia allied with the western Bavarian people against eastern, belligerent Magyar peoples; the area was Christianized under the initial Premyslid rulers who, echoing the cultural history of the Boii and Marcomanni, attempted to expand their control over neighboring lands; Bretislav I led a successful foray into Moravia and then attempted to annex Poland, which caused the German king Henry III to intervene and rein in Bohemian power.

Bohemian attachment to the Holy Roman Empire gave the land a high political status, which the Premyslid dynasty exploited well. Vra-tislav II (r. 1061-92) obtained the title of King of Bohemia, which was extended by Otakar I into a hereditary title. Under his rule the lands prospered and migrants from overpopulated German areas moved in, bring vital agricultural skills that transformed the poorer areas and mining skills that enabled the development of the silver mines and brought the beginnings of economic growth.

Under Otakar II, Bohemia grew politically and economically; it turned to annex territory in Hungary and pushed its lands to the Adri-atic Sea. In 1278 Otakar turned his armies to Austria with notions of further aggrandizement, but the kings of Hungary desired his curtail-ment as did the presiding Rudolf, count of the Austrian Habsburg dy-nasty. Otakar was defeated and killed in the battle of Dürnkrut, which also saw Bohemian power substantially reduced. His son played the diplomatic game well enough to revive Bohemian fortunes: Wencelas II (r. 1278-1305) rose to become King of Poland and Bohemian power was at its peak; however, following his death, his son, Wencelas III, was assassinated and the family dynasty ended.

In 1310 a new dynasty — the Luxembourgs — took over the throne. They expanded control over Moravia, Silesia, and Upper and Lower Lusatia and in 1355, the Bohemian king Charles I became Holy Roman Emperor as Charles IV; Charles founded the University of Pra-gue in 1348 and thereby fostered a center of high learning and art that is still maintained today. The Bohemian School of Art flourished under

Charles's patronage and while the artistic output waxed and waned with Bohemia's political fortunes, the legacy persisted through to the modern painters and writers of the 20th century. Meanwhile, under Charles I, Prague became the capital of the Empire for awhile. Its nobles, however, were wary of centralization. In the late 14th century, Smil Flaska penned a tract called the *New Council* in defense of the rights of the nobility against the Crown, assumedly tapping into political misgivings but also providing for the continuity of a cultural tradition against central control that echoes through Bohemian history.

But religious disputes generated a new form of cultural dissension in the 15th century. Throughout history, the Bohemian lands were torn by internal dissension amongst its ruling classes; now a religious twist was added that both supplanted the desire for independence from external powers and added to internal factionalism. The source of disputation emanated from a capable cleric, Jan Hus (who was a follower, incidentally, of the nationalist theologian John Wycliffe of England, whose teachings eventually led to the creation of an independent Anglican Church under Henry VIII). Hus was a popular local man and wrote in the native Czech, following an old tradition begun by the ninth century Czech Saints Cyril and Methodius, who penned tracts in the local tongue to counter the influence of Germanic priests. Hus was burned at the stake for his "heresy" in 1415 and wars ensued between the Bohemian Hussites and their Roman Catholic compatriots; external Catholic powers of course got involved and the procession of violence in the name of God continued for a century till it sparked off the Thirty Years War.

The conflict between the Protestants and Catholics climaxed in 1618 in the Protestant revolt against Catholic Habsburg rule; but military defeat ensured the removal of Bohemian political independence for three centuries. Nonetheless, the independent spirit of the Bohemian people could not be extinguished. Protestantism and nationalism were suppressed and German became the universal language of education, yet the Czechs persisted in their demands for autonomy. The Romanticist period saw a revival in Czech nationalism and in 1848, the year of European revolts, the Czechs and Moravians attempted but failed to secure independence from the Habsburgs. The momentum continued into the 20th century when the Slovaks and Czechs were granted independence following the Versailles Treaty (1919). However, the presence of so many German-speaking Czechs gave Hitler an excuse for German occupation in 1938. Following the Second World War, a brief independent interlude was cut short when Soviet Russia expanded its influence in the area; in 1993 Czech and Slovakia separated, with the Bohemian territories belonging to the western half of what is now the Czech republic.

The continuity of some themes in Bohemian history underlines the strength of cultural beliefs in connecting generations with not just the recent past but also the distant past. The medium is ideas, which are sublimated as well as articulated in a society's language and in the history it teaches its new generations as well as the expectations it entrusts. The particular manifestations of the Bohemian striving for independence is unique but the general influence of the past on the present is not unique; similar histories can be told of many peoples: the Irish, for example, retained a dream and desire for independence that nationalists could readily tap into, especially following the effective martyrdom of the leaders of the Easter 1916 uprising.[45] Transplanted cultures often take with them vestiges of their previous existence, as the impact of immigrant cultures into the United States testifies.[46] What is of great fascination is the process by which hitherto mutual enemies turn into patriotic allies in their new homeland: its most visible form is the American story of the European migrants, a story that is beyond the remit of this book but which points us to the possibilities of peaceful settlements.

The next chapter expands on an important implication of the dynamic aspect of culture — namely that war can be seen as an unintentional development, a spontaneous convergence on a destructive institution.

NOTES

1.   *On Aggression*, p. 222.
2.   *The Ethics of War*, pp. 109-110.
3.   "Culture" is also usefully defined by Rand as "the sum of the intellectual achieve-
     ments of individual men, which their fellow citizens have accepted in whole or in
     part, and which have influenced the nation's way of life. Since a culture is a complex
     battleground of different ideas and influences, to speak of a "culture" is to speak
     only of the dominant ideas, always allowing for the existence of dissenters and ex-
     ceptions." Rand, *Philosophy: Who Needs It*, p. 205.
4.   Hayek postulates that: "It may well be asked whether an individual who did not
     have the opportunity to tap such a cultural tradition could be said to even have a
     mind." *Fatal Conceit*, p. 23. Consider also the plight of feral children.
5.   Hayek, *Law, Legislation, and Liberty*, vol. 1.
6.   Hayek, *Fatal Conceit*, p. 23.
7.   E.g., against intra-specific physical violence as with the howler monkey.
8.   In a simplistic reading of human nature, hedonists and utilitarians argue that man's
     actions are motivated solely by pain and pleasure. To increase learning, therefore,
     would entail increasing the pleasure involved in learning, or increasing the pain
     involved in not learning. Those rules that advance the long term benefits of the indi-
     vidual, vis à vis a member of a society, should thus supersede those rules that do not
     advance them However, while this thesis offers a simple explanation of many
     things, its failings lie in the positivist rendering that would have pain and pleasure
     measured. Such concepts — such entities even — are purely subjective phenomenon.
9.   The conditional is added, since evolution is not necessarily always "right" in the
     sense of producing the best — over adaptation of certain traits can result in a spe-
     cies' demise, for example the Irish Elk (extinct circa 500 BC) had antlers of up to
     4m wide.
10. This is the general thrust of Friedrich Hayek's philosophy, summarized in *The Fatal
     Conceit*.
11. Dawkins coined the term "memes" to express a cultural equivalent of "genes". *The
     Selfish Gene*, ch. 11, noting the useful properties for propagation as "longevity, fecun-
     dity, and copy-fidelity." p.194.
12. Different emphases may be placed on the extent that cultural forms evolve because
     of a specific environment versus sublimated expectations and rules of behavior that
     have evolved over hundreds of generations — both are explanatorily determinist,
     with the latter permits some notion of volition to enter group choices over genera-
     tions. The modern path in this methodological direction is provided by Vico.
13. For example, Ruth Benedict's school of "cultural psychology" asserts that cultures
     form theories of reality which condition the human mind. Such theories entail forms
     of epistemological relativism or polylogism; they ignore the universality of human
     reason. Often they are derived from Hegel's philosophy which asserts the primacy of
     cultural relativity.
14. White, for example, deems any links made to the human organism in the study of
     culture as not only irrelevant, but also wrong: "In short, the differences of behavior
     from one people to another are culturally, not biologically determined. In a consid-

eration of behavioral differences among people therefore we may regard the biological factor as a constant, and hence eliminate it from our calculations." Leslie
White, quoted in Dobzhansky, *Mankind Evolving*, p.74.

15. Yet has been held by various ideologies such as Marxism and Nazism.

16. Belittling racist conceptions of other peoples, or general misconceptions or a lack of
knowledge concerning the intelligence or tenacity of others has often caused disas-
ters on the battlefield, from the infamous Roman loss in Germania in AD 9 (Battle of
Teutoburger Wald) to the pitiful defenses at Hong Kong and throughout the Far
East against the supposedly ignorant Japanese in 1941.

17. The complementing historical hypothesis is that proto-human wars began as purely
cultural phenomena prior to the evolution of language and reason.

18. Simple example: nodding for yes.

19. I am intentionally ignoring the logical primary biological reaction for ease of elucidation here. For example, if a conflict situation arises, the body responds quicker
than the mind in increasing adrenaline, etc; but a person's body can also be trained
not to so react.

20. Although the success of individual adaptation is no guarantee that the general culture as embraced by the tacit and explicit actions and reasons of the majority will
be accepted at large. Arguably, the extent to which individual adaptation and innovation is acceptable is a function of the culture's general predisposition to new
ideas, if the majority of people are conservative, the innovative individual has a
harder time disseminating his new ideas, strategies, or products.

21. Lorenz, *On Aggression*, pp. 22-23

22. One of the most disturbing characteristics of the modern battlefield is the use of
child soldiers, who can be armed with very light machine guns at a very low cost.
Cf. Michael Ignatieff, *The Warrior's Honor*.

23. Cf. Mises, *Theory and History*, pp. 303-308.

24. Just as the outcome of a match between two soccer teams cannot be predicted from
what previous scores have been.

25. Meeting a new culture prompts a reorganization of the rules and codes of conduct
and the expectations people have of each other. This is obvious when a new culture
is encountered as Margaret Mead's experience of the Manus illustrates: "[W]hen
Margaret Mead first observed the Manus, their society seemed stable, even stag-
nant, and the people safe in supposing that they should always maximize the de-
lights of trading, quarrelling, and being in the right, and should fear the vengeance
of their ancestors for failure in these activities. That was the communal choice. But
when Manus life was disturbed by World War II, and change began to seem possible, it turned out that many people had not been satisfied. And, as some of Margaret
Mead's informants explained to her, they learned from the American soldiers that
people mattered more than property." Mary Midgley, *Beast and Man*, p.295. Cf. Mead,
New Lives for Old, 1956, pp. 177-8

26. Kant in *Perpetual Peace* argues that commerce provides one of three causal factors for
two nations to converge more onto peaceful than belligerent intercourse. The other
two are a growing universal acceptance of the rights of other nations' citizens fostering understanding of separate cultures, and the desire for security and welfare
lead different groups to form alliances and treaties, which are less likely to fall
apart, as Doyle comments, if a nation is predominantly politically liberal (i.e., ac-

cording to Kant, it is republican, acknowledges cosmopolitan laws, and seeks peace treaties with other liberal allies). Doyle, "Kant, Liberal Legacies, and Foreign Affairs", pp. 225-232.

27. "However and wherever war begins, it persists, it spreads, it propagates itself through time and space with the terrifying tenacity of a beast attached to the neck of living prey...War spreads and perpetuates itself through a dynamic that often seems independent of human will...If war is analogous to a disease, then, it is analogous to a contagious disease. It spreads through space, as groups take up warfare in response to warlike neighbors...it is a form of contact that no human group can afford to ignore or disdain." Ehrenreich, *Blood Rites*, pp. 132-133.

28. The expansion of commerce to undermine belligerency is also the premise of Kant's "Perpetual Peace" in *Political Writings*; later proponents included the Manchester School of Free Trade of Richard Cobden and John Bright.

29. Eighteenth century philosophers from Rousseau to Voltaire to Godwin admonished war for being initiated by those who did not have to pay the costs of life and destruction. Those who fought were of the ranks who also produced the wealth by which wars were often fought.

30. The "solution" is that the American seamen will try to shoot the Kamikaze pilot down and the Kamikaze pilot will try to kill himself by slamming his plane into the ship. The perversity of this example is that death for the Japanese pilots was valued over life: honor and prestige would come from a successful suicidal mission; in the typical game theory examples, the pay-off reflects a simplistic hedonist vision of human nature, that man seeks pleasure and attempts to avoid pain. The values of a suicide squad can be mathematically incorporated by game theory by including the protracted value of "life" and "eternal pleasures" in the hereafter, but valuing death certainly negates hedonistic principles that should support a secular existence!

US/Japanese	Die for Japan	Live for Japan
Shoot Kamikaze	100, 100	100, -100
Do not shoot Kamikaze	-100, 100	-100, -100

31. Especially the economists of the free-market school as opposed to mercantilists and even Keynesians.

32. "But the state is an individual, and...in its individuality, must generate opposition and create an enemy...Admittedly, war makes property insecure, but this *real* insecurity is no more than a necessary movement." Hegel, *Elements of the Philosophy of Right*, §324, addition G (trans. Nisbet).

33. Although the people themselves might not take up the sword, as Sir Thomas More envisioned in his *Utopia*, and the Vortigern of post-Roman Britannia, was apparently forced to do by hiring the services of the mercenary Hengist and his army, cf. *The Isles*, Norman Davies, pp.164

34. "To introduce into the philosophy of War itself a principle of moderation would be an absurdity." Clausewitz, *On War*, Book 1, Ch.1.3, p.102

35. Mead, "War is only an invention", p.270-1.

36. The origins of cultural change may be less obvious when cultural change comes from within. Internal cultural change happens when new religions, new philosophies, new codes of conduct, or even music and theatre, are generated within a soci-

ety, or new ideas may be prompted by exogenous or endogenous shocks to the economy — from population growth or decline, from the failure or expansion of the harvest, or from technological change. But once the new technology, for example, is grasped and used or accepted by the general populace, then the technology becomes a vehicle for the original idea of what it was primarily destined to be used for as well as a host of unforeseen developments in purpose and use. For example, the expansion of railroads and communications in the nineteenth century created an avalanche of social change and a corresponding expansion of new uses and products. The evidence of change can also be very apparent when societies are torn asunder as different groups attempt to deal with new ideas or new cultural demands in different ways. When reasoned argument and discourse fail, or agents demand quicker solutions to social ills, riot and even civil war may result.

37.　Johnson, *The Offshore Islanders*, p.49. Johnson argues that the uncivilized values of the Vikings, who invaded Britain between 865-878 AD, eventually led to their demise; and the same can be said of the Mongol invaders (1207-1227), for internal divisions eventually meant that the momentum of the initial successes of the Genghis and Kubla Khans evaporated.

38.　A feasible reason for this is the lack of genetic disparity in humanity, suggesting that genetic drift has been common; love can transcend cultural barriers.

39.　J.S. Mill, "Civilisation", p.122. The economist, Ludwig Mises, for example, writes: "With the exception of a small, negligible number of consistent anchorites, all people agree in considering some kind of social cooperation between men the foremost means to attain ends they aim at. This undeniable fact provides a common ground on which political discussions between men become possible. The spiritual and intellectual unity of all specimens of homo sapiens manifests itself in the fact that the immense majority of men consider the same thing — social cooperation — the best means of satisfying the biological urge, present in every living being, to preserve the life and health of the individual and to propagate the species." Mises, *Theory and History*, pp. 37-38

40.　Hoppe, *Democracy: The God that failed*, pp. 4-5

41.　If a position on the philosophy of mind is to be explained, it is that the particular content of the mind is ultimately dependent on the senses, on experience, and on reflection and conjecture from that experience, but also that the brain has evolved "programs" or the "hardware" for abstract thinking. Humans may thus possess innate predispositions to say the acquirement of language and even to curiosity, but such development and expansion of the particular content of the mind can only occur if an infant has been treated appropriately — being dependent on human contact an obvious requirement. As the human mind develops in the individual, not only explicit, linguistical commands are learned, but more is learned in the realm of tacit ideas generated from observing the conventions and attitudes in others, which in turn prompt the forming of implicit conclusions from facts, events, relations, and actions in the world. Something doctors finally seem to becoming round to accepting is that just as the organs of individuals differ in size, ability to cope with various ailments, etc., so to are human brains. But one thing that is often amiss in the debate that sometimes surfaces in the popular media is the possibility that the brain may also be developed by conscious effort, as any muscle can be affected by conscious intention through exercise. Some people may be born with the capacity to assimilate other languages quicker than others, or to do mathematics or learn a musical instrument quicker, yet they may not exploit this innate talent, while others may "train" their brains to learn an instrument through hard work, etc.

42.   The boundary between what is tacitly understood and what is explicitly understood is most certainly not definable or definitive. Knowing how to do something is often very different from knowing the process involved (e.g., consider tying shoe laces). This entails that when we come to understand the causal nature of war, we will not find a single definable cause, for there will be overlapping elements and conditions between what people may explicitly articulate and what they may actually do without conscious deliberation. One of the joys of humor or poetry for example, is enunciating what is often believed or understood tacitly — exploring the language of things that are "just done" through metaphor and insinuation. While we may readily recognize the effect and reason for the success of a joke concerning cultural behavior, we should not hesitate to pursue analogous thinking into other realms of human action.

43.   *From Dawn to Decadence: 1500 to the Present, 500 Years of Western Cultural Life,* Barzun, xviii.

44.   A review of Vaclav Havel's writings should convince the reader of the sustained independence of mind and culture that Prague has generated.

45.   Following the first executions, de Rosa comments on the change in Dublin's reaction from one of antipathy towards rebels to one of sympathy towards nationalists. "Already that most feared of critics, the back-street balladeer was writing songs that were being sung the length and breadth of Ireland." De Rosa, *Rebels: The Irish Rising of 1916,* p. 480. De Rosa emphasizes the lack of cultural understanding on the part of the British in their relations to the Irish, underestimating their own sense of independence and unique culture; it is a mistake often committed by occupying or invading powers.

46.   For an excellent history of the impact of particular cultures on various areas of the globe, cf. Thomas Sowell's *Conquests and Cultures.*

CHAPTER NINE: Unintentional War [1]

Cultural developments are the product of social interaction — of intercourse involving numerous people: their actions, speech, mannerisms, reactions, and so on. Moreover, cultural developments are forged not only at a given time and place, but also over time: a meeting between two people has repercussions not only in the time in which they talk and trade, but also in the repercussions that continue over time in the people's thoughts and memories. A brief encounter between two people (à la Noel Coward) can have long-lasting implications — and the impact of battles and wars of course can make or break states,[2] peoples, families, and individuals.

Since every encounter has immediate and long term ramifications, the meaning of an event can alter over time. Similarly, the stories we tell of past events alter and generate new, unintended meanings; however, a single meeting also involves communication and a convergence onto understandings that do not have to be uttered or expressed. Indeed, tacit understandings enable cooperation and hence enable increased production. Hume provides an excellent example of the workings of pre-rational, tacit mechanisms converging onto mutually benefiting rules, using the image of two men rowing a boat to illustrate the spontaneous emergence of conventions; the results of such convergence need not be articulated, or even be articulable: "Two men, who pull oars of a boat, do it by agreement or convention, tho' they have never given promises to each other."[3] They reach their destination — one can imagine, without a word being needed on how to row or where to row. A gesture suffices and the process of mutual aid gathers pace: the resulting rule or mode of behavior "arises gradually, and acquires force by a slow progression, and by our repeated experience of the inconveniences of transgressing it."[4]

Accordingly, what arises in cultures may not be the product or even the intention of a single mind, but the outcome of a plurality of intentions and actions. Although this theory is used by many thinkers to explore the beneficial institutions that have arisen spontaneously,[5] it can also be used to explain the genuine possibility that war may have emerged without any conscious intention on the part of early societies. Such products of interaction may also be said to remain embedded in implicitly supportive matrices of social interaction, language, ethics, and political assumptions because it has generated an internal dynamic of its own. This does not imply that man does not choose war, or that war chooses him: determinism is still to be rejected for what persists in human cultures are ideas and beliefs, and these are in turn learned and assimilated and acted upon volitionally by individuals.

The evidence from ethnology is that war is an unintended consequence — a product of a variety of cultural and economic factors. War seemingly originates as a solution to inter-societal conflict over resources and population pressures, or as an extension of sport or ritual;[6] arguably, war does not *originate* as the product of an articulated policy but as the result of many interacting factors that converge onto and then sustain forms of collective violence. Many anthropological theories touch on this cultural aspect of war's origins.

For instance, McDougall notes that the tribes of Central Borneo were constantly at war with one another and, if an intelligent chief were to be asked why, "the best reason he can give is that, unless he does, his neighbors will not respect him and his people and will fall upon them and exterminate them."[7] One can imagine that through seemingly benign intentions to encourage respect for the chief, the institution of the chief — and the expectations of office — had to show powers in putting down other tribes. Perhaps this was first done with insults and then with spiraling violence.[8] The descendants inherit something none of them would have wanted — a culture of incessant war and fear. The question for anthropologists is what particular factors prompted some communities to turn to collective violence.

Barbara Ehrenreich argues that the development of human warfare corresponds roughly with the global decline in large animals, a point at which humans began hunting animals more effectively, probably as a result of inventing spears and axes.[9] From over-hunting the traditional game, she argues, the propensity to hunt may have turned against humankind itself. At the same time nomadic populations began settling to farm. War may be the unintentional product of over-hunting and of rituals that turned from productive uses (hunting) to destructive uses (war). However, the benefits of war would still be evident, either in the form of acquiring others' property, women and herds, or in the obvious implication that if such values were not defended militarily, they would result in the annihilation or assimilation of the group.

Regardless of its initial origins, war, Ehrenreich observes that war is a contagious phenomenon, and Doyle concurs; "war — is basically a set of epidemics become, in the larger perspective, endemic to the international state of war."[10] An act of aggression has to be defended against and/or revenged; once begun, for whatever cause or motivation, it has a tendency to gain its own momentum — over and above the capacity of participants to control it. War thus becomes an evolving institution and it influences and may even dominate the linguistic, political, moral, and economic direction societies take.

Accordingly, the philosophical problem is that war may result from a two-pronged unintentional consequence. Firstly, from ideational formation in which beliefs are formed and internalized in meanings and expectations of a group, and secondly from internalized customs. Neither may be removed piecemeal without affecting a whole matrix of what may turn out to be detrimental unforeseeable consequences and on which entire sub-matrices of activities (including war) may depend. This means that attempts to abolish war by political means alone are bound to fail or be vulnerable to pre-rational, culturally dominating upheavals and rejections of rational discourse. War became, and remains, immersed in the tacit and behavioral expectations of most societies.

Ideas that are no longer productive or beneficial to a community do not disappear abruptly once they are challenged by reasoned or enlightened argument.[11] Language — with its emotionally evocative powers — may, for a time, sustain institutions which cooler thinking deems inapplicable or undesirable: for example in calling wars "glorious", the casualties of wars "collateral damage", or implying that men become "real men" through fighting.[12] Against such notions General Sherman declared: "There is many a boy here today who looks on war as all glory, but, boys, it is all hell."[13] Yet the glory of war was not undiminished by the horrors of the US Civil War nor the First War; in fact, the latter unleashed a century of intensive and increasingly total war.

What this implies is that a conservatism is necessarily present in cultural development and in the articulation of arguments — not only in the sense that new ideas take their time to penetrate the minds of other people, but also in the sense of the slow adaptation of words and the worlds of intentions and feelings they secure. Language, and hence cultural traditions, permit the succession of ideas over time that nobody truly intends, nor truly can define, nor articulate fully. The origins of war lie beyond the pale of reason, and its abolition may therefore be beyond man's intellectual capacity.

Theoretically, a possible solution to abolish war lies in a gradualist approach to the alteration of the matrices of meanings attached to words through a concerted effort to apply a more explicit definition of their meanings, and through changing the ideational rules and expectations people have of each other and of the world, i.e., through alterations in tacit as well as explicit beliefs.

For example, that war has been called a "glorious activity", whose participants are to be hailed as heroes, may be assailed with the consequences of war so readily communicated by modern media methods. Arguably, the glorification of war that was prominent prior to the First World War could be said to have steadily declined in recent decades: war's cultural-linguistic support has changed, at least in some quarters of the West, in the face of the evidence of war's brutality on our TV screens; on the other hand, this is counteracted no doubt by the proliferation of computer games in which young children can make the most graphic "kills" and the real computer and remote images of rockets that hit distant, anonymous targets and buildings in the recent technological developments since the Gulf War (1990-91) that mimic the computer games available in main street arcades.[14]

The application of explicit reason to the implicit, unarticulated, tacit values and expectations that are subsumed in language can unravel the origins of particular cultures' decline into collective violence. However, words, theories, and explanations are not sufficient: that is, what is called the political rationalist line of positively engineered laws or exhortations and appeals to man's reason cannot generate peace. Only counter-cultural practices acting alongside reason can thoroughly undermine war's appeal. Here, free traders and classical liberals[15] propose the expansion of commercial activity, which reaches into the tacit conventions that spontaneously form between people through trade, and which promotes such transformations to the peaceful life on deeper and more permanent levels; Kant writes, "the *spirit of commerce* sooner or later takes hold of every people, and it cannot exist side by side with war."[16] Accordingly, for such writers the spread of the appropriate civil values that emerge from trade, especially that of trust, acts to ameliorate the almost endemic joys of war.[17] The extension of commerce also acts to reduce the threat of war by bringing people into a mutually beneficial matrix in which the cost of waging war against those with whom one trades increases substantially.

Internalized customs thus may continue to sustain undesirable institutions such as war. Customary reactions to perceived threats that some of the group would eventually like to jettison may never be discarded if the actions and interactions of the members of the group sustain their existence. That is, so long as people continue to converge or fall back onto a particular custom or tradition, behavioral or institutional norms and mores may continue over generations. In the theories of war's origins, the employment of surplus males may have prompted the perpetuation of war as a displacement for their energies.[18] At the individual level of interaction, people will support those rules and institutions that are seen to be and/or have proven, or are assumed to have been proven to be, beneficial to the group over the long run. In times of crisis, the pull to older forms of behavior that sustained the group in the past becomes evident. In peacetime though, such reasonably benign actions may foster and maintain institutions inimical to peace.

If ideas lead to wars, and if ideas are formed from observation, imitation *and reflection* formed in a cultural-linguistic framework whose nature is partly the result of unintended effects, then plausibly the ideas and behavioral norms that support war are transmitted across generations. There is then a temporal lag in social change, which means that the realm of tacit knowledge (held in pre-linguistic, pre-rational, or non-rational forms) can be a continuing source of aggressive war. Opposing the attempts of governments, philosophers and campaigners to abolish war, the greater body of humanity may continue to give indirect as well as direct support to warfare through the cultural momentum that originates in a group's deep past. If this is true, then humanity falls into a sociological trap and war can never be abolished by design.

The arenas over which tacit and explicit knowledge hold sway are not mutually exclusive. Explicit, articulated forms depend much on unarticulated forms of knowledge. Nonetheless, explicit arguments may influence the customary actions of people by pointing out contradictions with other rules and expectations they have, or showing their obvious uselessness.[19] Reason — in the sense of the application of consciously articulated argument (logic) — should not be discounted, but its remit is very much limited by the intransigence of a people unwilling to lift their minds up from the cultural morass they have fallen into, as well as by the cultural inertia that the tacit and inter-generational transmission of knowledge fosters.

When we consider warfare, it can be reasonably argued that it arose originally as a cultural institution that met group needs. War itself, as well as the content of how wars should be waged (the rules of engagement), evolved as a solution to pressing problems — of territorial rights, of population delimiters, and of resource use. Regardless of the different theories that have been proposed concerning the biological benefits of what can be called "primitive war", and regardless of the independent validity of each proposition, we can entertain the general conclusion that initially human war originally evolved as *"a product of human action but not of human design."*[20]

At the level of "low primitive war" — of unarticulated, pre-rational, non-political war — war is wholly an unintended enterprise, in the sense that it is a purely cultural phenomenon which falls below the extent of articulated intentions. As such, low primitive war bridges the gap between animal and human war and is probably only relevant for proto-human groups. For high primitive war, articulated beliefs may invoke war's necessity: each foray or battle may be organized and deliberated over. But what is implicit is that the participants may not be in a position to justify warfare or to account for its requirement, except by invoking atavistic reasons — noting that it has always been the case.

War becomes, in this analysis, an institution that has survived the test of adaptability, for it has proved a successful institution for some groups, at some times. It has meant their survival, and even their expansion. It has assisted the successful warring group to transmit its own cultural structures and reproduce its own members successfully.

However, a shocking implication of this is the apparently repugnant conclusion of moral positivism: that "might is right".[21] For if war has proved successful for a group, then why should a belligerent group entertain peaceful conduct with its neighbors? And is the retort that aggressive war and other forms of parasitic behavior are inherently self-destructive, and are illogical on evolutionary principles, sufficient to prove their inefficiency? If aggressive war is a parasitical enterprise, then, like any form of parasitism, it requires the continued existence of those forms of activity or of life that allow the parasite to live — in the case of war, enemies. Yet war need not be a parasitical enterprise, especially if we take Ehrenreich's hypothesis that war evolved following the demise of communal big game hunting: the complete destruction of the enemy would be a counter-productive act if valuable assets could continue to be acquired through permanent and periodic warfare. This complements the hunter's strategy of ensuring enough game are left over to secure their exploitation for future hunts. However, the retort is that, as Ehrenreich notes, the advent of weaponry and long range weapons for hunting led to the overkill and extinction of some species, and the same threat arises with human war. Its innate destructive momentum may overwhelm any benefits that may be had from limiting war and limited warfare. But while animal and primitive war could hardly become so exploitative as to annihilate the hosts (for that would prove *ipso facto* self-destructive), war above the military horizon of public armies and long-range weaponry could become so self-destructive, as the inherent logic of the Cold War testified.

Following this implication further, any possible limits to total war evaporate once permanent forms of government are created. Wars enacted by governments — "true wars", in the literature — are highly organized, Clausewitzian *political affairs*. Armies are created that fall under the general rules of organization and whose deployment and engagement in warfare are defined intentionally by the government. War, with its reasons, extent, and aims, is now "above board", as it were: why a war is declared, and what are its objectives, are verbalized and hence are amenable to reasoning and political processes. Political or "true war", in contrast to primitive war, *is* the result of articulated design (although its origins lie in the spontaneous evolution of cultural institutions). But here is the optimist's escape clause: if war is the result of human design, it follows that its abolition *is within human capacity.*

Nonetheless, what people desire from government is not always enacted out by government. The rules of organizing the government's jurisdiction need not comply with the expectations held by the people.[22] Or vice versa. This means that war can be let in through the back door of even the most rationally codified of states, for it is an institution that has generally been culturally successful and which has seeped into tacit and behavioral expectations, and thus it continues to be *tacitly* expected of governments to implement, even if reason proves its inherent destructiveness. Government leaders may easily rekindle — or exploit as demagogues — the cultural framework of which they are a part; and it is these unarticulated expectations, as well as explicit thoughts, beliefs, notions, and conjectures — i.e., the cultural-philosophical matrix of society — that converge unintentionally onto a traditional acceptance of war as the "proper" solution to international problems.

In summary, the implication is that war is a result of the general evolutionary processes of cultural and ideational selection, one that has proved successful in the past to some groups and may well do so in the future. If governments are subject to the pressures of public opinion, as David Hume maintains, the demand for war is "voted on" by the general population through implicit as well as explicit support. Hence war continues to exist, regardless of the well-intentioned objections of the few who may oppose it.

Nonetheless, a government is able to wage war regardless of the (tacit) cultural affinities of the people. A government is typically in a position to use, or rather abuse, its status as possessing a monopoly on the use of force to enslave citizens for aggressive war, as the Taliban and other "rogue" regimes have shown themselves to be highly capable of doing. Edmund Burke reflected that "tyrants seldom want pretexts",[23] for they can usurp the power of government that is invested in them for their own purposes. But the most successful tyrants are those who tap into the latent expectations their cultures possess, stirring old enmities and the desire for glory or self-identification in war.

In complex societies, the means of successful adaptation permit individual members to pursue their own ends, which in turn foster the dissemination and transmission of knowledge through market and cultural institutions. War becomes a counter-productive institution that no longer meets the demands of complex societies: its existence becomes increasingly costly in terms of alternative uses and attractions. However, the potential for war's maintenance is high — considering the cultural lag that exists because of the tacit, pre-rational agreements and expectations we make of one another. And this is especially so if the external situation — the presence of aggressors and bellicose states — maintains the need for a militant aspect. (Incidentally, against the neo-Kantian optimism that man is predisposed towards peace and that democracies do not foster belligerent attitudes or do not go to war,[24] one only has to look at the American Civil War or more recently to the popular election in 1990 of Slobodan Milosevic: democracy implies rule of the majority, and the majority are often the greatest harbingers of old ideas and traditional expectations and hence the greatest conduits of aggressive foreign policies and war.)

When man began to settle and farm the lands, he unintentionally set his progeny on the road to what we now know as civilization — urbanization, writing, the broadening and deepening of the division and specialization of labor, the rise of codified rules and more systematic international trade, and so on. But in very few areas of the globe could that advancement proceed without some threat or violence of war. That has meant the culture of war has persisted. In the next chapter, we examine the added complexities generated by the interplay between civilization and culture.

Notes

1. Elements of this section were published in "Is War a Hayekian Spontaneous Institution?" in *Peace and Change*, January 2002.

2. On war's effects on the state, cf. Bruce Porter's *War and the Rise of the State*, summary in Ch.2.

3. David Hume, *A Treatise of Human Nature*, p.490.

4. David Hume, *A Treatise of Human Nature*, p.490.

5. Adam Smith coined the useful metaphor of an "invisible hand" to express the beneficial results of self-interested action. Cf. *Wealth of Nations*. A similar phrase is also found in ancient Chinese philosophy, cf. Roderick T. Long, "Rituals of Freedom: Austro-Libertarian Themes in Confucianism", working paper for Austrian Scholars Conference, 2002, held at http://www.mises.org.

6. Cf. Keegan, *History of Warfare*, pp.24-60

7. McDougall, "The Instinct of Pugnacity", p. 34.

8. Keegan explores the ultimate extrapolation of a total war culture on the Easter Islands, which led almost to the natives' extinction, *History of War*, pp.24-28

9. Barbara Ehrenreich, *Blood Rites*, p. 120.

10. Michael Doyle, "Kant, Liberal Legacies, and Foreign Affairs, Part Two", p.351

11. Witness the revival of religion in Western Europe in the early to mid-Nineteenth Century following its demise in the Eighteenth and its Age of Reason.

12. Ehrenreich, *ibid.*, 127

13. Quotation from a speech given in 1880.

14. Cf. Ignatieff, *Virtual War*.

15. E.g., David Hume, "Of the Jealousy of Trade" in *Essays Moral, Political, and Literary*; Immanuel Kant, "Perpetual Peace"; Adam Smith, *The Wealth of Nations*; David Ricardo, *Principle of Political Economy and Taxation*; Richard Cobden, *The Political Writings of Richard Cobden*.

16. Kant, "Perpetual Peace", p.114 (trans. Nisbet)

17. Kant, in his "Perpetual Peace", employs the pacifying tendency of trade; however, his argument rests on the *inevitability* of progress (i.e., a historicist conception of history) which entails that man is not free to make mistakes and to retun to earlier forms of barbarity — as he indeed did in the 20th century.

18. Ehrenreich, *op cit.*, Ch.7

19. For example, superstitious rituals fall into both categories: they contradict the physical sciences in their attempted explanations of natural phenomena, and conflict with modes of living that presume the world to be a place not inhabited by demons and ghosts. Nonetheless we can recognize that superstitions, mythologies, and religions evolved and continue to meet human needs. The popular forms were successful -in the sense of being accepted popularly, for they were able to meet some of man's latent expectations and curiosities. But they become outdated or outmoded when other, more successful explanations that reflect the nature of reality better are proposed.

20. Quoting Adam Ferguson, in Hayek, "Dr Bernard Mandeville (1670-1733)", p.96.

21. For early theories and criticism of the 'might is right' theory, cf. Plato's *Republic*, trans. Alan Bloom, and the conversations with Thrasymachus 338c ff.

22. Although it the fabled long-run of economists, all government's powers are dependent on the support of the population. Cf. Hume, "Of the first principles of government", in *Essays Moral, Political, and Literary*, p.32

23. Burke, *Letter to a member of the National Assembly*, 1791.

24. Cf. for instance, Doyle "Kant, Liberal Legacies, and Foreign Affairs," and Rawls, *The Law of Peoples*. The Ancient Greeks and all those influenced by their political debates (including the Founding Fathers of the States) retained a healthy mistrust of democracy; after all, as Plato was wont to remind us, democracy condemned Socrates.

CHAPTER TEN: Between Culture and Reason —
Civilization and War

It has often been argued that man's move towards a civilized life causes war[1] — that the initial shift to a sedentary existence, or to more complex forms of law and government, produced the economic, political and social factors that brought war upon an unsuspecting humanity (or a humanity guilty of choosing civil life). Civilization, according to its critics, taints human nature, bringing out the worst of human vices as men fight over artificial values such as property, money, and national borders. Before civilization, the story goes, there was no war, no famine; the animals conversed and lived peacefully side by side, man was a vegetarian and Eve was truly obedient. In short, life was sweet.

The implication of blaming civilization for war is that peace can be achieved by curtailing urbanization and its trappings: only by returning to a sedentary existence can the necessary counteracting measures for abandoning warfare be developed. That is, man must return to his prelapsarian state in the Garden of Eden, and peace will follow. On the other hand, Thomas Hobbes famously describes uncivil life (the state of nature) as solitary, poor, nasty, brutish and short,[2] and sees the formation of permanent government (his Leviathan) as the route to peace. But for many, especially Jean-Jacques Rousseau, who condemn the advent of civilization, the life of the "noble savage" is far preferable: only there are man's natural feelings and intuition unencumbered by artificial values.

The two great thinkers posit two disparate views of nature. For Hobbes, it is an unremitting hell; for Rousseau it is heaven. For Hobbes, war is endemic in the state of nature; for Rousseau, leaving that state brings war. The actual situation is more complex, of course.

The roots of war are multifarious and are derived from all aspects of man's nature. The cultural and biological remnants of past social systems that support war may linger on in his adaptation to a settled, sedentary and then urban life. Yet civilization also prolongs man's life and expands the opportunities for individuals and communities to enjoy a more variegated and extended life, but not for all. Some — most certainly a minority — choose not to enjoy the freedom civilization offers, while others, in some cases because of the political system they are in, are unable to access the benefits civil life affords.

But philosophically, whether man is "happier" now than he was in the Paleolithic cannot be proven; is a person happier at this moment than he was during a moment last week? All that can be said is that according to the general assumption that most people prefer more to less[3] — more life, more products (whatever their nature), man is better off today. But that cannot resolve whether he is happier or not, for the contents of the mind are personal and unique and not accessible to research. However, civilization — and especially industrial civilization — has presented more opportunities for man to pursue his happiness (and whatever criteria that entails): a longer, healthier, life, more leisure time and more products to enjoy. Yet the peace and wealth of civilized life is not only vulnerable to war, many still attack it for being the root *cause* of war.

Aside from those philosophers who applaud the state of nature or the edenic golden age, others point to archeological evidence that prehistoric war apparently emerges with the advance of civilization.[4] However, the lack of evidence for pre-historic war does not mean that war did not take place, for wooden weapons are not likely to survive and stone implements used for butchering animals could also have been used in hand-to-hand fighting. Alternatively, others blame the extinction of big game, which resulted in the need to settle down to farm, rather than civilization, per se, for war.[5] Accordingly, war is said to originate from hunting patterns that are then culturally transmitted into inter-societal warfare with the evolution of settled life.[6] Hunting and farming are often blamed for man's belligerence — yet it was not a meat eater that turned Europe into a cauldron of total war in 1939.[7]

On the contrary, civilization brings a plethora of opportunities for economic and epistemic expansion that the "state of nature" does not. While it must be recognized that it also brings the possibility of "unleashed boundless violence,"[8] civilization produces more goods than the uncivil state; it is when those goods are usurped by warriors or states for belligerent rather than peaceful purposes that war takes on the horrendous breadth witnessed in the 20th century.

The hypothesis that civilization is the cause of war is misplaced. Wars certainly occur below the "military horizon" of sedentary existence,[9] and they occur in the animal kingdom. What civilization offers is an intensification of the energy and resources that can be channeled into wars.[10] Even if it can be established factually that war did emerge with civilized society and that prehistoric man was generally a peaceful beast, it does not necessarily follow that war can be abolished by returning to a more primitive existence — were that at all possible.[11] War, once initiated, may have its own cultural and political dynamic and momentum that straddle the generations and bind them to the past; but removing the initial cause may not remove the present cause. Returning man to a state of nature in which money, property, trade, technology, and education do not exist would not only extinguish five billion lives or so (for we would have to return to the low populations that the pre-developed world could sustain), but neither would it necessarily abolish war. The reconstituted "eco-friendly, pacifistic, vegetarian, new stone age man" would take with him many of the ideas and beliefs that now sustain his understanding of the world — but even if the "pure" in heart and mind (the elect) could begin again in a communist society, conflict would soon arise. The reasoning is as follows: in a unpropertied world, factors of production would still need to be deployed to produce food and shelter, and the resulting produce would have to be distributed by a mechanism other than price signals. Without price signals, no economic calculation by producers or consumers could take place.[12] The deployment of factors of production (land, labor, capital) would be ordered by command rather than exchange. A command economy could not rationally distribute resources in the sense that although resources may be channeled according to political or moral criteria, the lack of economic calculation (normally set by prices on markets) entails production and consumption are blind to the real costs.[13]

The unintended or even intended results of the political directing of commodities generates frustration and arguably creates conditions for conflict. This is especially so in heterogeneous nations in which particular groups hold political power over ethnic minorities and can thus withhold production or consumption opportunities from them. Command economies must distribute resources according to non-economic criteria; unless the command economy has a global reach, they must recognize property rights by claiming all resources as belonging to their own particular jurisdiction. In a system of nationally defined command economies, the lack of resources in one area and the inefficiency or nonexistence of trade between political units cannot but generate generate economic and political frustration that again easily turns to war.[14] In a system without national or property boundaries — i.e., a state of anarchy — there would be nothing to stop marauding bands from pillaging the more economically productive peoples. The vision of humanity enjoying the fruits of civilization without its institutions is a romantic vision that on a closer look cannot be sustained.

But to dispel fully the myth that civilization brings war, it is worth examining its nature.

NATURE OF CIVILIZATION

Civilization can broadly be characterized, in political terms, by the rule of law, the existence of private property, the formation of institutions of arbitration (courts, government), and the minimization or absence of violence, the objective control of force. Socially, it can be characterized by the existence of permanent settlements and an extended division and specialization of labor, and so on.

Civilization per se does not cause war, for the rule of force is inimical to the essence of civilization. Civilization — and the extension of property rights — pacifies man and prompts him to look to cooperation and to the future, rather than to violence and the present:[15] nonetheless, what civilization produces may be used for martial purposes when expropriated from private producers, especially if the dominant ideology of a people seek value in war.

Liberalism[16] asserts that all civilizations rest on peaceful cooperation. Peace within and without a group's borders is necessary for the benefits from the advantages of cooperative effort to flow, whereas a constant fear of war and predation raises the costs that must to be borne in terms of defenses and preparations. In turn, civilizations tend to foster and cultivate values that emphasize peace and cooperation, in which capricious violations and crimes by individuals are condemned by common rules of conduct favoring the just use of force by a neutral government. Such is the logic of the modern liberal theory of government in which the rule of law supersedes the rule of the arbitrary monarch, the warrior class, or the mob.[17] Liberalism is rejected by a variety of schools that stress the repressive aspect of civilization. Romanticists, for example, claim civilization represses natural instincts and divert man's energies into destructive tendencies; socialists argue that capitalist civilization is a rationalization for the oppression of one class over another; environmentalists emphasize civilization's destruction of natural resources.

Those who reject liberalism may see anti-social behavior as symptomatic of civilization's artificial constraints. Liberals, however, define criminals as those who seek to overthrow or exploit the product of peaceful society, who wish to undermine the conditions of civil life. Rather than earn their income, they seek to take and steal their income through force and fraud. Such actions are not conducive to civilized life, and *a fortiori* criminal activity abroad in the form of aggressive war — the plundering of others' resources — is not conducive to enjoying the gains of cooperative enterprise from international trade. War and crime destroy capital and diminish man's ability to produce for the future, which is evinced in war-torn nations struggling to produce beyond the bare sustenance and therefore deplete the population of its ability to survive: famine in such areas is endemic and the population live a precarious existence.[18]

Extended and open societies enjoying a broad division and specialization of labor and the ensuing profitable fruits of industry are often targeted by belligerent predation. A cultivated field makes an easy and attractive target for a nomadic group, permitting nomadic tribes or a warrior class to exist parasitically on groups who have settled down or who are enslaved to produce. A famous case is that of the Spartans, who lived vicariously on the economic activity of the *helots*, who worked the land and produced the economic product required for the warrior race;[19] ultimately, their parasitism came to an end as the once successful warrior culture became inflexible and unable to change in the face of their enemies' strategic adaptations. Inflexibility — so inimical to civil life — dooms societies, whether they are pre-civilized groups or highly developed urbanized cultures. Flexibility is begotten by pluralism and individualism; together with the concomitant conditions of freedom and the rule of law, flexibility and adaptability are crucial for civilizations that need to continue developing and adapting to new problems. But is the civilizing process sufficient in itself to end or to limit war?

Immanuel Kant argued that modern liberal (free, republican) societies will, as if through a Smithian invisible hand, generate a sufficient peace between them that will spread internationally.[20] The internal biological and cultural dynamics of civilization, he thought, will be sufficient to abandon warfare: civilizations have more to lose from war than they have to gain, and the reach of mutually beneficial commercial interests will diminish the incentives for war.

There is much hope in this viable argument and one that underpinned the optimism of the Manchester free trader, Richard Cobden, in the mid-19th century plea for the end of war through the expansion of commerce.[21] Nonetheless, civilizations do go to war — often for atavistic purposes and motives that linger on in their cultural make up or for ideological reasons. Thus it is important to distinguish between the definition of civilization as encompassing the intensification of the division and specialization of labor within a framework of peace, and the implied ethical standard: that civilization entails the abandonment of force. Elaborating on Kant's theories for perpetual peace, Doyle argues that liberal (civilized) societies do not wage war[22] — by definition. When they apparently do, Doyle conveniently redefines them as illiberal, since a liberal (civil) society does not wage war; however, he glosses over the many wars which democratic nations have actively participated in and not always from reasons of self-defence.[23]

Economically speaking, any civilized society is capable of waging war when the economic product of civilization is usurped and exploited for military means. Whether the war is for aggression or for defense, civilizations are taken into war by a belief in war's efficacy, its justness, or its necessity. War in turn generates conditions for its survival: states adapt and organize for war and in doing so make later wars easier to organize. Wars affect the nature of civilization by generating centralized bureaucracies and states, which are then in a position to exploit social resources for the advancement both of the state and of war.[24]

Regardless of the economics of war, which requires a separate volume, what is of interest to the philosophy of war is that a civil society may retain uncivil beliefs in the efficacy or value of war, such as the philosophy of might over right, the support of the arbitrary or unlimited use of force, the goal of economic (imperial) aggrandizement, the glorification of tyranny and of heroic warriors, and so on, as well as a host of cultural relics from ages past in which war was a glorified and successful institution. What must be rejected at this point is the theory or the implied theory that with the advent of civilization and the state, man becomes a thoroughly rational animal and relinquishes his prior cultural reactions and structures,[25] but this also must lead us to a skepticism of programs that seek peace through man's rehabilitation, re-education, or other forms of social engineering that emanate from writings across the political spectrum.[26]

With the rise of civilization, it is true that more destructive weapons were invented as a result of the extended division and specialization of labor. But the purposes to which they are put are not in any sense determined by the existence of that division of labor or by the private property, cooperation, and markets that made the wealth possible. The purpose of any product is governed by what people think it ought to be used for — once expropriated by the officers of the state, it may be deployed militarily for defense or for aggression; and herein lies the rub for civilization, for many historical echoes of war's usefulness may reside within its walls.

It would thus be wrong to suggest that the advent of civilization brought forth more destructive forms of warfare. The fundamental forms of warfare available to civilized and non-civilized societies remain unchanged as economies develop, deepen, and grow. Undeveloped and developed societies both could enact indiscriminate and total warfare in which no restraints are employed. It is also not historically accurate to claim that civilization developed "civilized warfare" with its codes of just conduct: just and fair rules in war are known to non-civilized and to civilized societies.[27] Nevertheless, such rules are more likely to develop in wars between similar societies[28] that can agree to — or perceive — the mutually benefiting restrictions on the extent of war. Such a perception comes more readily to a society that already possesses a deeper conception of the longer term consequences of actions than one that seeks only present gratifications.

In the case of wars between different civilizations,[29] common rules of conduct have no mutually beneficial basis to develop, except from self-imposed restraints. Restraints are less likely in wars between different civilizations, since the combatants are not likely to envisage peaceful cooperation with their enemies and the enemies are often morally de-humanized: that is, they are not considered part of any utilitarian calculus. Both civil and uncivil forms of society have enacted policies of unlimited warfare and scorched earth, sparing none and destroying everything; and both forms of society have been guilty of the most atrocious acts of war, as well as having acted to mitigate some of war's excesses. But why wars occur, and why they take the particular forms they do, ultimately rests on peoples' ideologies, not on the generation or advancement of civilization. Ideas give people purposes; effects do not.

Civilization itself is thus not responsible for war or for its conduct. It confers benefits on humanity by unleashing individual talents through the extended division and specialization of labor. As many are wont to note, civilization has invented the most destructive technologies — from gunpowder to nuclear arsenals, but it has also invented the most creative technologies and the means to combat illnesses, to educate, and to extend life expectancies and reduce mortality rates.[30] What is crucial is what we do with the product of civilization, and while that does demand an ethical and political analysis of the nature of the good life, for our purposes here, the remnants of determinist thinking are to be rejected: civilization itself neither pacifies man nor turns him into an envying belligerent. It is in the realm of his thoughts that his actions are governed from.[31]

War is predominantly the result of ideas, not of the environment or the technical state in which people exist. Often, the ideas supporting and motivating men to war are inimical to civilized life, which demands peace and the rule of law; such ideas, as has been gleaned from the previous chapters, motivate pre-rational conceptions that men have of one another — the tacitly held and culture-specific beliefs that may lie beneath the surface of articulated argument but which are roused by demagoguery or threats to the commonweal.

Ideas that support warfare can be divided into those whose purpose is to support and defend civilization and peace from predation and aggression, and those whose purpose is to violate the fabric of peace and disrupt the fragile bonds of mutually benefiting markets and institutions. Some philosophers see no differences in war's purposes, denying that aggression and defense are separable categories (rationalizing, say, that war is endemic to human relations), but in doing so they belie a criticism of the values and benefits of civilization — of peace, security and progress. It is not without irony that the political rationalist theory of war often depends on the assumption that civilization generates war and that wars are the product of the ruling politics of the relevant groups. This theory is critiqued in the next chapter.

Notes

1. Dyer, for example, observes: "[A]ll the wars and the massacres, the ruthless application of power and the unrestrained cruelty of the victors, were implicit in the invention of civilization." Dyer, *War*, p.33
2. Hobbes, *Leviathan*, p.186
3. Mises, *Human Action*, Part One: Acting Man.
4. Leakey, for instance, records that "[b]eyond the beginning of the [prehistoric] agricultural revolution...the depictions of battles virtually vanish." Leakey, *Origins*, p.233
5. Ehrenreich, *Blood Rites*, pp. 118-119
6. Similarly, Fagan comments that; "warfare can be rejected as a primary cause of civilization without much discussion since large military conflicts appear to have been
a result of civilization, not a direct cause of it." Fagan, *People of the Earth*, p.426
7. Adolf Hitler.
8. Dyer, *op cit.*, p.33
9. Fagan, *ibid.*, p.426
10. I.e., the expanded division and specialization of labor characteristic of civilizations
produces greater amounts of wealth that may be exploited for war.
11. Demographically, such proposals would imply reducing the present population of
around 6bn to around 1m.
12. Cf. Mises, *Socialism*, Part II, "The Economics of a Socialist Community."
13. For example, imagine a centrally planned system desires to produce more cars for
the poor. What materials should be used? What size should the car be? What fuel
should it use? How efficient should the engine be relative to other criteria such as
speed and internal comfort? How much labor and capital should be diverted to car
production and away from health? The matrix of potential resources and their com-
binations cannot be comprehended without prices: a price, generated by the demand and supply for a given product, presents a socially formed signal of its relative
scarcity and utility to the engineers working on a car. Without prices, they do not
know whether they are overusing or underusing a particular factor of production or
material.
14. For example, Germany's population substantially grew in the 19th century, but its
people were barred from migrating to the British colonies or to other areas of low
population density. The concomitant pressures (lower domestic wages and hence
falling relative standards of living) in the face of migratory barriers created a dire
problem that could be solved either by permitting free migration or by German
aggression against the barriers. Such pressures added another causal layer to growing German militarism that finally burst forth in 1914.
15. Cf. Hoppe, *Democracy: The God that Failed*, on the nature of time-preferences and civilizing actions. Ch.1
16. Both modern and classical liberalism subscribe to the view that civilization requires
peace and that stable political conditions with a neutral government are necessary
to support social and individual development within the confines of a civil community. For an exposition of a classical and modern conception of liberalism cf. Mises,
Liberalism and Rawls, *The Law of Peoples* respectively.
17. Although Hoppe, in *Democracy: the God that Failed*, offers an interesting economic

analysis of the benefits of monarchy, namely that monarchies are likely to possess a longer view of the future than democracies, which are inherently present-oriented; accordingly, stable monarchies are more likely to be conducive to economic growth than democracies. Hoppe criticizes both for their potential to usurp private resources and argues for a property owning republic.

18. E.g., Ethiopia in modern times or the Germanic states during the Thirty Years War.

19. Interestingly, Plato uses the Spartan kingdom as a blueprint for his *Republic* — the warrior élite are replaced by a philosophical élite and the class system is based not on race but on ability, but the general division between classes is to remain.

20. Recently promoted by Michael Doyle "Kant, Liberal Legacies, and Foreign Affairs."

21. Which contrasts with the vociferous imperialism of the art critic John Ruskin!

22. Doyle, "Kant, Liberal Legacies, and Foreign Affairs, Parts 1 and 2."

23. One could include the American Civil War, the Boer War, the Boxer Rebellion, and the Korean and Vietnam wars; however, each of these examples are controversial – the fact that a democratic nation goes to war does not in itself invalidate Doyle's claim, for what is important is the reason the nation goes to war: for illiberal purposes, such as aggrandizement, or for liberal purposes, such as to halt a genocide or extended self-defense?

24. Porter, *War and the Rise of the State.*

25. Reflecting the subtle but pervasive theory that with civilization man became a completely rational animal Dawson writes: "The *cultural* balance of power, in which most human societies had been trapped for thousands of years, was replaced by the *political* balance of power, which has endured to the present day." *Origins of Western Warfare,* p.38 It is a subtle criticism, but balance of power political theories assume the rationality of the political process; Clausewitz, the most famous modern proponent of the doctrine, espoused that war is the continuation of politics by other means, and many modern historians, such as Michael Howard, nod their aggreement. The theory is examined and rejected in the next chapters.

26. Anarcho-libetarians, Marxists, and other utopians are often in agreement that if only X changes then Peace will follow. For anarcho-libertarians that may involve an 'understanding' of the innate oppressiveness of the state; for Marxists an understanding of class consciousness. Utopian philosophers seek perpetual peace in redesigning man and/or his institutions rather than looking at his present nature and history and learning from his mistakes and successes. Cf. Thomas More, *Utopia* for an excellent blue-print for the perfect society, as one capable mind saw it.

27. By non-civilized societies is meant those which do not possess writing and/or a permanent form of government, or a settled community. For a history of just war practices and theory, cf. eds. John Kelsay and James Turner Johnson, *Just War and Jihad: Historical and Theoretical Perspectives on War and Peace in Western and Islamic Traditions.*

28. What Veale calls "secondary types" of war. *Advance to Barbarism.*

29. What Veale calls "primary types" of war in *Advance to Barbarism.*

30. Stephen Clark, a thoughtful critic of industrialism and environmentalism, comments, "I am certainly so far a man of my time and place that were I faced with a direct choice between industrialism and romantic naturism...I would choose industrialism and hope, unhopefully, that we would – somehow – avoid

catastrophe." *The Political Animal*, p.100

31. Man's environment certainly plays its role in *what* he thinks about, as does his historical facticity, but he is still free to direct his thoughts and to act upon his values. No environment produces a homogeneous set of responses and values.

CHAPTER ELEVEN: Rationalism and War

> Let our conjectures, our theories, die in our stead! We may
> still learn to kill our theories instead of killing each other.
> — Karl Popper[1]

This chapter continues the criticism of single explanations of warfare focusing on those theories that claim war to be the product of man's faculty of reason — specifically, those theories that consider man is nothing but a rational animal.

The previous three chapters examined various shades of culturalist theories that assert that all human action is only understandable from and through cultures — indeed, that human action is indistinguishable from culture. While there is a great advantage to exploring the tacit beliefs and motives of people and groups, they do not *completely* explain causal factors in human action, ignoring primarily the effect of reason on ideas as well as the impact of biology on man's thinking and societies. In turn, the biological thesis was seen to be lacking in its exclusion of culture and reason. This chapter criticizes the reductionist theory that all human action is resolvable into rational (explicitly articulated) acts — that is, the rationalist theory of war.

The proper aim of a philosophy of war should be to draw all three aspects of human nature together to provide a more comprehensive understanding of war's origins and nature, rather than relying on monistic explanations: hence a strict rationalist thesis of war is rejected, since it attempts to explain warfare without reference to any cultural or biological factors and relies solely on man being a rational being that can articulate all of his beliefs, and that acts upon those he explicitly chooses to act upon.

Much in the human realm, as we have seen in the previous chapters, is the product of internalized thinking — of emulation, and of mutually beneficial arrangements that form without need of articulation. Reason thus cannot stand alone as the sole cause of war.

Nonetheless, the importance that reason plays in war, and generally the universalism to which rationalism appeals, is supported — but guided by an acknowledgement of such limits. Reason provides man with a very capable means of understanding himself and the world, and relieves him of the delayed duration of biological adaptation and even cultural adaptation to new environments, ideas, and behavioral patterns. Man possesses the ability to perceive the effects of an action, and while omniscience or certitude is certainly not a corollary of reasoning, the attempt to understand the world, the self, others, and all the relevant interactions and principles governing life, does provide humanity with its most useful and powerful tool of survival and progress.

When articulated ideas superimpose themselves on man's cultural heritage, that culture will change and adapt, especially if those ideas are more conducive to survival and human flourishing than traditional norms. When men reason that war is not in their interests, the effect on culture can be far-reaching; but it can also be shallow, permitting the alternative blast of war to once again "stiffen the sinews and lend the eye its terrible aspect" (Henry V). The rationalist dream of peace through reason alone must, on this account, remain only a dream.

THE RATIONALIST THEORY OF WAR

Rationalism is the term given to a broad range of theories that emphasize the importance of reason in man's affairs. Succinctly described, the rationalist theory of war assumes all interaction to be dominated by articulated argument — a theory that is often connected to the weighing of the calculated benefits and costs to waging war. The initiating rationalizations for war may be embedded in religious and mythical explanations,[2] but as the state becomes increasingly secular, so the justifications, rationalists may argue, become more concerned with and explained by *Realpolitick*: the costs and benefits of war as they fall on the state. The state is the primary unit of analysis for such rationalists, although not all rationalists are statists.

Most rationalists consider political war to have emerged historically with the rise of the state, hence state and war can be chartered historically in the development of the great ancient civilizations of Egypt, Sumer, the Indus and Yellow River valleys.[3] Some rationalist theorists blame man's reason and civilization for war, whereas others believe that the application of reason (or of better, more logical or sound reasoning) is man's escape route from war and that it is the lack or misuse of reason that creates war. In other words, these rationalists may accept other causes of war (e.g., the prompting of emotions), and conclude that war's origin lies in the lack of rational control over the aspects of man that ought, in a civil society, to be subservient.

But in general, the rationalist theory of war declares that war is solely the result of articulated arguments and *political deliberation* — of reasoned argument or utilitarian consideration concerning wealth or power, i.e., concepts allegedly resoluble into materially accountable units. It is captured in the political realism of Machiavelli,[4] for instance, and the present historian Michael Howard describes it as such: "However inchoate or disreputable the motives for war may be, its initiation is almost by definition a deliberate and carefully considered act and its conduct, at least at the more advanced levels of social development, a matter of very precise central control."[5] Clausewitz is the essential and most influential military thinker in this light, describing war as the continuation of politics by alternative means.[6]

Rationalist wars can accordingly be defined as predominantly the deliberate policies of permanent state organizations, whatever form they take; and in turn the edicts and policies of governments are derived from the articulated, concrete designs and ambitions of those in power. Hence the explicit appeals to act on the part of a government are assumed to be pitched to man's capacity to reason and to his consideration of his proper (rational) interests.[7]

As a general theory, the rationalist theory of war appeals both to those of a utilitarian bent, who argue that the good is derived from the calculus of costs and benefits as they relate to man's happiness or pleasure, as well as to political realists, who see life as a constant power struggle in which the cleverer should (or do) rise to positions of hegemony and for whom power rather than pleasure is the true standard.

However, as an ethical theory, rationalism also emphasizes the need for open and critical discussion of problems over violent solutions,[8] since the employment of one's reason entails the antithesis of deploying force.

Nonetheless, what is sometimes underplayed by rationalists is that explicit verbal argument and rhetoric can motivate people *away* from cultural processes that converge on conflict resolution, or, in other words, away from the principles and values of social cooperation toward destructionism. In other words, explicated, logically reasoned out beliefs can promote war and aggression: reason can promote anti-reason.

This is because articulated argument is a two-edged sword: explicit reasoning may offer explanations and justifications which may ultimately be complementary to life, or it may offer rationalizations that negate human life. Pure rationalists may deny that reason could be inimical to life, arguing that reason can resolve *any* potential conflict of interests.[9] Nevertheless, while reason's inherent nature is to appeal to universalism,[10] the explicit manipulation of language may produce emotive, pre-rational, and highly parochial effects in the audience: such is the art of rhetoric.[11] "On, on, you noblest English. Whose blood is fet from fathers of war-proof! Fathers that, like so many Alexanders, Have in these parts from morn till even fought And sheathed their swords for lack of argument," cries Shakespeare's Henry V, stirring his men into action through atavistic rhetoric.[12] The use of words is not confined to exploring logical niceties. Language is meant *to invoke* visions and dreams, *to motivate and rouse* men to action. Nobody went to war over ¬P, but plenty have gone to war for the glory of their nation, their flag, their home, the desire for heroic immortality, or to avoid losing face.

Various forms of political idealism — the primacy of political and philosophical ideals over the lives of men — may be said to have caused wars from religious crusades to independence movements and wars of imperialism. A great many doctrines — religious and secular — have emerged in history that demand the sacrifice of the individual to the ideal. "Philosophical concepts nurtured in the stillness of a professor's study could destroy a civilization," writes Isaiah Berlin[13] on the consequences reason can have on human action. The impact of ideas is taken up later, following an outline of rationalism.

Some who appeal to the universalism of rational thinking argue that if humans were to act reasonably — i.e., according to the dictates of reason — wars would never occur again, since reason discloses the futility of war. The implication is that the pursuit of war is by definition an irrational (or unreasonable) pursuit, which in turn suggests that the agents involved are acting irrationally.[14] But reasoning — the use of articulated arguments that may propose excuses or putative justifications of cultural demands and expectations, as well as cogent, universal theories of the world, self and other — may nonetheless fall short of logical soundness or moral coherence. Although we admit the limitations to rationalism in that reasoning may prompt non-reasonable behavior,[15] given the presence of tacit forms of knowledge, can we accept that reason is a dangerous tool that threatens, say, mass annihilation?

It can be argued that reason may disengage us from what might prove to be better methods of adaptation — biological or cultural methods, that is. Peter Singer offers a useful analogy of an escalator: once reason is engaged, its upward path is unlimited;[16] he suggests the possibility that conceptual, articulated thought, permitting a speedier means of adaptation, potentially loosens the links a simpler creature has to its needs and hence to its potential for survival.[17] This is a plausible contention; but it also fosters what Rand terms a "tragic sense of life" — a pessimistic view of man's greatest endowment, namely his reason that takes humanity away from its allegedly "more natural" roots. (Interestingly, this kind of thinking echoes the condemnation of human nature — specifically man's ability to choose and reason — epitomized in the Fall of Man myths, in which the enactment of choice leads to humanity's secular burdens, and by implication leads to war.[18] It also finds a recent and influential proponent in the guise of Jean-Jacques Rousseau, who begins the modern assault on reason and who seeks man's salvation in the return to nature, where his compassion rather than his reason would rule and so produce peace.[19])

Singer's "escalator of reason" symbolizes that articulated thought adapts quicker than cultural and especially biological processes. To paraphrase Malthus's theory of population: conceptual thought expands geometrically, whereas cultural beliefs adapt arithmetically. For those who criticize man's reason to some extent or other, it is this lag that poses a danger for humanity, for man may not culturally adapt quickly enough to the expansion in knowledge and technology which provides him with increasingly powerful tools.[20] The argument becomes particularly worrisome in an age of nuclear weaponry; if instincts have not biologically adapted to match the greater power conferred by wielding the simplest of long-range weapons, humanity may be dangerously far behind the mentality required for controlling the use of nuclear weaponry and its technology.[21]

Cultural structures (the tacit and explicit ideas supported by individuals in their daily lives) thus may not match the achievements of reason. If culture provides the first learned order of creating inhibitions against killing and warfare, reason advances knowledge to a higher level. Reason is free to some extent from traditional frameworks of reference and thus it offers new vistas from which to view the past, present, and future.[22] Although reasoning (i.e., logic, imagination, conjecturing, theorizing) permits humanity to envisage the consequences of actions and to comprehend errors in behavior or in institutions, cultures that uphold war as a solution to inter-societal problems may take their time to catch up to the realization that war is ultimately inimical to human life or counter-productive to the values sought. As we have seen, vestiges of feudal or aristocratic martial notions, or a cultural inertia in favor of violent resolutions, may plague and retard the ability for a society to forge the conditions required for the extension of the complex order of civilization.[23]

The ability of reasoned argument to maintain the peace depends not so much on the power of the argument as it does on the power of the traditions and cultures within which the argument is made and the change that reason may effect. Where peace is not a tradition, it is unlikely to be accepted by argument alone. Reason is insufficient to guarantee peace.

This can also be seen by looking at the vehicle of logic, which can also be used for non-peaceful ends. It is sometimes thought of reason that its results must be innately peaceful to humanity — that all can see the answers and solutions to the world's ills. This is the vision the European Enlightenment gave the world in the 18th century, one that was wholly optimistic in man's ability not just to understand but also to control his world. Yet logic and reason are employed by people — in fact, by individuals. They are not self-sustaining edifices to which mankind must bow in obedience; and being employed by people means that they can be channeled into rationalizations — putative justifications for action or inaction, war or peace.

Nonetheless, we can optimistically counter that the sometimes subtle distinction between sound reasoning and rationalization[24] can be uncovered through a thorough-going critical analysis. But often, in war, the opportunity for critical analysis is rejected. In the modern state, this is enacted primarily through clamp downs by officials on criticism or on the free flow of information.[25] This certainly happens in democracies as well as what Rawls calls "outlaw states".[26] Ostensibly, the more centralized a democratic state is, one would expect the easier it would be to control information flows, but the size of the government does not however guarantee how information is controlled (just as its stock of weapons does not tell us how they will be used): what is more important is the political culture of the nation towards free expression, i.e., the dominant and relevant ideas regarding the values of discussion, the perceived understanding of facts by the majority, the historical effects of similar policies in the past, and so on.[27] Nonetheless, a reaction to restrain information flows need not be lain at the door of any statist conspiracy to hide the truth, and may indeed be understandable from the point of view of exigency and emergency: in war there is evidence that groups experience a collective rush to close ranks and thereby incidentally close possibilities for intellectual critique in the push to consolidate defensible values.[28]

The rhetoric of war often *prima facie* appeals to reason. But in the name of seeking the universal stance of ethical impartiality, what it commonly succeeds in doing is to stir ancient cultural prejudices, latent martial values, the cohesiveness of the group, the herd mentality, and the defensive mechanisms of the tribe. Wars justified on, say, forms of moral relativism, racial, religious, or cultural antagonisms, or from mercantilist or *Lebensraum* economic policies, are examples of such rationalizations. These may stem from other cultural norms assuming either a moral and political supremacy over other nations, or indeed a deep seated feeling of inferiority or vulnerability to invasion. Both, arguably, played their role in German aggression in the two World Wars of the 20th century: the fear of Russian aggression and of being sandwiched in by France and Russia, as well as myths of Germanic or Teutonic purity and supremacy. Great Britain pursued wars around the world in the 18th and 19th centuries on the assumption of its own moral correctness[29] rather than any sense of fear of invasion of its own territory, whereas

American Cold War policy reflected, in part, a fear of communism's spread around the world and hence a fear of attack and invasion.

POLITICAL REALISM

The rationalist theory of war is often (although not necessarily) connected to a realist political theory of war that assumes that the state and its officers are solely the agents of warfare and that the attainment of power (wealth, land) is war's purpose.

> A ruler, then, should have no other objective and no other concern, nor occupy himself with anything else except war and its methods and practices, for this pertains only to those who rule.[30]

War's origins and nature are then deemed reflections of state policy,[31] and once initiated, war is deemed wholly subservient to political considerations and its direction, as the famous writer of *On War*, Carl von Clausewitz assumes: "We see . . . that under all circumstances War is to be regarded not as an independent thing, but as a political instrument."[32]

For Clausewitz, even though war necessarily and always takes on its own nature (for it possesses an inherent tendency to escalate to "absolute war", and hence the overall control of politics can never be complete[33]), politics remains the master to which war refers.[34] [35] In a similar vein, the historian Michael Howard writes:

> [I]n general men have fought during the past two hundred years neither because they are aggressive nor because they are acquisitive animals, but because they are reasoning ones: because they discern, or believe that they can discern, dangers before they become immediate, the possibility of threats before they are made.[36]

If power is the end of war and power can mean survival as much as aggrandizement, realists explain war's origins by balance-of-power theories, that is, by the interplay of kings and princes on the world's stage, each seeking power, each determined to improve his position in the pecking order, and to insure against the rise of alliances or powers that would threaten his own status. "Don't forget your great guns," wrote Frederick the Great to his brother, "which are the most respect-able arguments of the rights of kings."[37] Balance-of-power theories are perennially popular amongst historians and theoreticians[38] as offering useful explanations of why wars arise.[39]

Realists stress the interplay of state relations or of the relations of power within the state. Realism typically rests on a particular theory of the nature of the state and its officers: internally, the state's reins may be the object of power brokering, while externally, the object of power may be the aggrandizement of the state, the protection of its interests, or the conquering of others. Theorists differ on whether any morality but the attainment of power plays any role at all in human affairs (Machiavelli), or whether it is merely lacking in the international sphere (Thucydides, Hobbes). But they agree that the international sphere is either ruled by, or should be ruled by, nothing but national self-interest.[40] Realists thus see power governing the cause and the form of international politics and hence see the origins of war in the striving for power or in its maintenance against others' designs.[41]

The reliance on "national interests" implies that balance-of-power theorists refer solely to political wars and thereby do not include primitive or non-state wars (or do not consider them wars as such).[42] Wars, Howard argues, are solely the province of the foreign affairs of *states*, which implies that only states may wage wars, all other forms of collective violence coming below the requisite military horizon.[43] For example, political war for Michael Howard begins with Frederick the Great and the *Staatspolitik* of which it was a function, but this ignores his own reference to Sparta and its wars.[44]

But the interpretation of what constitutes a state and hence the emergence of *Realpolitick* is a small problem besetting Howard's rendition of balance-of-power politics. It does not in itself undermine the theory that war's origins are to be found in the diplomatic games statesmen play, and the repercussions of those games for other states, in their pursuit of power. As Raymond Aron argues, in a realist vein: "The stakes of war are the existence, the creation, or the elimination of States."[45]

There are four assumptions to the typical balance-of-power theory derived from political realism: states cause wars (e.g., Rousseau); states are individuals (e.g., Wolff); states naturally reside in fear of one another (e.g., Hobbes, Hegel); and the decision to go to war is rationally or politically made (e.g., Clausewitz).

The cause of war is accordingly either the existence of an international arena of independent states and/or the fear that pertains to their conceptions of each other. The decision to go to war as a rational choice describes the process that states use to weigh the pros and cons of waging war. Those that seek power are supposed to engage in consequentialist reasoning, deliberating over what would be the best policy for their pursuit. Accordingly, traditional morality is relegated to a luxurious obstacle or is abandoned, as Machiavelli advises, *in toto*.

In the international sphere, realism implies that attempts to create an over-arching morality or to foster peace through international treaties are ultimately pointless.[46] They may have their use in securing some values for the nation, but once those purposes are exhausted, the pretence should be abandoned. The reality of the situation, realists argue, is that power rules the world's affairs — or should do, and the rules of this game are to ensure one's own nation is sufficiently powerful to avoid being taken over. Behind any façade of peace the international order is essentially anarchic — wars may not be waging, but their threat is ever present.

There is a division between positive and normative realism here — positive realism describes the state of affairs, i.e., the world is ruled by power, whereas normative realism claims that this ought to be how the world is ruled.

DESCRIPTIVE REALISM[47]

Descriptive realism commonly holds that the international community is characterized by anarchy, since no overriding world government exists to enforce a common code of rules. This anarchy need not be chaotic, for various member states of the international community may engage in treaties or in trading patterns that generate an overarching order of sorts, but most theorists conclude that law or morality does not apply beyond the nation's boundaries (Machiavelli holds that it does not apply within either).

Arguably, descriptive realism complements the Hobbesian view of the state of nature that the relations between self-seeking political entities *are* necessarily a-moral. Hobbes asserts that without a presiding government to legislate codes of conduct, no morality or justice can exist:

> Where there is no common Power, there is no Law: where no Law, no
> Injustice . . . if there be no Power erected, or not great enough for our se-
> curity; every man will and may lawfully rely on his own strength and art,
> for caution against all other men.[48]

Without a supreme international power or tribunal, states view
each other with fear and hostility, and conflict, or the threat thereof, is
endemic to the system.

A second proposition entails that a nation can only advance its
interests against the interests of other nations, which implies that the
international environment is inherently unstable.[49] Whatever order
may exist breaks down when nations compete for the same resources,
for example. In such an environment, the realists argue, a nation has
only itself to depend on: a view that Rousseau, following Hobbes, pro-
poses.[50]

Either descriptive political realism is true or it is false. If it is true,
however, it does not follow that morality ought not to be applied to
international affairs. What ought to be does not always follow from
what is. A strong form of descriptive political realism maintains that
nations are necessarily self-seeking — that they can only form foreign
policy in terms of what the nation can gain — and cannot, by their very
nature, cast aside their own interests. However, if descriptive realism is
held as a closed theory, this means that it can refute all counter-factual
evidence on its own terms and any attempt to introduce morality into
international affairs would prove futile. For example, evidence of a nation offering support to a neighbor as an ostensible act of altruism is
refuted by pointing to some self-serving motive perceived by the giving
nation — it would increase trade, it would gain an important ally, it
would feel guilty if it didn't, and so on.[51]

Examining the soundness of descriptive political realism depends
on the possibility of knowing political motives, which in turn means
knowing the motives of the various diplomats and officers of the state.
The complexity of the relationship between officers' actions, their motives, subterfuge, and actual foreign policy (never mind the rewriting of
the history afterwards!) makes this a difficult if not an impossible task.
Logically, though, the closed nature of descriptive realism implies that a
contrary proposition that nations serve no interests at all, or can only

serve the interests of others, could be just as valid. The logical validity of the three resulting theories suggests that preferring one position to another is an arbitrary decision, i.e., an assumption to be held, or not, depending on the whim of the thinker. This reduces any philosophical soundness of descriptive realism: it is not a true or false description of international relations, but an arbitrary assumption that cannot be proved true or false. That weakens its merits as a theory both philosophically and with respect to historical investigations.

That the present international arena of states *is* characterized by the lack of an overarching single power (a world Leviathan) is an acceptable description.[52] Evidentially, war has been common enough to give support to political realism: there have been over 200 wars and conflicts since the signing of the Treaty of Westphalia in 1648. The seemingly anarchic state of affairs has led some thinkers, following Hobbes, to make comparisons with domestic anarchy when a government does not exist to rule or control a nation. Without a world power (or effective world power), they may reason, war, conflict, tension, and insecurity have been the regular state of affairs; they may then conclude that just as a domestic government removes internal strife and punishes local crime, so too ought a world government control the activities of individual states, overseeing the legality of their affairs and punishing those nations that break the laws, thereby calming the insecure atmosphere in which nations find themselves.

The "domestic analogy" is the presumption that relations between individuals and relations between states are the same. The 18th century jurist Christian Wolff, for example, holds that: "since states are regarded as individual free persons living in a state of nature, nations must also be regarded in relation to each other as individual free persons living in a state of nature."[53] Such an argument however involves the collectivization of individuals into a single mass and/or the personification of states: that is, individualism is necessarily abandoned by dressing the state up in terms of personalities. Realism often describes nations as "individuals" acting upon the world stage to further their own interests, but behind the concept of "France" or "South Africa" exist millions of *unique* individuals, who may or may not agree with the claims for improving the national interest. Those nations are controlled by individuals in power who hold privileged positions over the lives of the citizens, but who do not *embody* the nation-state and all of its values.

Some, rejecting the domestic analogy, claim that the relationships between states and their civilians are much more different than those between nation states, since individuals can hold beliefs and can suffer whereas states cannot.[54] Or those who emphasize the distinctiveness of nations may reject the domestic analogy, arguing that the citizen has duties to the laws of the land but a nation cannot have any duties beyond its borders. If the domestic analogy does not hold, arguably a different theory must be proposed to explain the state of international affairs, which either means revising political realism to take into account the more complex relationship between collectives and individuals or moving to an alternative theory of international relations.

PRESCRIPTIVE REALISM

Prescriptive political realism argues that whatever the actual state of international affairs, nations *should* pursue their own interests — i.e., power. This theory resolves into various shades depending on the standard of the national interest claimed and the moral permissibility of employing various means to desired ends. Several definitions may be offered as to what ought to comprise the national interest. More often than not, claims invoke the need to be economically and politically self-sufficient, thereby reducing dependency on untrustworthy nations.

The argument supporting the primacy of self-sufficiency as forming the national interest has a long history. Plato and Aristotle both argued in favor of autarky on grounds of securing a nation's power.[55] Nations, they both reasoned, should only import non-necessary commodities that can be prohibited or lost, if war arises, without much loss to the community. This economic doctrine has been used to support political realism through the economic theory of mercantilism, which is a form of economic nationalism — that is, the unit of analysis for economic study is not global, city, or individual wealth but national wealth. In the 18th century especially, political theorists and mercantilists maintained that political power could only be sustained and increased by reducing a nation's imports and increasing its exports.[56] The common proposition between the two positions is that a nation can only grow rich at the expense of others: namely, that if England's wealth increases, France's must concomitantly decrease. It was a guiding support to the imperialist expansion of Great Britain during the 19th century and had the intellectual support of some of the West's great thinkers including, at an important junction in intellectual history Montaigne: "That the Profit of One Man is the Inconvenience of Another", he titled his Essay Number 21.[57]

This influential tier supporting political realism is, however, unsound. Trade is not exclusively beneficial to one party: it is mutually beneficial, otherwise trade would not take place.[58] "I will venture to assert", wrote David Hume in the 1750s, "that the encrease of riches and commerce in any one nation, instead of hurting, commonly promotes the riches and commerce of all its neighbours; and that a state can scarcely carry its trade and industry very far, where all the surrounding states are buried in ignorance, sloth, and barbarism."[59] Hume's challenge to mercantilist thinking was put into a more analytical framework by Adam Smith and David Ricardo, and it forms the basis of international trade theory and much of micro-economics today.[60]

Nonetheless, the political realist may admit the benefits of international trade and retort that despite the gains that can be made, nations should not rely on others for their sustenance, or that free trade ought not to be supported since it often implies undesired cultural changes. The arguments against free trade are ancient and often repeat the same reasons adumbrated by the Ancient Greeks; they gained particular momentum in the 18th century in the writings of the legal scholars Samuel Pufendorf and Emmerich de Vattel who both asserted the nation's right to decide what is in its interests to import and export rather than leave it to the market.[61] It is often argued, for example, that trade may constitute a dangerous weakening of military (or cultural) strength, which requires an increase in domestic production to promote national security. In that respect, the nation's political interests are defined as lying over and above any material benefits to be gained from international trade.[62] The essential philosophical point is that the nation is the unit of analysis rather than some narrower or broader collective.[63]

Political realists are often characterized as a-moralists (who claim that any means should be used to uphold the national interest). But a poignant criticism is that the definition of morality is being twisted when we assume that acting in one's own or the nation's interests is immoral or amoral at best. It is unfair to claim that any self-serving action is necessarily immoral. The discussion invokes the ethics of impartiality that requires brief attention. Those who believe in a universal code of ethics argue that a self-serving action which cannot be univer-salized is immoral. However, universalism is not the only standard of ethical actions. Partiality, it can be claimed, should play a role in ethical decisions. Partialists deem it absurd that state officials should not give their own nation greater moral weight over other nations, just as it would be absurd for parents to give equal consideration to their chil-dren and others' children.[64] But if morality is employed in the sense of being altruistic, or at least universal, then political realists would rightly admit that attempting to be "moral", in that sense, will be detri-mental to the national interest or even for the world as a whole, and therefore morality ought to be ignored. But, if morality accepts the va-lidity of at least some self-serving actions, then *ipso facto* political real-ism is a moral political doctrine.

However, normative realism can be refuted on four levels.

First, not all wars involve power, and power does not have to be incorporated in the existence of a state. States may form with the devel-opment of settlements, but alternative social systems are also available to humanity. Anarchist and communist thinking assert that a state is not required for society, but, what is more important, wars evidently occur between pre-state and non-state societies.[65] Man's exercise of control over nature is a much more vital deployment of his time and energy than is the exercise of power over other men. Progress depends on the existence of peaceful relations between men and the ability for mutually beneficial structures and exchanges to develop, and progress intensifies man's capacity to enjoy a life of quality; warfare destroys that capacity and hence the capacity for man to control his environ-ment and the primary needs for his existence.

Secondly, states are erroneously considered as individuals on the international arena.[66] This is characteristic of both Christian Wolff's political positivism (Wolff is considered the father of legalistic modern political rationalism) and Hegel's collectivism that regards the state as society incorporated. Wolff writes:

> Nations are regarded as individual free persons living in a state of nature. For they consist of a multitude of men united into a state. Therefore since states are regarded as individual free persons living in a state of nature, nations must also be regarded in relation to each other as individual free persons living in a state of nature.[67]

And Hegel assumes the state to be the moral absolute: "In the Government, regarded as an organic totality, the Sovereign Power or Principate is . . . the all sustaining, all-decreeing Will of the State, its highest Peak and all-pervasive Unity."[68] Both are false descriptions of states, for states can also rightly be considered as tools to defend society from external and internal threats or as corporative bodies composed of individuals who are presented, or usurp, tools for securing law and order. Whether the state itself is a source of war or not cannot be answered simply without considering the intellectual and cultural context it presides within; Howard, for example, is keen to lay the blame at the door of the State: "It is hard to deny that war is inherent in the structure of the State."[69] The Hegelian underpinnings of Howard's musings become evident in such remarks. He continues:

> States historically identify themselves by their relationship with one another, asserting their existence and defining their boundaries by the use of force or the imminent threat of force; and so long as the international community consists of sovereign states, war between them remains a possibility . . . [70]

The statist thesis is a more extreme offshoot of the positivist jurists who assert that the head of the state assumes the personhood of the collective over which they have power (and as such it is not a very modern theory at all) — hence the term "England" can refer to the country and to the monarch. If the state is construed as an individual in the moral, legal, and political sense, then the balance-of-power concerns that Howard has in mind are actively promoted, for statesmen will view their remit as pursuing the national interest, regardless of moral norms or cultural affinities that may exist between groups or Rawlsian 'peoples'. Such pre-rational elements — as well as the host of commercial interests that may entwine two groups — are often rejected in the cool logic of *Staatspolitick*, in which the figurehead deems his or her interests to be the nation's and vice versa, and the voluntary, individually driven interaction of commerce and social intercourse are ignored (except when they make themselves heard in defending their interests) or not considered.[71]

That is not to say that the voluntaristic actions of any society can be ignored by the state in its foreign policies, but when such actions are collectivized into a common whole, the subtle commercial and social intercourse across boundaries cannot but suffer. What is important here for our analysis is that political realism ignores the complex arrangements that spring up from such interaction and which may or may not complement a nation's foreign policy as designed by balance of power theories — Adam Smith criticizes the 'man of system' who sees whole peoples that exist as mere pawns on the chessboard for his political entertainment.[72] Contrary to the alleged power of the machinations of individual politicians or bureaucrats who can control or plan society from the top, knowledge is highly decentralized and its extent lies beyond the capacity of any individual or committee to comprehend.[73] The fear most statesmen possess of individual initiative is that the implied decentralization of power cannot be controlled by legislation or the dictates of bureaucrats. At the limit, the strictest totalitarian systems cannot gain access to the individual's mind, which, as many Christian thinkers have noted, remains free.

The personification of the state into a single personality is often a rationalization for mongering economic power into a martial political body, as do all metaphysical theories that assert the organic nature of the state or nation. This can be seen in Hegel's metaphysics of the state, but it is an old theory that rests on the political identification of the state as the most important unit of analysis. Once the theoretical justification of the state as individual is made, realism and its balance of power policies flourish; the problem for realists is, however, that a nation's interests diffuse across peoples and time and cannot either be added together or rendered into a single allegedly common interest. The humanist and liberal philosophies from Erasmus to Rawls have tended to play down the role of the state in favor of examining and extolling individuals or cultures, regardless of their national affiliation.

Thirdly, balance-of-power politics are employed through the medium of producing a fear of others,[74] which reaches into not only cultural prejudices that may linger in beliefs and language but even into biological reactions to perceived threats.[75] Howard emphasizes Thucydides' observation that it was Spartan fear of Athenian power that precipitated the war — and no doubt it was. But often fear does not act alone: it connects to other thoughts and virtues such as glory or identity and prestige, which act in concert to produce a martial mentality, and fear alone does not itself lead to war, for fear can make man inactive or the attempt to create an atmosphere of fear can be rejected and even laughed off or countered by other passions: "In time we hate that which we often fear."[76]

The fear of others' activities that is characteristic of balance-of-power politics is no doubt a causal condition of warfare when it is considered to be part of a viable threat, but it is not a metaphysical inevitability (*pace* Hobbes) to which humanity must resign. Fear, although a primordial reaction, captures and combines with a complex belief concerning the nature of the threat: fear arises from an anticipation of pain or from ignorance of a situation that can be wholly imagined by complex thoughts, and can thus be justifiable or not. Ignorance of others' intentions no doubt can lead to a fear of them, but a nation ought not to go to war through fear alone. War must be justified by referring to what exactly is prompting the fears, before acting to assuage those fears. More important, fear is not the only predisposition or even reaction men may have regarding others' intents. A perceived threat can readily be mocked and dissolved through a variety of methods other than recourse to violence and war. Individually, we learn how to diffuse threats as young children, and the same principles may be said to govern how statesmen react to threats of violence against a nation's borders such as bluffing, counter-threats, appeals to reason, gestures of friendship or cooperation, applying to third parties, etc. Again, the simplistic, reductionist method that seeks one explanation for war's origins must be rejected. In such a complex, adaptive, thinking being such as man fear never can act alone as a driving impulse.

The final problem with realism's balance-of-power theories rests on the notion that political power is a necessary and sufficient condition of human relations.[77] That is, it assumes that any form of relationship existing between individuals or institutions is necessarily political and can only be described as involving power as an inevitable element and a necessary component. Reason is therefore to be deployed to examine the power relationships and to prescribe, à la Machiavelli, how power is to be secured and maintained.

Against this presumption, the contrasting importance of cooperation can be asserted, as can be the argument that cooperation does not require political deliberation. In terms of biological evolution, cooperation remains the sole form of effective adaptation, since, at the limit in evolutionary principles conflict, parasitism, and violence in general are logically self-destructive.[78] The Cold War (1945-89), infused with a matrix of logic in which the West attempted to curtail Soviet expansion, seemingly illustrates the realist vision of war. Yet other ideological motives were also at play, especially the desire to curtail the ideological expansionism of Marxism. Indeed the Cold War can also be seen as a clash between two visions of "manifest destiny" — the Soviet model, drawn from Marxist historicism in which capitalism was considered to be necessarily doomed to collapse, and the American model, which sprang from nationalist 19th century historicism and from President Wilson's goal to make the world safe for democracy.[79] The complexity of motives renders the simplistic two-dimensional game theories of the Cold War ineffective: moreover, the religious intonations involved in crusades and jihads cannot be modeled well in the game theories of rationalists — their rhetoric stirs pre-rational and instinctual juices that are positively irrational on secular terms. And more importantly for the philosophy of war, they act as a reminder that violence and war are not wholly rational, economic, or materialist endeavors, and evading those aspects does not produce a good theory of international relations or of the balances of power, as the Vietnam War testifies (see below).

Each of the four aspects of realism offers an unsound position on which to base an explanation of war's origins, but the theory remains effective to the extent that people use it to explain and predict human affairs, that is, to the extent that men and women live by the idea and view the world as a system of competing and conflicting power bases. But, like all theoretical doctrines, it is not a doctrine that must be held by any sense of necessity.

Nonetheless, political change in other countries can pave paths to war, and it is wise for officers of the state to maintain a vigilant watch for such developments. It would be imprudent for a government not to examine cautiously events abroad and not to listen to the advice of those who warn against other nations' power plays. Here we can agree with Howard's advice:

> Sophisticated communities . . . assess the implications that any event taking place anywhere in the world, however remote, may have for their own capacity, immediately to exert influence, ultimately perhaps to survive.[80]

Hence, in an international arena of sovereign states the balance-of-power theory is a useful guide to examine others' actions with interest and to avoid misunderstandings and war; but it does not in itself explain why wars occur except to the extent that people believe the world to be characterized by balance-of-power considerations.

The gravest criticism of balance-of-power theories that can be explained using (any) historical example is that they portray a two-dimensional and timeless view of people and cultures, as if, as Smith noted, they were pawns on the chess board or counters on a war-game, to be shifted at will. But people, especially those who have a long history of living in an area, maintain cultural structures that are rarely considered in balance-of-power politics in which history is bunk and what matters is the *present* power distribution. Ignorance of history — and hence of the cultural echoes and momentum that linger on in a people from ages past — undermines most balance-of-power theories, and it can be added, most foreign policies that are based on such shallow analyses.

The Vietnam War presents a good example of the depth of war's roots in man's cultural and hence political framework, which was ignored by balance-of-power considerations when the West got involved. The same story can be told of any military "hot spot"; one just has to review the history of the area to sense the martial momentum that is sustained in areas regardless of the teachings of reason, game theory, or the finer balancing acts of treaties and alliances. The temporal depth of man's beliefs cannot be ignored — ideas and expectations cross the generations to hamper or strengthen a community of individuals.

The following application of the philosophy of war to the Vietnam War should not be considered as a definitive or exhaustive explanation of its causes or description of its affairs. Such tasks are for the historians. Instead, it attempts to bring to the fore the cultural momentum that sustains war; while history does not repeat itself in the literal sense, the extent to which a people are wedded to a way of life predisposes them to act in similar ways in different periods.

THE FAILURE OF REALISM: THE VIETNAM WAR

The failures of political realism manifest themselves in all attempts by man to impose an ideal state of affairs or balance of power on the world.[81] This, of course, includes all forms of social engineering, of which the balance of power is a corollary: power is to be distributed and balanced according to particular individual's perceptions of the distribution of power.[82] After World War Two, American foreign policy was dictated by an allegiance to realism as well as the underlying optimism of rationalism — the foreign policy goal to "make the world safe for democracy" as President Wilson had put it.[83] The historical context of the target peoples for whom democracy was to be safely installed or protected was thereby missed in the grand and noble vision presented for which men were to fight and die on foreign soils.

As the Second World War was closing, President Roosevelt picked up the Wilsonian baton to demand freedom from colonial rule for the peoples of French Indochina. In mentally carving out the rights and ownership of lands following the war, Roosevelt was emphatic that a century of French rule must end: imperialism belonged to the past. Instead, America, he proposed, would take over as liberal guardian for a quarter of a century. He even offered the task to China, who categorically turned down the request of ruling such a difficult and complex land — they had had first hand knowledge of Indo-China, and it was an area that they knew would resent being ruled.

Self-determination — the proper liberal policy — ironically did not cross Roosevelt's mind, despite the Vietnamese's long history of independence against Chinese and other attempts to rule them.[84] Control passed back to the French once the invading Japanese were defeated, but then Roosevelt died in office and the American diplomats wished to appease France in the face of de Gaulle's threats to lean towards communism by offering support and later aid.[85]

Interestingly, while the superpowers talked about the post-war world, French and British forces cooperated against the Japanese with the Viet-Minh resistance, who were an assortment of nationalist and communist fighters. The Vietnamese, it turns out, had often taken to fighting for self-determination and had bested their powerful neighbor the Chinese. This was something American advisors either missed or did not take into consideration as important. Self-determination should have been a value of obvious moral and political worth to America, which had gained its independence in a baptism of fire against Great Britain in the War of Independence.

The realist foreign policy was, however, tinged with a defective premise concerning the equal worth of persons, for the Vietnamese were not considered equals in the racial scheme of things, which meant their advice, warnings and protestations went unheeded.[86] Accordingly, their own vision of themselves, their culture, their past, was not something to be valued according to this skewed vision of *Realpolitick*. It was also motivated by an emotive crusade against Communism that further weakened the need for a proper analysis of the situation. By ignoring the peoples of the land and their history, and even their own proclamations to secure self-determination for the peoples of the world, American theory collided with the reality of the situation, which is truly an ironic twist for *Realpolitick*: the realism of balances of power that supposedly should be *realistic*, playing on the strengths and weaknesses of people, their powers and resources, as well as their vision of themselves. The truth is that such a philosophy is inherently unrealistic, for it overlooks cultural and historical depths that ought to be plumbed for understanding.

The superficial but attractive rationalism of rights was what Edmund Burke warned against in his *Reflections on the Revolution in France*. Burke's warning that the cultural situation of the French was not being considered went unheeded, as did his prescient remarks that the 'liberal' revolution would turn sour. "The fresh ruins of France," he wrote, "which shock our feelings wherever we can turn our eyes, are not the devastation of civil war; they are the sad but instructive monuments of rash and ignorant counsel in time of profound peace." At the time American ambassadors of their own revolution, men of such stature as Paine and Jefferson went to France to assist in the enlightened overthrow of tyranny and thereby missed the plot:[87] France's situation was very different from America's. The mistakes were repeated in Vietnam, exacerbated by the American-European view of the Vietnamese as morally and politically unequal, a fatal error in any estimation of an ally or enemy.

Similar to Bohemian history prior to the Thirty Years War, the Vietnamese paraded a culture of autonomy and heroism against greater powers. It would be wrong to reduce the Vietnamese defense of their lands and of the north's attack on the south as purely 'ideological' in the communist sense,[88] for what counts as the apparent rationalizations for aggression or defense should not be held as the entire reason for so acting.

Ho Chi Minh allied his cause to Communism giving him international support, and his allegiance also reflected the times — the overthrow of colonial administrations was marketed as inherently Marxist, or more correctly Leninist. Yet the rhetoric of the ideology was infused, necessarily so, with the sufficient admixture of stirring reminders to the Vietnamese people of the justice of their cause. Rhetoric and demagoguery make fools of game and balance-of-power theories by plumbing pre-rational and irrational depths that lie latent in a people's understanding of who they are, of their cultural identity, their sense of belonging, their vision of their past and destiny.

The depth of Vietnamese sense of independence goes back two millennia. A distinct Vietnamese ethnicity emerged around 200 BC. It was originally annexed to China, but leader Li-Bon temporally regained local control in 541. In 939 in the north, so troublesome to French and American attempts to contain incipient nationalism in the 20th century, the Vietnamese of the Annam territory freed themselves from Chinese control. They also attacked the southern Vietnamese area of Champa which precipitated a century of war between north and south. The familiar sounding maneuvers should come as no surprise: during the Vietnam War, the north once again attacked the south — and both sides dealt with each other in a brutality that can only emanate from centuries of mistrust or latent hatred.

The southern Champa also waged war into neighboring Khmer — modern day Kampuchea, or Cambodia — which again recurred following the Northern victory over the South in 1975. In the century of warfare between Annam, Champa, and Khmer, the North usually had the upper hand successfully invading the south and repelling counter-invasions as well as attempts by the Khmer to invade. Champa and Khmer also fought each other continually.

In the 13th century Annam and Champa briefly united to repel Mongol invaders, who, under the leadership of Sogatu, advanced easily through Annam but was halted in Champa; the Cham proceeded to wage a guerrilla war against the occupiers. The Annamese successfully repelled a second wave of Mongols that captured Hanoi; Sogatu retreated in the face of a joint attack on his forces and was killed by the Cham. The Mongol Emperor, Kublai, agreed to halt invasions in return for Vietnamese recognition of his suzerainty; once the external threat had evaporated the two old enemies could once again exchange punches. Annam annexed Champa in 1312, but then they combined to meet a Thai invasion; that out the way, the Cham rebelled, forcing out the Annamese.

Peace only came with economic exhaustion. Once the economies were back on their feet, the two could once again try their best. Che Bong Nga of the Cham succeeded in capturing Hanoi in 1371, but full victory, as it was for both sides in this protracted inter-ethnic struggle, was beyond his grasp. The duel was interrupted by a Chinese invasion of Annam in 1407, which was then repulsed before the fight could continue. This time, the Annamese under Le Thanh Ton conquered Champa in 1471.

The 16th century was beset by civil wars and attempts at secession by the northern Tonkin subjects of Annam, and Champa once again freed itself from northern control. The Annamese dictator Trinh Tong rose to re-unite most of the country and impose some stability by 1592. Two dynasties of rulers now faced each other: in the north the Trinh family, allying with the Dutch, and in the south, the Nguyen, who were being supported by the Portuguese and the new technologies they imported. After successfully repulsing a Trinh invasion, the Nguyen built defensive walls to the north of Hué, half way up the country in an area that was to resound with battle once again in the Vietnam War. In 1673 the defenses had proved impenetrable and a peace accord between North and South Vietnam was signed, recognizing the Linh River as the natural boundary. Frustrated at their attempts of conquering the South, the North proceeded to displace its bellicose cultural momentum by invading and annexing parts of neighboring Cambodia (1739-49) and Siam.

In the second half of the 18th century, Siam repelled both Vietnamese and Burmese invaders and drove the Vietnamese out of Cambodia. In 1773 civil war broke out in Vietnam resulting in the elimination of the Trinh family and the ascendancy of Nguyen Anh, with Siamese support, to the position of *Gai Long*, or Emperor in 1802. Siam and Vietnam played parent to Cambodia in return for peace, but then a Cambodian rebellion allowed the Vietnamese to strengthen their control over the protectorate (1812). However in 1824, the French were beginning to upset the locals on the east coast following persecutions of Christians. French warships annihilated a Vietnamese navy in 1847; this was followed by sporadic bombardments by the French throughout the 1850s.

Setting up a garrison in Saigon and defeating a siege party, the French gradually expanded their control of the area taking advantage of internal Vietnamese unrest. In 1883 the Vietnamese acknowledged French dominion, as they had in the past briefly acknowledged that of the Mongols. But for a decade between 1885-95 the French had to deal with widespread revolts and guerrilla warfare before establishing a peace on the nation by virtue of their technological supremacy.

A foretaste of the intransigence of the people did not frustrate the French assumption of continual superiority with the Vietnamese, who had, once the time seemed ripe, shrugged off the Chinese, the Mongols, and Siamese. The nationalist movement, as it was now termed in Twentieth Century parlance, centered around the person of Ho Chi Minh. Ho led a delegation to the Versailles talks in Paris in 1919 to secure his nation's independence, only to be turned away by the great powers. Ho reverted to a pseudonym, Nguyen Ai Quoc, and became a charter member of the French Communist Party in 1920, before heading to Moscow for lessons in the fashionable ideology.

Tuchman summarizes:

> Protests and risings against French rule began with its inception. A people proud of their ancient overthrow of a thousand years of Chinese rule . . . who had frequently rebelled against and deposed oppressive native dynasties, and who still celebrated the revolutionary heroes and guerrilla tactics of those feats, did not acquiesce passively in a foreign rule far more alien than the Chinese.[89]

The French quashed the first modern uprising in 1930, which then went underground. During the war Ho Chi Minh pulled together rebels into a united nationalist force that aided the West against the Japanese. Once the war ended, Ho's party declared Vietnamese independence. The French attempted to re-establish full colonial control, but were ignominiously defeated at the battle of Dien Bien Phu in 1954 and thereafter ceded colonial control. Prior to the battle, European rationalism and political arrogance blinded the French to the reality and the depth of the situation they were in: "contempt for an Asian enemy was typical of the ethnocentrism of commanders schooled in the colleges of Western Europe and America, rather than the hard school of guerrilla warfare in the jungles of Indo-China."[90]

General Henri Navarre rested on French technological superiority and the presumed ignorance of matters military on the part of the Vietnamese. But the French were quickly outnumbered and outmaneuvered by the Vietnamese who used French bicycles to get transport their supplies of Russian and Chinese arms, and the French superior technology of planes and tanks became worthless as low clouds encumbered flights and mud trapped the tanks. After a three month siege the Vietnamese overpowered the French fort. A Conference established a national division at the 17th Parallel — the ancient 'hot-zone' to the north of Hué.

By that point American foreign policy was supplanting French — aid and materials were flown in to halt the Communist-nationalist victory. In effect, America had bank-rolled the French defense, but America had also undermined Western efforts to control Vietnam by sponsoring a coup led by Ho to overthrow the pragmatic Vietnamese Emperor.[91] But as the French pulled out, America became involved in constraining what they thought might be a communist take over of South East Asia; not an unnecessary fear given the history of Northern Vietnamese aggression against the South and neighboring countries, although the fear was couched in the modern parlance of balance-of-power concerns.

Eisenhower acquiesced in realist fears, side-stepped democratic obligations to set up elections, mumbled about defending freedom, and finally committed America to defending South Vietnam.[92] In 1961 the North invaded the South — not much had changed in the past millennium! Following American cease fire in 1973, the North conquered the South, enacted brutal ideological policies against the "consumerist South" and promptly invaded the traditionally soft target of Cambodia to the West (1977, 1979) and repulsed a Chinese incursion in the North (1979). Meanwhile the South began insurgencies against the Communist regime. In 1989 Vietnam withdrew from Cambodia

Although the Vietnam war is reported as an ideological flashpoint in the Cold War in which Communist North succeeded in taking Non-Communist South, the history and culture of the land presents an intractable cultural-political rhythm that cannot be ignored. North and South have fought persistently for over a thousand years, periodically breaking and even uniting to dismiss foreign intervention, before returning to the brutal feud. Ethnic, religious, and ideological divisions amongst the Vietnamese complicate the parochial alliances, but the fundamental tensions that existed between the Champa and Annamese have not faded — their masks may have changed but their mutual mistrust and bellicosity has not.

The new dimension of political ideology may have deepened the intensity of the violence between the groups (i.e., the social engineering policies to denude the South's cities of its population, a policy mirrored in Cambodia to genocidal proportions), but as the times have changed, so has the vocabulary and justification of occupation. In the 1990s, the Communist Party watered down its adherence to ideology as it turned its gaze on the economic benefits of market globalization and trade.

This cursory review of Vietnamese history and the background to the Vietnam War should amplify the principle that people are not wholly rational beings — each of us is immersed into a cultural context that cannot be extracted easily or at all from who we are, never mind ignored in international relations. Reason, whether deployed to claim the need for peace or for an equal balance of power, possesses a shallowness when compared to the momentum cultures often have.

CONCLUSION

Thus far we have explored biology and culture to reach into man's political demesne. Here war is the product of ideas, and ideas, once they reach the level of the intricate complexity of philosophy, do not lose their ability to affect man's destiny and hence his desire to wage war.

Ideas are never disembodied thoughts, for they are attached to individual people who may or may not act on them. In the matrix of war's causation, war's origins lie deep within man's history — to some extent within his biological constitution but more importantly within his cultural systems of languages, rules, and morals. The thin veneer of reason may in turn kindle the flames of war in the games that politicians play with civilians' lives; reason cannot guide man's actions totally, for its rules of logic and generalization may be employed to produce the most convoluted as well as the most simple of philosophies and theologies, those general systems of thought that crowns man's intelligence. Explicitly articulated philosophy presents the final tier in the hierarchy, or the final element in the great causal matrix of war.

But, as with the other elements, philosophy does not reside in isolation and in mutual exclusivity to the demands and needs of culture, individual wit and intelligence, or man's body; nonetheless, because it may theoretically run free of any attachment to this world, philosophy can produce systems of thought that are at once inimical to man's life and destructive of his relations with others and the world. Rousseau's description of the man of philosophy who rationalizes his way out of going to the aid of another in dire need is a most useful reminder of man's ability to lose his mind to Ideology.

The next chapters relate more complex theories that have been advanced over the ages to war and attempt to root out the primary philosophical premises assumed — we enter the arena of political idealism, political and philosophical descriptions of war's nature and purpose.

Notes

1. Popper, "Natural Selection and the Emergence of the Mind", p.152
2. Cf. Dawson, *Origins of Western Warfare*, p.40
3. Cf. Dawson, *Origins of Western Warfare*, p.37
4. Cf. *The Prince*, and *The Art of War*.
5. Howard, *The Causes of War*, p.12 For Bertrand Russell, the very existence of politicians and diplomats is sufficient to raise the probability of warfare: "In every nation, by the secrecy of diplomacy, by cooperation of the Press with the manufacturers of armaments, by the desire of the rich and the educated to distract the attention of the working classes from social injustice, suspicion of other nations is carefully cultivated, until a state of nightmare terror is produced . . . " From "War: The Cause and the Cure", p.18
6. "To conduct a whole war, or its great acts, which we call campaigns, to a successful termination, there must be an intimate knowledge of state policy in its higher relations," he writes in *On War*, p. 68, Routledge Kegan & Paul, 1968 edition.
7. However, nuances arise within the rationalist camp. Some deny that the capacity to reason, or its method, is universal — such people emphasize either the plurality of rational methods (polylogists) and divide between who they think the élite possessing proper reason consists of. Cf. Chapter Fourteen.
8. This is the philosophy of rationalist liberalism.
9. E.g., Ayn Rand's "objectivist" philosophy.
10. Thomas Nagel presents a succinct view of our ability and the limits we face in seeking universality. "An objective standpoint is created by leaving a more subjective, individual, or just human perspective behind; but there are things about the world and life and ourselves that cannot be adequately understood from a maximally objective standpoint, however much it may extend our understanding beyond the point from which we started." *The View from Nowhere*, p.7
11. Rhetoric toys with language to evoke pre-rational responses from an audience. Pure rationalists may retort that it is therefore not an exercise in reason, but the possibility of a completely disembodied language (as conceived in a pure mathematics or a pure logic) is limited when it is acknowledged that each word, each enunciation and articulation, is intimately entwined with the passions and the host of pre-rational beliefs, motives, and predispositions every individual possesses.
12. Shakespeare, *Henry V*, Act 3 Scene 1.
13. Quoted in Henry Hardy, "Editor's Preface", p. ix, *The Power of Ideas*.
14. As Ginsberg claims: "In one manifestation or another, the cause of war is the irrationality of man. [Whereas] armed with reason man ought to be able to master himself." Ginsberg, "Philosophy vs. War", p. xvi. And Lorenz argues: "[T]he same human faculties which supplied man with tools and with power dangerous to himself, also gave him the means to prevent their misuse: rational responsibility." Lorenz, *On Aggression*, p.206
15. To which universalist rationalists reply that reason cannot, by definition, promote non-rational ends. This position is emphasized by Thomists and Ayn Rand.
16. Singer, *The Expanding Circle*, p.88
17. Lorenz concurs: "Knowledge springing from conceptual thought robbed man of the

security provided by his well-adapted instincts long, long, before it was sufficient to provide him with an equally safe adaptation." Lorenz, *On Aggression*, p. 205

18. Cf. Pagel, *Adam, Eve, and the Serpent*. It is a position held and made popular by St Augustine amongst others.

19. Cf. *Discourse on the Origin of Inequality*, and *The Social Contract*.

20. Midgley rightfully argues that: "Intelligence, even with all the powers of culture at its disposal, has certainly never enabled our species to clear out its vast cavern, to uproot all the pre-existing emotional structures and start again. And this is probably just as well, since intelligence would not have the slightest idea how to generate a whole new set of emotions to replace them." Midgley, *The Ethical Primate*, p.181

21. This fear leads to the strong political demand that nuclear weaponry should not fall into the hands of societies that would not be trustworthy owners of the technology — what constitutes trustworthiness requires a separate work, but generally it can be accepted that liberal democracies are inherently more trustworthy in their international relations than autocratic dictatorships; although this is a generality and not a principle, as the actions of France's unilateral nuclear testing in the 1990s readily show. (Cf. John Rawls, *The Law of Peoples*).

22. "We may think of reality as a set of concentric spheres, progressively revealed as we detach gradually from the contingencies of the self." Nagel, *A View from Nowhere*, p.5

23. Groups that remain wedded to conflict and warfare cannot develop economically; wars in Eritrea, Yugoslavia, Cambodia, and so on, this century show how quick capital is to leave war zones, and with the flight of capital goes any chance of sustaining a population, never mind progressing economically. The division of labor, writes Mises, "would never have been allowed to develop to the point where, in case a fight really did break out, one would have to suffer privation." *Liberalism*, p.25. That is, the threat of war reduces investment plans and shortens the production process — people will not overextend their resources and economic activity if war, or any kind of potential violation of their rights, is expected.

24. Rationalization is defined as offering spurious reasons or self-interested reasons for an action; it can also be conceived as evoking rhetorical flourishes that ferment pre-rational motives and dispositions. Shakespeare's Falstaff (e.g., *Henry IV Part I*) presents an excellent archetype who persistently rationalizes.

25. Maintaining closed borders governs the ability to ensure a monopoly on the free flow of information; "porous" borders, with valleys, gullies, rivers, etc., can sustain a flow of information and goods from abroad. Saddam Hussein is able to exploit the less porous borders of Iraq for controlling the state's flow of information, where as Milosevic, finally toppled in October 2000, was unable to dam the cracks surrounding him.

26. Rawls, *The Law of Peoples*, pp. 4, 80-81.

27. For example, Churchill's Minister of Information, Brendan Bracken (1941-45), shifted the balance away from the hype that had characterized the British government's coverage of the First World War towards permitting criticism of the government and away from false propaganda, knowing that credibility was more important than mendacity. Lysaght, "Churchill's Faithful Chela", in *History Today*, Volume 52, February 2002, p.44. Also, "the British now carefully avoided the grave mistake which, committed in the other war, had caused them no end of embarrassment –

the fabrication of atrocity stories out of whole cloth." Whitton and Larson, *Propaganda*, p.41.

28. The mass feelings generated by war are not necessarily destructive, Ehrenreich comments, but are akin to those felt for religion with its overtones of sanctity: "To say that war may be, in an emotional sense, a close relative of religion is not to pass moral judgment on either of these ancient institutions. We are dealing with a very basic level of human emotional experience, which can be approached just as well at, say, a labor rally as at a nationalist gathering or a huge outdoor mass . . . . This is one of humankind's great natural "highs" and is, perhaps paradoxically, as likely to be experienced at an anti-war demonstration as at a pro-war rally . . . . All "minor" differences (as, for example, of class) disappear when compared to the vast differences (construed as moral, cultural, and sometimes racial) that supposedly separates us from the "jerries", the Communists, the Arabs, or the Jews." *Blood Rites*, pp. 15-16. The closing of ranks is low cultural cum instinctual reaction to external aggression, and the flight to solidarity certainly raises the costs of individualism and criticism.

29. As well mercantilist philosophy that sought to corner world markets and to keep out competing European nations such as the French.

30. Machiavelli, *The Prince*, trans. Russell Price, Ch. XIV, p.51-2

31. Howard: "States may fight . . . not over any specific issue as might otherwise have been resolved by peaceful means, but in order to acquire, to enhance or to preserve their capacity to function as independent actors in the international system at all." Howard, *The Causes of Wars*, p.14

32. Clausewitz, *On War*, Ch. 1, §27, p.121

33. As interpreted by Gallie, *Understanding War*, p.58

34. "War is . . . a wonderful trinity, composed of the original violence of its elements, hatred and animosity, which may be looked upon as blind instinct; of the play of probabilities and chance, which make it a free activity of the soul; and of the subordinate nature of a political instrument, by which it belongs purely to reason." Clausewitz, *On War*, Ch. 1 §28, p.121, italics added.

35. However, political theory is itself pluralistic, and different schools of thought offer competing analyses of war. The various political schools — classical, jurist, realist, psychological, etc., have their own conception of the origins and nature of war; because of this plurality, the political rationalist doctrine is thus too broad to be of use as it stands, unless the theories are analyzed in turn for their strengths and weaknesses, which is beyond this work's jurisdiction. Wright, *A Study of War*, pp. 1378-9

36. Howard, *op cit.*, p.15

37. Letter to Prince Henry, April 1721. In *The Dictionary of War Quotations*, p.58.

38. E.g., game theorists who envisage international politics to be an extended form of the prisoners' dilemma. However, life does not come complete with numerical values attached to the various and complicated situations that arise, and neither are most moral problems "dilemmas" — they too have intricacies and complexities that can hardly be mathematically modeled, for the ethical choice depends on a host of considerations involving right, good, virtue, self, others and duties.

39. Howard acknowledges that the theory goes back to Thucydides' comment that;

"[w]hat made war inevitable was the growth of Athenian power and the fear this caused in Sparta." Thucydides, quoted in Howard, *The Causes of Wars*, p.10.

40. The pursuit of self interest can be a moral goal; often it is derided and cast aside as an amoral value by definition, but this is to avoid a proper philosophical analysis.

41. Realism is the subject of some of the best literature and dramas (e.g., Richard III), as well as the popular understanding of Machiavelli's politics, and the theory comes in a variety of forms, even a Marxist form.

42. But there is nothing in the logic of realism to extend it to civil wars, guerrilla wars or even gang warfare.

43. Howard erroneously interprets Wright's definition of civilized war as commencing after the Medieval ages. For Wright, civilization and hence civil or political wars stretch back to the period of writing and of a rudimentary state. Cf. Wright, *A Study of War*, Ch.VII, and Howard's quotation on p.13: "Medievalists will perhaps bridle at the application of the term "primitive" to the sophisticated and subtle societies of the Middle Ages . . . ", which is not what Wright has in mind at all.

44. Howard, *The Causes of Wars*, p.13.

45. Raymond Aron, *Peace and War: A Theory of International Relations*, p.7 Howard also draws on this quotation, *ibid*, p.14. Similarly, Howard uses Rousseau's theory, arguing that "if one had no sovereign states one would have no wars", although the absence of states, he agrees with Hobbes, might not entail peace either. Howard, *op cit.*, p. 11.

46. Cf. Rousseau's skeptical comments in *L'état du Guerre*.

47. Elements of the following were first published on the *Internet Encyclopedia of Philosophy* under "Political Realism".

48. Hobbes, *Leviathan*, Part I, Ch. 13 "Of Man", and Part II, Ch. 17, "Of Commonwealth"

49. Steven Forde, "Classical Realism", p. 78.

50. The economic theory behind this thinking is that the resources of the world are to be distributed rather than produced, hence if one nation gains more resources, it is at the cost of another nation. This conveniently complements the economic theory of mercantilism which invokes much balance-of-power theorizing. Both were the dominant political models of the Eighteenth century, and one sees echoes of it in American post-war foreign policy of containment. This ancient and erroneous view of production and distribution resounds through the centuries as an explanation and a justification of war.

51. These are standard examples in the analogous case of "psychological egoism", which holds that a person can only act in their own interests.

52. Attempts by the UN to become such a power are marred by the political partialities that are endemic in the organization. Cf. Robertson, *Crimes Against Humanity*, p.49 and *passim*.

53. Wolff, *Jus Gentium Methodo Scientifica Pertractatum.* §2, p. 9.

54. Gordon Graham, *Ethics and International Relations*.

55. In contrast to the common assumption that Max Weber promulgated that the industrial revolution stemmed from a 'Protestant work ethic', it must be noted that Martin Luther was a vociferous opponent of foreign trade, believing that his compatriots should make do with their rough woolen clothes rather than import finer cottons and silks. "I do not see that many good customs have ever come to a land

through commerce." Quoted in Irwin, *Against the Tide*, p. 21.

56. Cf. in particular the influential writings of Thomas Mun in *England's Treasure by Forraign Trade*.

57. Montaigne, *The Essays*, p. 82.

58. People often regret the trades they have made because of new knowledge that comes to light, or from a feeling of being pressured into an exchange, but apodictically when a trade takes place both parties are at least as well off as their previous position.

59. Hume, "Of the Jealousy of Trade", in *Essays Moral, Political, and Literary*, p. 328.

60. Cf. Jacob Viner, *Studies in the Theory of International Trade*.

61. Cf. Irwin, *Against the Tide*, Ch. 1.

62. A discussion of the ethics or even of the pragmatism of such an approach is beyond the remit of this work.

63. Cf. Rawls on defining 'peoples'. He prefers to focus on peoples rather than states because, "just liberal peoples limit their basic interests as required by the reasonable. In contrast, the content of the interests of states does not allow them to be stable for the right reasons," state are, after all, he notes, "always guided by the basic interests." *The Law of Peoples*, p. 29 and p. 28.

64. Lafollette, "Personal Relationships", in *A Companion to Ethics*, pp. 328.

65. The state is not a necessary causal condition of war. Many wars are indeed fought by states, but many also do not involve states as such, as Scottish clan wars or North American Indian wars, and so on, exemplify.

66. This conception of states as individuals is prominent in political philosophy, as Charles Beitz notes: "Perceptions of international relations have been more thoroughly influenced by the analogy of states and persons than by any other device. The conception of international relations as a state of nature could be viewed as an application of this analogy. Another application is the idea that states, like persons, have a right to be respected as autonomous entities." Charles Beitz, *Political Theory and International Relations*, p. 69. This perception applies only to the modern world however and is thus historically narrow as well as shallow.

67. Wolff, *Jus Gentium Methodo Scientifica Pertractatum*, trans. Joseph Drake, §2, p.9.

68. Hegel, quoted in Popper, *Open Society Vol.II*, p.45

69. Howard, *op cit.*, p.25

70. Howard, *op cit.*, p.25. Cf. also Hegel: "It is as particular entities that states enter into relations with one another", *Philosophy of Right*, §340. "Individuality is awareness of one's existence as a unit in sharp distinction from others. It manifests itself here in the state as a relation to other states." *Philosophy of Right*, §322

71. Noel Coward poignantly and humorously reminded the British during the war, "Don't be beastly to the Germans" for after all the war had to end and trade and friendships would have to be renewed.

72. Smith, *Theory of Moral Sentiments*, pp. 233-234,

73. Cf. Hayek, "the whole idea of 'central control' is confused. There is not, and never could be, a single directing mind at work." *The Fatal Conceit*, p.87. This is a particularly useful principle for comprehending the origins of war: war is never the result of a single individual declaring war, war is a collective enterprise involving great numbers of people who agree, individually, to follow their leader.

74. Fear is assumed to be — explained to be — a necessary condition of war. Realists may contend that it is also a sufficient condition.

75. Bertrand Russell in one of his essays claims that the instinct of fear is the cause of war. This is not the only cause that he asserts in his pamphlets and letters on war, but for the purposes of elucidation, his comments are useful: "Man as he is can only be explained by man as he was, and never by man as we would like him to be — the wishful thought of the pacifist. He is the product of thousands upon thousands of generations of savage and bloodthirsty progenitors, who have bequeathed to him his instincts. Fear, the most potent of all, is the sentinel of barbarous and civilized man alike; it remains the oldest of protective mechanisms, and becomes manifested in every child before the end of its third month." Russell, "Fear as the Ultimate Cause of War", p.30 And he argues that the sacrifices demanded of individuals cannot be attributed to a desire for conquest, rather the desire is found in fear, "the principal motive with ordinary citizens." Russell, *ibid.*, p.30

76. Shakespeare, *Antony and Cleopatra*, I. iii

77. The philosophical basis of this is found in Hegel's master-slave thesis that is assumed to be logically a necessary and sufficient condition of all human relations, and whose origin is assumed to be in the structures of human consciousness. Hegel dubiously concludes that people are determined to strive to dominate one another. Nonetheless, the master-slave theory relies on cooperation -that the slave cooperates with the master, but the overriding characteristic is the uncooperative function of domination.

78. Hegel acknowledges this in his master-slave theory in which he asserts that recognition of the self requires the continued existence of the other. Nonetheless, a permanent state of "terror" (Sartre) is expected to exist between the relations of people remains. Hegel's master-slave thesis proffers support of militarism, and militarism is not conducive to peace but is an attempted justification of war. Yet the master-slave theory is not a brute inalterable fact of existence -it can be rejected and other theories of inter-social relations accepted. The proposals of Christianity, humanism and liberalism, for instance, propound the unification of humankind, rather than its dissolution into castes.

79. The term "manifest destiny" came from John O'Sullivan in 1845 to explain America's goal to secure Texas and Oregon.

80. Howard, *op cit.*, p.14

81. All utopias are the product of single minds, who, while themselves are part of the great linguistic and cultural heritage of their own upbringing, attempt to remove themselves from that tradition to begin anew. The attempt is futile, for what passes as the ignorance of the present generation may serve ends the author is wholly unaware of; utopias are often the product of immature minds, striving to improve the world by stint of their own genius or cravings for power over others. To butcher a wonderful quotation by Mark Twain: in our youth we amazed at the world's ignorance, but in our maturity we are amazed at how more intelligent it has suddenly become. "When I was a boy of fourteen, my father was so ignorant I could hardly stand to have the old man around. But when I got to be twenty-one, I was astonished at how much the old man had learned in seven years." Attributed by *Reader's Digest*, Sept. 1937. Utopias do, however, guide our policies and thinking and therefore can impact on choices; their failing is to presume the primacy of explicit reason

over biological and cultural logic that both act to educate and to help man survive and flourish in the form of reactions and tacit knowledge that evolves.

82. Bismarck, German Chancellor , certainly proved a capable

83. A similar mentality underpinned some policies of the British Empire, which were enthused with a Protestant righteousness.

84. Tuchman, *The March of Folly*, p. 235. The same criticism is leveled against British policies towards Ireland by De Rosa in *Rebels*, when British and Irish soldiers were fighting for Belgium's right, regardless of the merits and demerits of the idealistic nationalist rebellion, to determine its own affairs, the same right was not acknowledged in Dublin.

85. Tuchman, *The March of Folly*, p.237

86. "Finding expression in the terms "slopeys" and "gooks," it reflected not only the view of Asians as inferior to whites but [especially] of the people of Indochina." Tuchman, *The March of Folly*, p.241

87. Cf. Conor Cruise O'Brien, *The Long Affair: Thomas Jefferson and the French Revolution*, p. 102ff.

88. Keegan refers to the war as "an unavailing ideological war", *History of Warfare*, p.381.

89. Tuchman, *The March of Folly*, p.238

90. Geoffrey Regan, *The Past Times Book of Military Blunders*, p.80.

91. This was the work of the anti-colonial Office of Strategic Services which ironically attempted to set up a left-wing regime.

92. Initially, Eisenhower had said that he could not "conceive of a greater tragedy for America to get heavily involved." This changed to a worry of a "chain reaction" and of "falling dominoes" in the area, to his last statement on Vietnam: "The loss of South Vietnam would set in motion a crumbling process that could, as it progressed, have grave consequences for us and for freedom." Quoted in Johnson, *A History of Modern Times*, pp. 632-633.

From the manipulation of reason in the pursuit of parochial designs for power, we move to the great ideologies that sometimes grip minds and generate crusades, *jihads*, class wars and the like: the arena of political idealism. We reach the point where deep philosophies merge with political ideologies in the form of idealist movements that explain the past and drive the future.

Political idealism appeals to the highest faculties of men and women — to their reasoning capacities and incessant sense of curiosity and desire to know their place in life and to the possess an all-encompassing direction that explains life. Man has produced a variety of ideologies that aim to present all-encompassing explanations of life, the universe, death, and of course war. Such ideologies develop with, although are not mutually inclusive with, the great religions, and their origins are often found in the myths and rites of ancient lore;[1] they gain a secular twist with the advent of philosophical thinking. However, and this remains an underlying contention, the great religious and mythical explanations are not always wholly superseded by the advance of secular philosophy. To some extent they are swallowed up by philosophy, sometimes being regurgitated; occasionally older forms of thought are refuted, but ideas die hard and the cultural momentum of some ideologies lingers on to support new generations in their beliefs.

Political ideologies often are based on the same erroneous premise as balance of power theories, namely that they assume the possession of omniscience on the part of agents — usually leaders — who are assumed to be able to explain everything. Herein lies the greatest threat to an individual's life and also to a community's: for in presuming the infallibility of another, an individual renounces his life.[2] Systems of thought that demand the renunciation of critical reasoning to an ideology are demanding a philosophical obedience to its dictates (and hence demand a political obedience that may in turn forge a cultural predisposition to obedience[3]). In renouncing the efficacy of his own mind, the individual becomes a pawn for the wielders of the great ideologies and hence, if called upon, a foot soldier in its wars both ideological and real.[4]

Explanations and theories of politics are not in themselves dangerous, but when they demand the abnegation of the individual mind, of individual critical thinking, to the expositions (and solutions) of priests, princes, and politicians then the individual is lost and so too, ultimately, is his culture.[5]

The roots of political ideologies are not shallow. They reach deep into philosophical issues that provide an ultimate basis for an ideology's expansion and its limits. All political doctrines depend on a view of man (ethics and theories of human nature), a view of the universe (metaphysics), and a view of man's relationship between himself and the universe (epistemology). To provide, therefore, a more thorough understanding of war's rationalist origins, of how war emanates from man's intellectual creations, we must turn to these metaphysical roots.

This chapter expands on war's etiology into the territory of man's political ideas; but we do not proceed far if we merely discuss political theories without considering their intellectual roots. All political theories are dependent upon deeper premises — they are formed from assumptions on the ultimate nature of the universe, namely man's metaphysical beliefs that underlie some of the ideologies that demand whole scale obedience. In exploring how they relate to war, we pay particular attention to those of a *historicist* nature. In doing so, political theories of war's origins and nature become more comprehensible.

All political belief systems have metaphysical roots and it is to these premises that we turn.

METAPHYSICAL BELIEFS

Metaphysical beliefs deal with our understanding of the ultimate nature of the universe. Admittedly, most people have not heard of metaphysics, nor do they consider whether their metaphysical beliefs are consistent or coherent in any manner; nonetheless such ideas that they do hold have ramifications on how they behave or perhaps how, ultimately, they explain their actions or the nature of the world in which they act.

Ideas matter: they are not the sole causal springs of human action, for, as we have seen, biology and deep cultural structures in which ideas are sublimated into understandings play their part, but the effect of explicit ideas cannot be ignored. Accordingly, metaphysical beliefs are not merely abstract philosophical arguments that have no application to human reality, they are causally efficacious for human action. People act on their beliefs or presuppositions concerning their view of reality, regardless of whether these beliefs are liminally held or are explicated into intricate theories. Metaphysical beliefs underlie all ideologies; they are of the first order in terms of priority for understanding the world but they are intricately linked — individually through a person's psychology and socially through a culture — to political theories.

Succinctly, metaphysics provides our ultimate foundation of thought. Metaphysics provides the basis on which our explicitly argued for opinions rests; some people turn their minds to consider explicitly the nature of those grounding propositions, asking whether existence exists, or whether it is perceived or conjectured. Others may form a conception of the nature of reality, but not integrate it in any manner with their other beliefs, although the connections are often implicitly made; most, however, accept the guiding metaphysics of their culture, agreeing implicitly that there is a God, or that there is not a God, that reality is what you make of it, that it's all a figment of the imagination, and so on. Such non-thinkers merely parrot the thoughts of others they pick up from the pulpit or today from the television, or from the fiction and magazines they read (if they read!). It can be said that such people remain slaves to others' thinking in so far as they do not question;[6] however, the efficacy of some ideologies over time must give the philosopher pause to think. Not all is sundered by reason, not all erroneous theories are cast down by great geniuses never to shackle the human mind again.

The principle lesson drawn from the previous chapters is that man is much more than a rational animal: he is biological, and as such he evolves; he is a cultural animal, and as such he learns tacit ideas and behavioral norms through emulation and mutual reciprocities and these structures also evolve through continued interaction and development. Erroneous notions, in so far as they do not lead to the ultimate destruction of the group, do have a tendency to be culturally conveyed over the generations,[7] and the greatest error that an individual can make in his thinking, and hence the gravest error that a culture can propagate, is the denial of reality — that is, the negation of the extra-mental world of existence (the physical world). Metaphysical theories begin with an assumption or argument concerning the nature of the universe, and many deny its material reality in favor of various forms of idealism, in which the world (rather than our knowledge of the world) is constituted by our ideas of it; accordingly, the nature of the world is something that alters according to thought, and since each person will possess his own perception of the world, the nature of the world cannot ever be accepted as real or objective.

The ramifications for political ideologies becomes apparent. When an individual denies the reality of the material universe,[8] the reality of individuals is also questioned, and so too is their individual status of unique sentient beings deserving rights or dignity to forge their own identity and life. Socialist doctrines, for instance, presume the primacy of the group over the individual, and deny that the individual can have an existence apart from the group; the individual is therefore to be moulded into the group's identity — i.e., the identity that it should take, as seen from the perspective of the relevant author or politician.

For example, animal liberationist doctrines espouse the moral and hence ontological equality of mankind with the animal kingdom, and thereby, by raising the status of animals relegate humanity below that which it is capable of. Politically they wish the destruction of reason and complex cultures, which give humanity its edge on the rest of the animal kingdom, and prefer us to be wed thoroughly to our biological status.[9] Theocratic doctrines similarly reduce man's status, but this time as chattel of the gods or as penitent humble souls attempting to improve their status through life's ordeals. Metaphysically, most theologies support the existence of life after death and thereby, to some extent or other, reduce the importance of this life in favor of death. These examples — cast up to stir *thinking* — all deny some aspect of reality and hence produce theories that logically become removed from man's proper position in the universe as an entity that is individualistic, cultural and intellectual. From previous chapters we have noted that man is a biological being, but he is more than that, that he is a cultural being, and he is more than that; and so it is with rational man — he is capable of reason, but reason, whilst the *sine qua non* of his being does not exhaust his nature.

In tying metaphysical ideas to political ideologies we place ourselves in a better position for understanding war's origins as they emanate from man's thinking; just as man's nature has its hierarchy — from its biological basis through its cultural developments to its mental world — so too has the structure of thought: from basic conceptions of the universe (metaphysics) through how we understand the universe (epistemology) to how we ought to relate to one another (ethics and politics). Ideas matter and *so too does the structure they take.* When they are not consistently integrated in our minds, the culturally dominant notions — those that are repeated more often within a group — begin to govern other aspects of our thinking. That is why the belief that the individual is worthless and that this life is a mere illusion translates easily to the individual becoming a sacrificial object, in which his or her life is of no value, and who is to be deposed of according to the higher values set *by others.* If the individual believes he possesses no value, then what difference does it make if he is called upon to die for his country or for his God? Sartre would condemn the man who acts on behalf of others, but he would not condemn the man who authentically chooses his path whatever the value he seeks. But the psychological implication advanced here should not be taken as a simplistic explanation of Aristotelian *akrasia*.[10] The freedom to choose is exhausting and often wearying and sometimes being told what to do,[11] or falling back on older habits of behavior, is easier than forging an authentic choice, which requires a sustained and untiring effort. However, it is not the case that whole classes of people are subservient in their ideological formation and others — the élite — are active and challenging; a more reasonable approach is to describe ourselves as at times tenaciously dogmatic and at other times accepting of new thought, at times thoughtless and at other times philosophical.

In determining what makes people act the way they do, we refer to purposefulness; and to understand the individual's purpose and hence to be able to make comment on the means used, we refer to the ends the individual has in mind when acting.[12] No statement or proposition regarding human action can be made that does not refer to the ends aimed at: "The very concept of action is finalistic and is devoid of any sense or meaning if there is no referring to conscious aiming at chosen ends."[13] Humans act to achieve certain ends,[14] hence when they fight, their fighting is for a purpose; the specific purpose for which an individual may fight will differ across individuals and even across the same individual over time. What an individual desires as an end is a matter of thinking, of prioritizing values and of wondering how best to satisfy them.[15] The result is an idea invoking a value, an end and its means.

Ideas — learned concepts and abstracts — guide behavior and purpose. They are the primary causes of actions above the purely biological level acting through cultural structures as well as explicitly articulated reasons.[16] War is predominantly a product of man's ideas and the pursuit of ideas is *always* volitional. The acceptance of ideas may be pre-rational in the form of tacit agreements to traditions or conventions of belief, but in the case of *an articulated* agreement to wage war, the idea, the justification or rationalization, can usually be traced to previously considered notions of right and wrong; for example, to culturally evolved conceptions of the group's identity and also to philosophical ideologies and religions explicitly learned.

Explicit ideologies originate with particular thinkers — by definition. Intellectuals do not have to be a separate class of people, as Aristotle and Plato would have liked, for new ideas or insights may arise from any *thinking* person (entrepreneurs in the commercial world are a common example of this). It may be useful to employ the concept of a "class of intellectuals" whose thoughts seep down through a feudal hierarchy of those less able to think originally for themselves, and historical evidence may support this; however, it is better to consider the "class of intellectuality" as residing within each person.[17] Socially, the open society in which individuals are free to engage in their own pursuits as they see fit destroys the feudal pyramid model of influence, of those at the top casting their wisdom on those below; instead in a free society there are complex and interactive matrices — ideas emanating from a variety of sources subject to impersonal forces of acceptance and dissemination. The propagation of truths becomes therefore more socially egalitarian. The ideas of a village farmer may not proceed as far as those of an educated editorial writer, but his education is no guarantee of either the truth or the longevity of his musings, whereas the farmer's may be passed down through the generations in his locality. Nonetheless, when there is a political and cultural system that systematically demands obedience to intellectuals, theologians, or prophets, then the advance of particular knowledge from the body of the general public is less likely. Deference to "one's betters" complements an intellectual deference of the mind, which at once creates a more pliable public less able to exploit the advantages of particular and diffuse knowledge.

When a body of ideas attempts to supplant all other notions and seek the obedience of men's minds to its content, then the pluralism of ideologies and of knowledge and the search for and exploitation of particular knowledge is lost. When people give up their own reasoning for the sake of an ideological system then the most important factor of human maturation, epistemic progress, and economic development is foregone. The altar of ideologies has many sacrifices throughout history and can be a most belligerent god with whom man seeks glory and victory. Explicit ideologies are generated by man, but man cannot be changed to fit ideologies;[18] the great tragedies and wars of modern civilization have been dominated by man's attempts to force his contemporaries into ideologies.[19]

The most devastating ideologies in terms of their impact on human affairs and for the intellectual origins for war are teleological theories of history, i.e., *historicist theories*, that claim man is subject to great ineluctable laws of human development through time.[20] Teleological ideologies are philosophically predominantly metaphysical but they also impose on a man's mind epistemological, ethical, and political ramifications. To believe in the inevitability of history, of the war to end all wars for example, is at once to invoke predestination or fatalism (metaphysical arguments that claim "I cannot help what I do or what happens") as well as a belief concerning how one knows the fate of humanity ("What must be, must be"), and thereby how one should alter policy and behavior accordingly. The paradox is manifest: to believe in fate is to act according to that belief, but to act according to a belief is to choose a manner of existence. Before we look at teleological theories, it is worth casting a view over the status of metaphysical beliefs, which arguably, set the tone for a person's or a community's philosophy, for all political, ethical, and aesthetic theories are resoluble or are supported by metaphysical notions.

METAPHYSICAL BELIEFS AND WAR

To some, the universe is an evil place and the domain of evil forces subjecting humanity to a constant barrage of violence, anxiety, and pain. Man's lot is one of torture, anguish, suffering, and frustration. This universe is assumed to be fundamentally malevolent towards human life, and war is just one of the characteristics of this baleful existence. Pessimism and the stoical acceptance of the ills of the world reflect such a metaphysics.

The theory, whilst popular and influential, must be rejected if a sense of optimism and peace is to be propounded. We find the theory in the writings of Thomas Hobbes, for example. Hobbes postulates a material universe, whose underlying nature (in the state of nature) is inimical for human existence, for people cannot live peacefully in it without artificial structures:

> Hereby it is manifest, that during the time men live without a common Power to keep them all in awe, they are in that condition which is called Warre; and such a Warre, as is of every man, against every man.[21]

Hobbes's conception of the basic nature of humanity, and thus his primal conception of the universe as it is relevant for human action, is that in a state of nature humans are predisposed to war with one another — their values inherently conflict and without an arbitrating force, they will come to blows. The state of war will thus be a constant companion of humanity, and what seems to be peace is merely a lull before inevitable warfare. Implicitly, the universe in this conception is inimical to co-operation and to peace.[22]

The implication for Hobbes's 'malevolent universe metaphysics' is that war can never be abolished, for it is innate in nature. That is, if left alone, humans would fight an unceasing warfare with one another. They only co-operate out of self-interest to form a commonwealth that takes up their powers to arbitrate disputes and thus secure peace. The "Leviathan", or state, is created to quell the innate predispositions of people to wage war in the state of nature. Seemingly though for Hobbes, despite the viciousness of the state of nature, life can be considered a good thing that is worth preserving and defending against aggression, for the state is formed to preserve life.

Although it is to human nature that Hobbes looks, he proffers a materialist metaphysical theory of war. That human nature is considered depraved in its natural state implies in turn that the universe in which humanity finds itself is not natural or beneficial. Dualists, like Plato (and later St. Augustine[23]), point to the transcendental or supernatural dimensions of a heaven as being the proper place for humans (for Socrates, peace and knowledge is to be found in death, a theory that underpins many of the world's religions). Whereas monists, who do not split the universe into a material and spiritual realm to keep it as a singular entity, argue that contentment can be gained by supporting those institutions that minimize the incidence of war and arresting the supposed outbreak of human reactions to the universe in which people find themselves.

It cannot be doubted that humans commit the most awful crimes, but it must be asked what prompts them to evil deeds? The universe cannot be an evil place per se, since it has 'allowed, metaphorically speaking, life to evolve and to be sustained. Admittedly for most living creatures life is fraught with danger — a constant struggle against environment and predators, and Hobbes emphasizes this when he calls life "solitary, poore, nasty, brutish, and short." But life adapts, and through natural selection those forms and patterns of behavior best suited to living succeed in reproducing — that is Darwin's great insight. Hobbes's description of the "condition of Man of everyone against everyone" is thus reductionist,[24] for the universe 'allows' new adaptations to succeed through co-operation as well as conflict.

Humans can live peacefully, if they so choose to act, but in choosing a vivacious philosophy they should, to be consistent, remove the vestiges of malevolent metaphysics from their thinking. Cultures obviously take longer to adapt, but holding on to even a simple theory such as *la vita è bella*, reflects an obvious attachment to life in this world rather than a harking for life in the next.

Metaphysical descriptions do not remain idle in men's minds. Philosophically (at the level of explicit and articulated thinking, or at the level of presumptions tacitly accepted or embedded in the pre-rational structures of expectations and meanings) such descriptions influence man's actions. Assuming life to be woeful and plagued by violence or the conspiracies of others to frustrate one's goals sets the mood for conflict. Inner-city gang youth are submerged in a Hobbesian cultural metaphysics, as are the great warrior tribes of history who raise killing to an awesome nobility. This is certainly more so the case when a malevolent metaphysics is conjoined with a teleological vision of destiny: war then attends not just a description of the natural state of affairs but a driving purpose, a purpose that man *chooses* to accept as his "fate", for he is a choosing being.

TELEOLOGICAL THEORIES AND WAR

Teleological theories of war propose a particular metaphysical purpose or design to human events that allegedly overrides or denies volition. The ancient priests perceived designs and plans in the minds of the gods whom they were sworn to obey; but with the rise of secular philosophy, many of the gods became secularized and took on the names of History, Nation, State, Race, etc.. Teleological theories complement a variety of determinist theories that hold humanity subject to alleged laws of history or of eschatology; i.e., as belief systems they demand a person must give up control over his own destiny in favor of the destiny outlined in the theory. Nonetheless, the renouncing of will - to another or to an ideology — is and can only be a volitional choice.

The teleological theories critiqued here are historicism and eschatology; weaker versions admit some human control over their own destinies but characterize war as an independent institution that periodically gathers its own momentum outside of human jurisdiction. And when war is merged with an ideology that glorifies it as an independent creature with a will of its own, war takes on a demanding energy; this is especially true when war is applauded as a means to bring forth a new historical era in which peace or a golden age will rule.

HISTORICISM

According to historicism, the ideas people hold are impregnated in their minds by mysterious or metaphysical forces. Ideas are hence not freely chosen or freely created, they are either pre-established in all humans, or enter into human minds at predestined stages of the evolving story of humanity. The ideas may emanate from a divine source (Spinoza), from Universal Reason (Hegel), from otherworldly dimensions of pure forms (Plato), or from inherent characteristics present in humanity that predispose people to certain modes of thinking that fit a teleological plan (Vico).[25] Historicism is deterministic in the sense that all human events are foreordained and man's belief in free will is illusory: each event fits in to the general path humanity is destined to walk; and if it apparently does not, the ideologues will soon rationalize it so.

In the metaphysics of Heraclitus, the world is assumed to be in a constant flux, in which things necessarily change towards their opposites — hot becomes cold and cold becomes hot, for instance.[26] For Heraclitus war, or conflict generally, is such a catalyst of change, and without war humanity could not 'progress', as the historicist conceives of progression as a movement into the next, inevitable, stage of unfolding history: "One should know that war is common, that justice is strife, that all things come about in accordance with strife and with what must be."[27] Historicists may claim wars as evidence of the inevitable changes in all laws and minor conflicts as heralding the oncoming apocalypse that will bring forth the new age. Reasonably from such a vantage point, wars are to be greeted events. Indeed, H.G. Wells evokes such thinking when he declared the Great War (1914-18) to be the "war to end all wars": ideologically his words complement a host of Victorian assumptions concerning the inevitability of progress, but they also dig deeper into dominant millenarian theories that various Christians have periodically promoted from the Revelations texts. His words make sense in a cultural and ideological context in which progress is held to inevitable and in which progress entails the abandonment of war; the political factors surrounding the great powers' convergence to the First World War pale in significance and are effectively abandoned as causal explanations in the face of the millenarian call that *this* is *the* war to end all wars: what else could matter or be of use to explain the dawning of the new golden age of peace?

Historicism implies that all actions move *inextricably toward* a final end — the great purpose that lies ahead of all our actions. This entails that all actions are predetermined, that is they are set by the laws of history (the plans of the gods) and human choice is but illusory.[28] Fatalism errs as a philosophical argument. What actions we pursue are the result of preferences we make between courses of action, and making different choices alters the result of our actions, as well as the actions of others. We often deliberate over what will be the best course of action, and sometimes we err — and realize it. We are filled with remorse and disappointment at such moments that equally reflect the capacity for choosing. The fatalist attempt to explain human events should therefore be rejected.

But if by historicism is meant a weaker theory of destiny in which humans choose courses of action which then tie them into predetermined paths, then freedom of will can be partially rescued. But the acknowledgement of choice and of free will contradicts the tenets of historicism.

The destinal concept of history rests on many false assumptions. Firstly, it is assumed that certain "world historic figures" exist who can choose the destiny of humanity or of their nations.[29] Such a reading of history is very naïve and one no doubt an atavistic echo of ancient tribal cultures in which leaders were perceived as great men who chose the destinies of their people.[30] The actions and interactions of others form continually evolving cultural and political structures that unintentionally may counteract the decisions of the alleged historic figure. Secondly, making a choice does not always commit an agent to a determined course of action. Pulling the trigger of a gun does for the propelled bullet as it takes on its own trajectory and momentum, but assuming a policy of isolationism does not. The unfolding event of a bullet whistling through the air cannot be altered by the agent, whereas a policy of isolationism can be changed.

ESCHATOLOGY

Eschatological doctrines assert that the catalyst for the final war already exists, or that it may come about through the chaos of the war.

Historian Anatol Rapoport terms the first a "messianic" philosophy of war and the second a "global" philosophy.[31]

Messianic philosophies of war entail that some individuals — "prophets" — are able to access the principles governing the future history and development of the human race. For instance, the prophets may decry that a purge of the human race, or a war of the righteousness against heretics or the bourgeoisie may be "required", hence justifying crusades, class wars, and holy wars to unite humanity (or at least a part of humanity) under one ruler or faith. The forthcoming apocalypse or war will supposedly bring forth a better order. These premises support the theories of manifest destiny, and of the Nazi Master Race. What must be questioned are the premises on which the theory of messianic war rest.

The first premise is that the future of humanity is determined, which presupposes fatalism to be true. Since fatalism is false, it follows that the destiny of humanity is one of its own making; Sartre's existentialist motto, "you're free — you choose" aptly applies here. The second premise is that some individuals are able to comprehend forms or relations of knowledge that others cannot, hence they can set themselves up as prophets. This too is unsound reasoning, for knowledge, ultimately gained through the senses, is open to all to pursue. Prophets falsely allude to epistemologically dubious, unverifiable and unfalsifiable, non-empirical knowledge. Messianic philosophy entails a requirement to suspend rational judgment and to accept calls for war on the basis of blind obedience or faith. As such, it is an irrational demand, and irrationalist ideologies can support any type of policy or ethics including aggressive war or suicidal pacts as well as peaceful relations and mysticism.

Global eschatology asserts that the grand purpose will be disclosed in a final war. A war typically in which those destined to enjoy the fruits (of eternal life) are separated from those who are not. But why should war bring about the final plan of the universe or of God? Why should it not be a fantastic technological invention, or the overcoming of absolute poverty? Why should something destructive necessitate the final plan except to drive fear into the minds of those culturally predisposed to obedience?

However, if the ultimate plan is beyond human comprehension, why should man give global eschatological theories any consideration in the first place? "What will be will be" according to this doctrine, and what will be is not something we can possibly know. So, why worry? Secondly, it may be countered that it is obvious that humanity or the universe is following a path of sorts, since historians are capable of discerning trends in what has already happened, but the future is for the most part unknowable, and since it was unknowable to those in the past making predictions, it is unknowable to those now making predictions.

Accordingly, although we can look back into history and recognize the unfolding of a trend, we are incapable of extrapolating into the future, for our minds are assumed incapable of grasping the ultimate reality of the plan. However, this implies that any proposed global eschatology (the end is nigh!) is pure fantasy, or at best an unscientific stab in the dark; or, if some credence is permitted, it still does not follow that warfare should be the catalyst to unveil the hidden plan for we do not know what form it will take and can only know once it has happened, so again, why worry? The theory becomes a weapon by which to repress critical thought by generating a fear of life.

FREE WILL REVISITED

Man is persistently faced with an array of values, from which choices have to be made.[32] Choice is a volitional act and only the individual can choose which values ought to be acted on. The individual can rely on knowledge gained from cultural conventions for which values are socially acceptable, and from the sciences for which means are most efficacious for personal ambitions. Ultimately, only individuals can make choices based on their belief systems — man is free to choose. He is no less free to choose his basic ideological systems once he begins critically examining his thoughts, his background, the people around him, and his goals.

It is often said that an individual is the product of his time, that he necessarily reflects the grand beliefs in which his beliefs swim, and for the most part in each of us and for the most part in most of us that is true. Even the greatest innovative thinkers, the rebels, the entrepreneurs, are caught up in the swarm of the times (but say "no" to something): yet the fact that man can think implies that man can challenge at least some of his own beliefs with which he grew up.

It is implausible to assert the rationalist dream that man is able to challenge all of his beliefs, for many remain unarticulated or inexpressible, or in simple terms of economy some must remain unexamined or whose testing would quickly become costly or counter-productive. That much of our learned beliefs, rules of behavior, and expectations of others remains undisclosed is not an evil to be damned nor a box to be pried open — we may accept the fashion codes of our era and the behavioral etiquette of the dinner table, but that leaves us free to examine the broader articulated ideas that emanate from others' minds, from editorials, books, and music, and from the philosophies of the ivory tower intellectuals. We are free to examine historicist conceptions of our era — that it is allegedly necessarily leading us into the abyss of environmental destruction or the nirvana of the freedom from want; we are free to examine political drives towards globalization or isolationism; we are free to consider the moral justification or political efficacy of a war.

"The unexamined life is not worth living," commented Socrates in a call to awaken the minds of his contemporaries who often espoused beliefs and ideas without much consideration. In Plato's dialogues, Socrates draws attention to *explicit thinking*, to the meanings of words and ideas that typically do go unchallenged; his unnerving ability to challenge the presiding doctrines symbolizes for all of us our human capacity to examine and question, and thereby symbolizes our innate freedom to think and choose — if we are willing. The reaction against him manifested itself in a counter explication, that Socrates was corrupting the youth and introducing new gods;[33] his famous trial thus centered on a man's right to express himself, to challenge the given, and to attempt to explicate the hidden. The mob won, for the mob preferred to remain unthinking, that is, his prosecutors argued that they should not argue; the contradiction is manifest and the result tragic.

When the individual leaves the mind's explicit contents unexamined, in which he renounces his innate faculty to question, he renounces his mind to another. Thus a metaphysical doctrine, accepted critically or not, that man is subject to great ineluctable laws that require his body in the war to end all wars, the final apocalypse, or to secure the golden age, becomes a doctrine of obedience to the will of those who maintain a grip on man's destiny; he becomes a pawn for those who bother to inform us of the meanings surrounding his life and the destiny he pursues. Historicism demands that man *chooses* fate and in so choosing his actions become fated.

Above the deeply embedded biological reactions to stress and extreme conditions, and above the pre-rational learned codes of survival in our deep history, war is the result of ideas — of the tacit or explicit decisions made by people. Articulated ideas are philosophically examinable and may be unraveled for their metaphysical meanings To the extent that they deny man's ability to choose, they become doctrines of obedience. Teleological theories of man's ultimate purpose may accordingly affect how we behave and what goals we strive for, but most emphatically, if we accept a belief system that denies our freedom to choose or our freedom to examine, we forego our freedom and our life becomes someone else's to deal with.

The next chapter relates epistemological theories to war's origins and nature, following on from our conception of the general nature of the universe as proposed by metaphysical theories to related theories of how we know what that nature is.

Notes

1. Cf. *The Golden Bough* by Fraser.
2. In connecting a lack of critical thinking with a lack in ego-centric values, Branden writes: "How many people die in insane wars because they do not want to admit that they care more about their own lives than about some abstract cause that may make no sense to them? How many people give up their dreams and aspirations in deference to the needs and demands of others because they dread the charge of being egocentric? This is an open secret: almost everyone knows it and almost no one talks about it. Instead, we go on insisting that ego is the cause of all our misery." Nathaniel Branden, "Reflections on the ethics of selflessness."
3. In *An Intimate History of Humanity*, Zeldin reviews the impact of slavery on cultures, noting its subtle modern effects on individuals' conceptions of themselves and their possibilities and constraining human development across the generations. Ch. 1.
4. This is evident in today's most intransigent war zones as Hamas and Al-Qaeda terrorists literally give up their lives in obedience to their superiors.
5. Such is the fate of all forms of totalitarian systems from communism to theocracies to military *juntas*.
6. Cf. Zeldin's *Intimate History of Humanity* in which he observes and comments on intellectual passivity, especially pp. 6-11.
7. The self-destruction of a group is a very rare phenomenon; it requires a strict geographical or enforced isolation from other groups, otherwise dissenters may migrate. The Easter Islanders were close to a cultural self-destruction through internecine warfare when Europeans explored their islands (Keegan, *History of Warfare*, pp. 24-28) and incidences of collective suicide by various cults throughout the ages exemplify a political and cultural drive to die that overwhelms the members, often promulgated by a charismatic and controlling (yet suicidal) leader. The possibility of migrating to other cultures reduces isolation; however, viewed globally, the threat of nuclear war between the nuclear powers does not leave mankind that hopeful exit to a more benevolent place.
8. Again, this does not imply a denial of our knowledge of the universe or, metaphysically speaking, of reality, for our knowledge is always there to be challenged and expanded.
9. Some environmentalists claim that man's status is below that of the animal kingdom — he is a destructive virus or cancer who, in effect, ought to be eradicated for the sake of the world. Cf. Stephen Clark's critique of environmentalism in his *The Political Animal*, ch. 6.
10. "weakness" or "incontinence of will".
11. Zeldin, *Intimate History of Humanity*, p.11
12. Ends can be liminally held, for many of our goals are products of imputed desires from previous thoughts or from emulation within a social group.
13. Mises, *Theory and History.*, p. 284.
14. The ends may not always be specified in positive terms — "I want food", for they may be enunciations to remove a sense of unease — "I don't want to be hungry any more". However, a negative demand is essentially planless and of not much use to the agent, for it implies a metaphysical belief that wishing can remove unease. A

negative demand must be coupled with a positive demand for purposeful action. "I want food" lends itself to questions concerning which food and how should it be acquired. "I don't want to be hungry" lends itself to inaction.

15. This implies that the individual who does not think about purposes becomes human drift wood, flowing with the ocean currents of ideological and cultural change. Thinking about ends produces an anchor on one's purposes, or perhaps better still, a mooring line that can pull one towards the desired shore.

16. But the realms of thought and body should not be dichotomized. Thoughts can affect the body and the body can affect the thoughts. Biology and psychology meet as it were in psychiatry.

17. Just as the early classical economists spoke of economic classes of labor, landowners, and capitalists, the proper method is to understand that these classes may reside in a single individual, rather than a separate sociological classes as Marx held. A laborer may indeed be a landowner and a capitalist. For an interesting comment on the flow of ideas, Rothbard writes: "the cut and thrust of history itself, the context of the ideas and movements, how people influenced each other, and how they reacted to and against one another, is necessarily left out of the Few Great Men approach." "Introduction", to *Economics thought before Adam Smith*, pp. 10-11.

18. Ideologies to be wary of are those that begin to lament human nature, "Oh, if only man could be changed!"

19. Cf. Paul Johnson's *History of the Twentieth Century* for an examination of the effects of social engineering policies.

20. Popper provides the classical criticism of historicism in his *The Poverty of Historicism* and his *Open Society* volumes.

21. Hobbes, *Leviathan*, Ch. xiii., p.185.

22. The same metaphysical attitude is held by Santayana who believes that: "There is eternal war in nature, a war in which every cause is ultimately lost and every nation destroyed. War is but resisted change, and change must needs be resisted so long as the organism it would destroy retains any vitality. Peace itself means discipline at home and invulnerability abroad -two forms of permanent virtual war; peace requires so vigorous an internal regimen that every germ of dissolution or infection shall be repelled before it reaches the public soul." From "Soliloquies in England and Later Soliloquies", pp. 104-5, in *The Wisdom of George Santayana*, p.217. Both arguments are also anticipated by Cleinas in Plato's Laws, except, whereas Plato holds a dualist metaphysics, Hobbes maintains a materialist view of the universe. Cleinas asserts: "for what men in general term peace is a name; in reality, every city is in a natural state of war with every other, not, indeed, proclaimed by heralds, but everlasting." Plato, *Laws, 625ef*, trans. B. Jowett, p.189 Plato argues through the Athenian Stranger that peace should be the purpose of laws, not war, nonetheless we can comment on Platonic dualism as it relates to war, for Popper remarks that militarists often espouse the words of peace but practice war. Popper, *The Open Society and its Enemies: Plato*, p.259, fn. 33.

23. Cf. Copleston, *History: Vol. II, pp. 78-79.*

24. Indeed, Hobbes's philosophical campaign was to disclose an axiomatic method for comprehending all aspects of philosophy, an idea that came to the forty-year-old opsimath while perusing Euclid's *Elements*.

25. Kant's definition of war is also entangled in an historicist philosophy of history, for he believes that the actions of nature belie a teleological purpose for humanity. At the political level humans are inexorably involved in a natural process to create a federation of states. The means to this end, Kant explains, is warfare. War thus has a purpose in nature, and history is the reading of the exposition of this purpose. Cf. "Perpetual Peace."

26. Cf. "Heraclitus", in Barnes, ed., *Early Greek Philosophy*, pp. 114-5.

27. Quoted in *ibid.*, p.114.

28. Ironically, Hegel's concept of "world historic figures" who emerge to promote the conditions of change, and who, according to him, break the presiding laws, becomes an empty concept. They too are all part of the overriding laws of history, since they could not have acted differently.

29. Typically by breaching the presiding historical laws — but in violating the laws, a variety of paradoxes arise: was the violation 'inevitable' to usher forth a new set of laws, or was it a matter of shear will power by 'world historic figures' and other such Hegelian heroes, and if so is that choice open to all?

30. But then again, one must be wary of asserting a simplistic thesis concerning ancient cultures: just because archaeological evidence has uncovered burial sites with leaders festooned with riches does not necessarily imply that they did not require a 'democratic' consent from their people.

31. Rapoport, *ibid.*, p.15.

32. "The categories of value and action are primary and aprioristic elements present to every human mind." Mises, *Theory and History*, p.284.

33. Cf. Plato, *Apology*.

The irrationalist insists that emotions and passions rather than reason are the mainsprings of human action...It is my firm conviction that this irrational emphasis upon emotion and passion leads ultimately to what I can only describe as crime. One reason for this is that this attitude, which is at best one of resignation towards the irrational nature of human beings, at worst one of scorn for human reason, must lead to an appeal to violence and brute force as the ultimate arbiter in any dispute.

— Karl Popper[1]

Metaphysics provides the basis on which our thoughts are ultimately formed for metaphysics concerns our conceptions of reality. In the previous chapter we have seen that metaphysical theories underlie political theories — and that when a political theory is examined it possesses metaphysical roots that in turn explain why war is considered either a natural or unnatural experience for humanity. We can draw similar explanations from epistemological theories. Epistemology is how we relate our knowledge to existence and it too relates to man's reason, for here we generate theories that provide us with the wherewithal for discussing the nature of reality.

Epistemology is the study of how we know things, what the limits to our knowledge may be, and how reliable is our knowledge. It intimately relates to metaphysical conceptions of the nature of the universe, and while explicit doctrines may be examined individually for their lucidity and consistency, their connection to metaphysical *and* to ethical and political theories cannot be ignored. Epistemology is infused with language, and language is infused with cultural and political meanings that may motivate passion, action, violence, and war.

As with metaphysical theories, most people do not consider epistemology to any great extent, but that does not mean they do not possess some rudimentary epistemological theories that govern their attempts to gain knowledge. People may refer to common sense or to experience, or to simple rules of inference and deduction, to the thoughts of others or to faith; but in doing so, they invoke epistemology. All people qua rational beings possess implicitly or explicitly a philosophy — a set of principles or beliefs, passively accepted or explicitly reasoned, that guide their everyday actions. Their thoughts on how knowledge is gained will play a part in how they interact with others, and one aspect of interacting with others is war.

The philosophical study of epistemology seeks to generate some consistency concerning our knowledge. Here epistemological theories are related to beliefs on war, for arguably, some doctrines, especially those that undermine the individual's ability to reason for himself, do grave damage to the prospects of peace. What are termed "irrationalist doctrines" can easily turn men's thoughts to irrational pursuits, for where critical thinking is condemned, the seeds of war may be sown much easier; and where war flourishes, critical thinking and concerted cooperation for prosperity are systematically destroyed.

The culture of critical thinking that emerges with a civilization can be shallow and vulnerable to devastation. Civilization's fruits are intricate and the product of complex individuals and interrelations that evolve in peaceful, trading societies. The economic growth and the technology produced by such cultures promotes pacifistic arrangements — the "soft morals" of commerce. The thin veneer of materialism — of urban growth, power plants, skyscrapers, airports etc. — can mask latent cultural prejudices and animosities. In the 1990s, for example, the developed state of Yugoslavia returned to a brutality that shocked the West, when in the 1995 genocidal "ethnic cleansing" of Bosnians in Srebenica and Zepa, 8,000 or more civilian refugees were murdered. That incomprehensible massacres had taken place one year before in poorly developed Rwanda (leaving 800,000 dead) created a general revulsion throughout the West and prompted NATO eventually to intervene. That a modern nation had reverted to such barbarism was strongly reminiscent of the German reversion to ethnic hatreds and the genocidal campaign waged against the "non-Aryan" peoples of central Europe: in Nazi Germany, Rwanda, and Yugoslavia, state-sponsored propaganda had kindled myths of ancient hatreds in non-critical populations.[2]

Often in history brute force has emerged to steal or to destroy the effects of civilization. Sometimes, though, civilization often attracts the aggressor into settling down and learning the benefits of longer-term planning, enhanced security and the lifestyle those conditions make possible. Nonetheless, what often destroys civilizations is rarely war-fare — for advanced societies possess the skill, knowledge and tools to defeat a barbaric enemy — but internal discord in the form of an igno-rance of the values and philosophy that promoted growth and develop-ment and especially the demise of critical thinking and the concomitant rise of complacency. When a society undermines its own knowledge, by taking it for granted, or by undermining its validity and success, then a society collapses intellectually. War in turn can intensify the retreat to the myopic and aggressive existence of the savage that often begets war in the first place, by reducing a group's ability to see beyond tomorrow and hence plan for peace and cooperation with the present enemy. The destruction or shortening of the temporal horizon which man looks to in planning his life with himself and his neighbor stems from epistemological failings.

We begin with considering a general belligerent epistemological attitude that defines and shapes political and cultural life.

EPISTEMOLOGY AND ACTION

As with metaphysical ideas, the epistemological premises a person holds guides his or her behavior. And if behavior is partly the product of epistemological premises, it can be inferred that epistemological thinking can have influence whether people fight or not — whether they know they are fighting and for what, whether they can know how to abandon or contain war, and whether they are fighting a just war or fighting it justly and they can know such things.[3] For a person may claim ignorance of the justice of his or her actions, yet permit someone else (King, commander, President, community, mullah, priest, parent) to shoulder that epistemological and hence moral burden. A person may avoid responsibility for their actions by obfuscation of their re-sponsibility hiding behind epistemological rationalizations concerning their duties, knowledge, actions, and freedoms by renouncing their own critical disposition in favor of the judgments of others.

A division of knowledge certainly exists which civilization is able to exploit through the division and specialization of labor, but where choices are made concerning the lives of others and especially of doing harm to them, a strict examination of beliefs and their sources is required. It is not enough to claim in war or in peace, "I did not know," if the knowledge was easily accessible, or the conclusions embedded in the action or situation. In part, the need to take a look at how epistemology relates to war should be motivated by the failure of integration and understanding: that is, a failure of critical thinking when critical thinking is most required, e.g., when truck loads of people are being transported away in the middle of the night, when individuals disappear, when groups are forced to leave their homes, when state propaganda creates a hate campaign, or when innocents are being directly targeted.

Ignorance and rationalizations have their roots in moral failure, but moral failure is rooted in epistemological failure, and here too we find the sources of war at the center of human thinking.

Socrates argued that a person does not do evil knowingly, that it is impossible to knowingly do evil. That is not the argument here; on the contrary, doing evil (above the psychotic level of irrepressible irrational behavior) in groups in warfare stems from irrationalist thinking — or from not thinking at all, which amounts to the same thing, that is, from the rejection of cooperation and of reason in human conduct, and often from the rejection of personal responsibility for actions. This is this epistemological problem that is dealt with here and, in effect, the epistemological foundation of war.

EPISTEMOLOGICAL ELITISM

Relating epistemology to war is strengthened by considering the example of a society that believes true knowledge can only be held by a political élite. The desires of the citizens must be then deferred to the élite, who sees itself as the proper interpreter of the truth, whether it is called the truth of God, Nature, Science, or of the State. The élite shoulders the epistemological burden of thought and of justification — those below are thereby unburdened and devoid of the responsibility for the actions that they are told to pursue. Aggressive wars are thus the remit of those in control and are divorced from the citizenry of the nation. Accordingly, people are considered to be pawns in the games of kings and princes, yet if their servile status is challenged, and it is rightfully admitted that ordinary citizens have the capacity to judge political events, it follows that they should also shoulder some of the burden of power — that it behooves them to challenge their government's policies.[4]

The political implications of those theories that demarcate responsibility between the authorities and the civilians are obvious: since none but the select should pronounce on questions of knowledge, the majority become epistemologically subservient to the élite, which translates well into political subservience. One philosopher who expounded on the political implications of an epistemological dualism — or, more exactly, a tripartism — is Plato.

Platonic epistemology rests on the presumption that society is divided into castes that are characterized by varying capacities to think.[5] For Plato, only philosophers are assumed to know what is the Truth, and it is their duty to lead the other lesser mortals in all aspects of their lives for their own good.[6] While Plato did not accept the institution, slavery, for instance, is often justified on the patronizing assumption that the owners *know what is best for the slaves.* The same is true of feudal societies, in which those who hold a higher status claim a better understanding than those below. And if it is the wish of the élite to wage war, it is not the position of the soldiers to question the justice of it, as characterized in the following conversation from Henry V:

> *Henry*: I could not die any where so contented as in the king's company; his cause being just and his quarrel honorable.
> *Will*: That's more than we know.
> *Bates*: Ay, or more than we should seek after; we know enough, if we know we are the king's subjects: if his cause be wrong, our obedience to the king wipes the crime of it out of us.[7]

Bates's point is more than a political one, for it reaches into epistemological considerations. The presupposition he holds is that some individuals are capable of possessing the truth (kings), while others are not (peasants). It is not a coincidence that political systems that attempt to enslave others or reduce their political importance must do so on epistemological grounds as well. If a political culture is cultivated, i.e., one that is actively promoted by government officials that emphasizes obedience to authority (whether it is the authority of priests of civil servants), then the conditions for critical thinking are affected for the worse. Educational systems that emphasize obedience and uncritical acceptance of ruling theories are somewhat to blame for political shifts towards despotism.[8] Bertrand Russell rightly warns that if "democracy is not to be a failure, the ordinary citizen must be given more training in critical thought, and opportunity for pleasures less harmful than a sensational delight in violence."[9]

Theories which rest on differentiating the epistemological capacities of groups (polylogism) necessarily uphold forms of political collectivism. Such theories espouse that some groups possess true knowledge and others are assumed to be dependent on them for guidance. This collectivism is behind many rationalizations of aggressive war, since its epistemological premises create a political distinction between people.[10] Once the underlying assumption that people are differentiable according to their capacities to know is refuted, political collectivism collapses and a philosophical tier supporting forms of oppression and aggressive war by élites disappears.

If knowledge and its use are assumed to be the province of the individual, the political corollary is a form of egalitarianism supporting the equality of individuals to strive for truths and apply their knowledge as they see fit.[11] If man is assumed to be 'the measure of all things,' then it is to the individual that theories of epistemology must turn.

Arguably, only individuals can be said to know things, and only individuals can be said to learn things — that the product of cooperation between individuals is often greater than what could be produced individually should not lead one to infer that a collective knowledge exists to expand social effort. Knowledge is essentially diffuse — hence no objective reason exists to divide humanity into groups who supposedly have their own truths, who are dependent on the equivalent of a Platonic philosopher king or theocracy for knowledge and guidance, or who have their own sciences as the Nazis asserted of the Jews.

The political implications of epistemology are thus evident. Epistemological theories are, subsumed into causally efficacious attitudes.[12] Popper, for example, insists that the attitude of "critical rationalism" is conducive to peace, whereas an attitude of "irrationalism" is conducive to totalitarian systems and hence to warfare.[13] However it must be admitted that peace may also be maintained through the imposition of strict rules designed by the élite, that is a Hobbesian peace in which free and critical thinking are prohibited.[14] This of course would not in itself establish a free society, for a free society requires free enquiry, and free enquiry cannot exist or flourish in a strictly regulated environment.[15] An epistemological imperialism may sustain the peace, but it would not be conducive of flexibility and adaptability, which are crucial, indeed necessary values a society must foster if it is to progress or react properly to change.

Individuals can interact in two different ways.[16] They can communicate "rationally" as equals (i.e., with the attitude that the truth can be learned through discourse and recourse to empirical facts or that parties may mutually benefit from intercourse, for reasoning creates neutral standpoints or observational views), or they can determine to overcome the other's will through varieties of force and intimidation.[17] It can be accordingly inferred that the choice for each agent is to act "rationally" or to act "irrationally".

In irrationalist epistemologies, we find an origin not only to violent behavior but to war itself. Those who renounce reason as an arbiter of social problems (when they can be expressed verbally and hence are amenable to rational critique), even if they are peaceful in intent, become vulnerable to solving inter-social problems through the use of force; and force is ultimately inimical to progress and life in that it destroys the possibility of creativity and growth by undermining social cooperation. Moreover, those areas of the world that are renown for perennial violence exhibit a marked lack in the recourse to objective, impartial reasoning in their affairs — violence, which has often "resolved" matters in the past remains an easy solution to intricate political, cultural, or even legal issues. The continuing violence on the West Bank of Israel reflects not just hundreds but thousands of years of dour, persistent and brutal inter-social violence. Nonetheless, the use of force is not to be rejected, for force is necessary to defend the jurisdiction of peaceful intercourse from both domestic criminals and foreign aggression.

The two opposing epistemological attitudes have different implications for war. Since people possess different attitudes towards knowledge, they will have different conceptions of what kinds of relations and politics there ought to be, or to how far others may be trusted. Popper asserts that people should adhere to an attitude of critical rationalism that lends itself to peace, for "rationalism is closely connected with the belief in the unity of mankind,"[18] a theory that characterizes humanist philosophy reaching back to Aquinas and through Erasmus, Vitoria and Grotius to the modern world. However, on the one hand, we have seen in the previous chapter that reason can lead to rationalizations for warfare, while on the other hand, irrationalism does not necessarily condone warfare. The problem is that irrationalism is morally neutral, for it offers neither reasons for or against war (or, for that matter, living or dying). But this is what precisely leaves it exposed to challenge from those who believe force is a positive value; it may thus lend itself to feudal or totalitarian political structures, which is what Popper, writing in the Second World War envisions:

> Irrationalism, which is not bound by any rules of consistency, may be combined with any kind of belief in the brotherhood of man; but the fact that it may be easily combined with a very different belief, and especially the fact that it lends itself easily to the support of a romantic belief in the existence of an elect body, in the division of man into leaders and led, into natural masters and natural slaves, shows clearly that a moral decision is involved in the choice between it and a critical rationalism.[19]

Choosing irrationalism, we can surmise, panders to the roots of human conflict, whereas a critical rationalism[20] can only condemn aggressive war as being contrary to the life of social, reasoning, and reasonable people. As such it is against our "better" nature, as Kant argues: "Reason, as the highest legislative moral power, absolutely condemns war as a test of rights and sets up peace as an immediate duty."[21] Critical rationality necessarily holds peace as its political corollary, for war invokes force against reason, and as such it is inimical to thinking and hence to life. Reason demands the use of the mind and the mind cannot work well under threats of ill.[22]

But we do not remain in the high arenas of rationalism; throughout this work the various aspects of man's nature have been employed to suggest that we cannot solely rely on man's ability to reason to remove the desire for war. Reason is one means that must act in concert with cultural structures (most often being generated by commerce) that emphasize peace and cooperation over hasty recourse to violence.

The application of reason to human affairs denies the validity and efficacy of aggressive war. This position is supported by two related arguments. Firstly, reason demonstrates the futility of war in terms of its costs, and secondly the capacity to reason is an attribute that unifies humanity, from which it follows that all conflicts can be resolved peacefully by those who are willing to reason instead of fight. Incidentally, those who resort to aggressive force cannot adequately resolve conflicts, for defeating an opponent in war or in battle provides no assurance to gain truths, nor can it provide for a cooperative society that can reap the benefits of trade and divisions of labor.

IRRATIONALISM AND FAITH

Earlier, it was noted there that irrationalism claims the redundancy or weakness of reason as a means to understand the world. Instead, other forms of knowing are posited, such as faith, intuition, mystical experience, and so on. Such epistemological irrationalism is dangerous for it lends itself to the undermining of humanity's only possible means to peace — reason and its corollaries of cooperation; irrationalism is thus an epistemological source of war.

Irrationalism entails placing little or no emphasis on the capacity of thinking to relate to the world. Reason itself is considered to be an obstacle to knowledge and to human progress, instead the passions are invoked in various shades by the irrationalists. Some irrationalists, following an epistemological elitism, may argue that only a few people are capable of reasoning, while the majority — the masses — are governed on the whole by their passions.[23] Others may claim that the passions completely rule reason for all.[24] Irrationalists may thus differ on whether reason plays some or even no role in knowledge — e.g., "mysticism". Mysticism asserts that knowledge is not dependent on the senses or rational thinking, but is derived intuitively through non-sensorial or rational methods such as prayer, meditation, ecstasy,[25] and so on.[26] Popper summarizes that "mysticism attempts to rationalize the irrational"[27], and Rand defines mysticism as: "the acceptance of allegations without evidence or proof, either apart from or against the evidence of one's senses and one's reason[28] . . . [and] mysticism will always lead to the rule of brutality."[29]

Against Rand, it may be argued that mystics may attempt to uphold peace and non-violence as moral and political goals. Many faithful religious men and women have led peaceful lives and have fostered and taught the conditions necessary for peace between otherwise disparate and conflicting communities — their efforts, particularly on the personal level cannot be underestimated in advancing the cause of peace, yet their principle of resting belief on faith alone remains vulnerable against those who desire to manipulate others through intimidation or force: through the faith of violence or of naked aggression. A peaceful mystic may reply that this life is not important, that the next or the other world should guide our actions here, but that entails that life is not a value to be held above death; however, if life is deemed a value, it can be argued that forms of mysticism and the attitude of irrationalism must be rejected as inimical to the requirements of human life on this earth. Regardless of the merits or demerits of basing a political philosophy on an article of faith, the vulnerability of pacifist religious communities to external aggression underlines the need both for toleration and for the defense of religious opinions.

Other forms of irrationalism, such as a dogmatic refusal to accept new facts or to adapt to new situations also play their role both in war's origins and the art of war. The concrete repercussions of irrationalist epistemologies can be horrific, as seen in one particular form, namely that of epistemological conservatism, which can affect both a culture's and an individual's ability to adapt to new conditions, other cultures, new strategies, and so on.

Epistemological conservatism entails a stubbornness to change one's opinion in the face of reasonable doubt. In the context of military activities, Dixon points out that a main problem of military incompetence is a "fundamental conservatism and clinging to outworn tradition, an inability to profit from past experience (owing in part to a refusal to admit past mistakes). It also involves a failure to use or tendency to misuse available technology."[30] Dixon argues that in the First World War (1914-18) conservative attitudes meant, for instance, the refusal to take up the innovative ideas of tanks until 1916 and a refusal to change outmoded strategies such as the frontal assault.[31] On the first day of the Somme offensives fifty-seven thousand were casualties of this irrationalism.

Unfortunately, a strong behavioral tendency exists to support uncritical conservatism. Conservatism requires using less energy than rationalism, which requires a sustained effort to think.[32] As new ideas arise, rationalism's imperative is to consider them critically, whereas epistemological conservatism implies following what others are doing, or falling back on old bromides and platitudes — of how things used to be done. The incentive for upholding conservatism is that the new information will, by definition, be of a high informational content requiring an effort to analyze, for it threatens to return the agent to an earlier state of uncertainty and discloses the realization that he or she may have previously erred.[33] Rejecting effort — i.e. critical thinking — forms a conservative disposition in this sense: new information requires new thinking, and the uncritically minded will prefer to let new information go.[34]

Such epistemological conservatism does not augur well for any species. Biologically and culturally humans must adapt to their circumstances, and to accept an ideology that praises conservatism is not conducive to this requirement of flexibility. Edward Gibbon warns: "All that is human must retrograde if it does not advance."[35]

This is not to deny the validity of political conservatism as espoused by Edmund Burke and others such as Friedrich Hayek, who both rightly point to the individual's dependency on traditions and conventions. They note that the wisdom of the past is highly useful and it would be impractical and foolish to reject the efforts of previous generations ('no need to reinvent the wheel' proverb). But critical rationalism maintains that *traditions must not be deemed epistemologically sacred or inviolable*, otherwise society will stagnate and become vulnerable whenever the need arises for it to adapt to new forms of behavior — as the inflexible Spartans found to their cost at the battle of Leuctra 371 BC, in the face of an innovative opponent, the Theban Epanimondas. What should therefore be rejected are epistemological attitudes that repudiate critical thinking and the possibility of improvements for a better understanding.

Some forms of irrationalism as well as being essentially conservative in nature pander to faith, which implies that in terms of upholding the peaceful coexistence of society, faith must be rejected as an epistemological basis for action. As an extreme example of this kind of irrationalism, but one that should be noted, Hitler, who twisted the faith of the German peoples in themselves, their past and their myths, to evil ends, writes:

> Faith is harder to shake than knowledge, love succumbs less to change than respect, hate is more enduring than aversion, and the impetus to the mightiest upheavals on this earth has to all times consisted less in scientific knowledge dominating the masses than in a fanaticism which inspired them and sometimes in hysteria which drove them forward.[36]

Rather than invoking an *ad hominem* fallacy, the consequences of abiding by faith alone are evident in Hitler's argument: faith can lead to fanaticism and hysteria which are so easily manipulated by warmongers,[37] for faith rejects reality as an absolute and inserts a blind acceptance to theories without test or rational consideration. Again, the consequences of such a militaristic and belligerent faith, which the leaders can direct against whatever targets they choose — are apparent in the hijacking of planes for use as missiles against civilians in New York on September 11, 2001.

The employment of faith in philosophies and theologies is rarely asserted as a belligerent device to ensure docile masses follow the orders of a warrior élite. On the contrary, faith is deemed to transcend reason for the benefit of man; whereas reason, it may be argued, is bound by experience, by the evidence of the senses, faith permits an acceptance of things that reason may never be able to establish. "There are more things in heaven and earth, Horatio, Than are dreamt of in your philosophy,"[38] comments Hamlet.

Reason, it may be said, cannot teach humanity everything. Pascal notes that "the heart has its reason that the reason does not know."[39] Explicitly articulated arguments and theories cannot encompass all forms of human knowledge and hence all potential sources of human action. Cultures sustain masses of information that are learned (and are hence amenable to change), yet which lie below or beyond the capacity of man to articulate, or which are too cumbersome or refined to bother thinking out; it may thus be accepted that forms of faith, an acceptance of certain truths or more especially forms of behavior are necessary for life and for making choices. Indeed, the great religions invoke faithful acceptance of moral and legal notions through their codes and rites, which arguably perform very useful functions in accommodating masses of people to civilized life.[40]

But faith should not be deemed a valid short-cut to knowledge either. Faith is not in itself a source of knowledge;[41] it is a source of belief in things reasonable and unreasonable. While many people may ground their faith in a love of humanity, of peaceful cooperation and brotherly love, or in the acceptance of things that we cannot know but which are nonetheless useful for civil society, the epistemological motivation is based on a weak premise. Faith may easily ask the individual to suspend judgment in matters in which a critical assessment is paramount — to suspend the activity of the rational faculties and just to believe. Faith remains, however it is presented, as a leap into the dark unknown, the acceptance of things without proof. It is therefore vulnerable to more twisted purposes: to accepting the orders of superiors for example; to waging war for the greater good — by those who would manipulate the obedient faithful for violent ends.

One more plausible connection between war and thinking is the irrationalist notion that the world is a frightening place and that humanity's position in it is precarious. From this it is concluded that it is assuredly better to let things be: curiosity is therefore condemned as upsetting the 'natural' precarious balance or order. This connects well to the malevolent metaphysical doctrine that the world is inimical to human existence. Accordingly, the natural or social order should remain unquestioned. In its extreme version this position reverts to fatalism — the doctrine that individuals are powerless to change anything.

When such ideas are held by those who wield power or who control armies, the results are disastrous,[42] and through various historicist arguments a gullible population can be led into wars which it assumes are its rightful or only destiny.

CONCLUSIONS

Epistemological attitudes and theories are immersed into philosophical positions, moral, political, as well as metaphysical. When people are called to renounce reason and cooperation between peoples epistemological theories become dangerous ideas. The initiation of force is always the negation of reasoned argument, and since irrationalism involves a partial or whole rejection of reason, it can be maintained that civilized war, in which war is the product of political analysis, results from the abandonment of reason and of a succumbing to less unifying social structures such as violence, mob-rule, suspicion, and nihilistic forms of subjectivism.

It is the replacement of the war of ideas with the war of might. General Moltke commented that if his troops were allowed to think, none would remain in the ranks, and Hitler agreed: "I need men who will not stop to think if they are ordered to knock someone down."[43]

However, irrationalism is ultimately *parasitical* on rationalism, for irrational activity can only succeed where reasonable people have produced and live in cooperation with one another (just as thievery is parasitical on wealth production). Philosophically, the choice between being rational or irrational is not an arbitrary decision but one that is determined by the necessary (metaphysical) conditions of human life. For a human *to live* requires thinking — and the volitional effort made to think; and for thinking to be efficacious, the mind must recognize the independent, non-contradictory facts of the universe.[44]

Critical rationalism — the exertion of thinking and articulated argument where appropriate — is a metaphysically *necessary* epistemology for man's life. It should not be an arbitrary choice or an act of faith. The mind is the most important means of human survival, and it is thoroughly incumbent on humanity to be critically rational, and no "minimum concession to irrationalism" need be thus effected.[45]

The philosophical common denominator to intentional violence and organized aggressive war is a rejection of reason as a tool for communication and its substitution by force. Once an individual decides to underplay the role of reason, or to reject it fully in intercourse with society, conflict almost inevitably results. Irrationalist epistemologies provide no basis for the unity of humankind, whereas critical rationalism provides such a basis, for it provides the foundation for resolutions for people through discussion and argument.

The attitude of rationality with its accompanying structures of trust and cooperation is therefore the key to peace — and the attitude has to be chosen again and again, by each successive generation, indeed, by each of us every day of our lives: once it is abandoned in favor of forms of irrationalism then the path to violence is short.

Notes

1. Popper, *Open Society*, p.233-234.
2. The violence of Germans against compatriots during the 1930s stands in a stark contrast to the abilities of its intellectuals, composers, and artists; yet so accepting were the German people in the new faith of nationalism and the deification of the state that few rejected the path the nation forged. Besides, many of the intelligentsia class joined the Nazi party (e.g., philosopher Heidegger): "The Nazi death camps were conceived, built and often administered by Ph.D.'s" notes Fred M. Hechinger, "Educators Seek to Teach Context of the Holocaust." New York Times, May 15th, 1979; quoted in Peikoff, *Ominous Parallels*, p.16
3. The epistemological foundations of a person's beliefs as well as a culture's general assumptions concerning the right to freedom to think have ramifications for war crimes trials, for example the responsibility of soldiers to obey perceived immoral duties.
4. A moral discussion of the boundaries of this theory is beyond the scope of this book, but is planned for the second volume.
5. Hence Plato's "Republic" is construed as a blue print for a dictatorship by Popper in the *Open Society* volumes.
6. It can be countered that any subject or discipline necessarily becomes élitist, for those who study it the longest are those who are able to teach others. In terms of subject knowledge this is true to some extent. But in Kuhnian analysis of the development of scientific knowledge, the formation of a hierarchy begets a conservativism within the subject, since students are taught the accepted ideas of the elders. On the other hand, individuals who challenge the framework are usually self-taught or approach the subject from a different angle, which positions them to challenge a dominating paradigm. Examples of the absurdity of ideological conservativism are replete in history (e.g., the unwillingness of intellectuals to consider Galileo's or Darwin's theories). And it does not follow that élitism in a subject provides an individual with any political right to govern, or imbues in them a higher conception of morality or ability to be moral.
7. Shakespeare, *Henry V*, Act IV, scene i.
8. Similarly, educational systems that unintentionally destroy a child's ability to think logically and in an orderly manner undermine his ability to think conceptually and hence critically.
9. Russell, "Lord Northcliffe's Triumph" p.123
10. German Nazism, for instance, claimed support from racial polylogism to wage war on its neighbors and its own civilians claiming that the Aryan race ought to rule the rest of the world.
11. The Renaissance thinker Giadorno Bruno offers an heroic example of one who dared to question theological and political dogmas by postulating the possibility of life on other planets, for which he was burned at the stake. Randall, *Making of the Modern Mind*.
12. Popper, *Open Society: Vol II*, pp. 224-225.
13. Popper uses the term 'rationalism' to mean those epistemologies which rest on the validity of logical explanation and the senses to explain and know the world. For Popper then, the 'attitude of rationalism' entails intellectual reasoning as well as

seeking empirical evidence, for both are required for rational thinking. Popper, *ibid.*, p. 224.

14. Hobbes in his *Behemoth* blames the British Civil War (1642-51) on the plurality of opinions that led to people seeking to undermine the unity of the state.

15. As a contemporary counter to Hobbes's thoughts, compare Milton's classical defence of the freedom to publish in his *Areopagitica*, 1644.

16. Popper, *Conjectures and Refutations*, p.373

17. Popper does not mention using intimidation, perhaps because he includes it in the use of force.

18. Popper, *Open Society: Vol. II*, p.232.

19. Popper, *ibid.*, p.232.

20. One that is not thoroughly rationalistic in the sense that reason is deemed the only means of knowledge and communication, but which recognises the limits to articulated reason.

21. Kant, "Perpetual Peace", p.104.

22. Irrationalism can lead to peace only if agents agree to separate in the case of disagreement. Forms of irrationalism (as epitomized in political doctrines such as Nazism and Fascism, etc.) that pose threats to the life of reasoning beings should be unmasked on epistemological grounds for their errors and the dangers they pose.

23. A point that was not lost on Hitler: "The masses are like an animal that obeys its instincts. They do not reach conclusions by reasoning", quoted in Peikoff, *Ominous Parallels*, p.41.

24. E.g., David Hume.

25. I avoid terming intuition as irrational, for I do not consider it to be so.

26. Diodorus, for instance, characterized the Celts as mystical, pointing to their tendency to talk in riddles: "In conversation they use few words and speak in riddles, for the most part hinting at things and leaving a great deal to be understood." Diodorus, quoted in Rafferty, *The Celts*, pp. 32-33.

27. Popper, *Open Society Vol. II*, p. 246.

28. Rand, *Philosophy: Who Needs It*, p. 62.

29. Rand, *ibid.*, p.70

30. Dixon, *On the Psychology of Military Incompetence.*, p. 152.

31. Dixon, *ibid.*, p.86, p.81.

32. Thinking about something new requires effort, as Norman Dixon elucidates: "One of the particularly hazardous aspects of the relationship between information and decision processes concerns the revising of decisions. It seems that having gradually (and painfully) accumulated information in support of a decision people become progressively more loath to accept contrary evidence." Dixon, *op cit.*, p.30.

33. Dixon, *op cit.*, pp.30-31.

34. Ultimately, all shades of irrationalism fall back on conservativist epistemology. Even nihilism and mysticism, for what they propose in context can only be have gained by through the content of present knowledge.

35. Commonly found quotation, from *Decline and Fall of the Roman Empire*, 71.

36. Hitler, quoted in Peikoff, *Ominous Parallels*, p.49, *cf. Mein Kampf, 337-38* tr. Manheim 1943.

37. As also witnessed in the activities of Peter the Hermit in stirring up support for the

First Crusade (1195).

38. Shakespeare, *Hamlet*, 1.5

39. From *Pensées.*, quoted in Barzun, *From Dawn to Decadence*, p. 219.

40. Cf. Hayek, "the religious view that morals were determined by processes incomprehensible to us may at any rate be truer (even if not exactly in the way intended) than the rationalist delusion that man, by exercising his intelligence, invented morals that gave him the power to achieve more than he could ever foresee." *The Fatal Conceit*, Ch. 9, "Religion and the Guardians of Tradition", p. 137.

41. Interestingly, while Popper's arguments are useful in emphasising the relation between epistemology and political doctrines they themselves lack a good foundation. Popper gives the epistemological high ground to irrationalism, for he believes that the acceptance of critical rationalism is in itself an act of irrationality. cf. O'Hear, *Karl Popper*, p.150. And Popper: "the choice [is not] between knowledge and faith, but only between two types of faith." *Open Society: Vol. II*, p. 246.

42. Cf. Norman Dixon's examples, *op cit.*, pp.81-2, and 115.

43. Quoted in Rauschning, *The Voice of Destruction*, p. 97.

44. Peikoff vouches that: "If concepts refer to facts, then knowledge has a base in reality, and one can define objective principles to guide man's process of cognition. If concepts are cut off from reality, then so is all human knowledge, and man is helplessly blind." Peikoff, *op cit.*, p.330.

45. As Popper claims is necessary, *op cit.*, p.232

CHAPTER FOURTEEN: Conclusions on War and Peace

We have seen the origins of war emerge in humanity's deep past, natural instincts and reactions that evolved over millions of years in the prior species and our closer ancestors. Biologically, we have inherited a vast complexity of instincts that are not easily reduced to single explanatory variables, such as the instinct to aggression, or the instinct of fear. We apparently have inherited a few herd instincts as evinced by the behavior of individuals in groups in both football stadiums and in riots. Yet such instincts often overlap others that may counteract the prevailing herd mentality — a sense of sympathy for the victim of the mob, for example. The more belligerent actions apparently developed as mechanisms for defense and for the protection of the biological values and resources of individuals and tribes; as the complexity of the species increased, learned patterns of behavior and of reaction emerged that straddled the biological instincts and taught codes and rules of social behavior.

With the advent of speech and articulation, higher forms of culture emerge with more complex rules that may be tacitly learned and therefore become embedded in the manners and expectations of a group, but also which may by amenable to reason.

Arguably, rules and rituals evolved to protect and defend the group as well as to further its own interests;[1] these initially would just have been the ability of the group to prosper and propagate, but later to secure its own cultural identity against that of others. A sense of needing to belong to the group complements several of the evolved instincts, and it is hardly surprising that rhetoric reaches a man's ability to consider a moral or political situation from the group's prospects, but more importantly it fosters a powerful surge of solidarity with his fellow men ("Once more to the breach, dear friends"). The psychology of 'we' is empowering, for the weaker member can hide in the group's strengths, through which he can gain a self-assertiveness and identity that he would otherwise not get. However the persistence of psychological or epistemological collectivism, in which the individual relinquishes personal responsibility for his own thoughts, choices and destiny, diminishes the ability to form a strong self or personally unique identity, and hence, in Sartre's terms, acts in bad faith. Without such strength, the individual is more likely to flow with the crowd, and is hence more amenable to explicit political control, to follow orders and to not question the demands of officers (or corporations that seek war).[2]

If civilization and its vulnerable values for prosperity and advancement are to be protected, collectivism in all its forms ought to be renounced in favor of individualism. Individuals do not fight wars, groups do (although we should never forget that groups are made up of responsible individuals), and groups are led by demagogues who seek to exploit remnants of latent collectivism residing in the tacit and explicit culture of the people, although the possibility of a tacitly, spontaneously mobilized group cannot by discounted, especially if that group were continually involved in a situation that warranted a constant ability to act without explicit direction by 'great leaders'.[3] If such predispositions to unthinking collective activity (compared to cooperative activity) diminish, the roots of war will fade. On the other hand, individualistic 'enlightenment' is utopian. Some have argued that if we each, individually, have the moral sustenance to be individuals and not to fall in with the crowd, we would be less likely to wage war, which is a collective enterprise. But, as this work has emphasized, there is more to man than his individuality. Man is a social animal, he craves or seeks society; he comprehends the benefits to be gained from an extended division of labor and life in a peaceful company of friends. But he is also intimately connected to the group's culture — each one of us is a product of our time, our experiences, and of the culture into which we were born. That cannot be easily shrugged off. Indeed, as Hayek noted, a man without a culture can hardly be called a man. The utopian dream of anarchic individualists is beyond our reach: we are social beings and a social existence generates institutions that both benefit and hinder individual growth and fulfillment.

The development of political states, characterized by the rule of law to some extent or other, advances the capacity of the species to control its own destiny and to channel resources and people into cooperation for specific ends. The danger lies in usurping that power for aggressive and exploitative ends, of using the tacit obedience people give to the state's authorities for their own peace for ulterior immoral purposes. What must not be ignored is that civilization rests upon the advancement and maintenance of a broad and deepening division and specialization of labor, which cannot be the product of a single guiding intelligence; civilization is the on-going product of millions — it is not an invention.

The early cultural institutions that evolved to ritualize or regulate human intercourse would have supported the growth or at least the maintenance of such orders, particularly in private property, which assists so much the economic development of a society as well as removing confusion over who controls what resources and hence a source of intra-social friction. Yet philosophies that underplay or undermine the efficacy and indeed even the morality of private property do great damage to civilization and the hope for perpetual peace between men. The danger lies in the fact that war, which has a plurality of origins in controlling resource access or the identity of the group, developed into a highly organized institution that could be accessed or channeled into aggressive actions against other groups by the state. The supporting structures lie deep in the human psyche or in the cultural roles expected of the group to further its interests or to foster its sense of honor, and even in times of peace, such latent energies could be easily broached by external threats or the rhetoric of war mongers. The state rests in a position to usurp that power — hence the need to ensure that its remit is at once limited, regulated, controlled, and responsible.

The extension of sedentary life and of the leisure to philosophize permits man to both examine the conditions of his success as well as to turn the energies of his civilization into imperialism and war. One of the murkiest conditions of his success is the expansion of the division and specialization of labor, with its concomitant extension of production and hence of exchange. As trade increases, the desire for war should decrease.[4] This is an argument deployed by Hume, Kant, Cobden, and a series of pro-market economists in the 20th century, but the pacification of the market is *not a necessary development*. Against free market optimists, we may recognize the benefits of cooperative activity over non-cooperation, of the international division of labor over the parochial, yet rationally such beliefs may be confused or countered by competing visions of the self and other, especially if the other is foreign: rhetoric may fall back on the atavistic language of prejudice to produce highly complex theories rationalizing isolationism or aggression, some even using economic analysis to explain the ostensible economic rewards of war.

But in conjunction with economic theories, religious, political, moral and psychological theories may all pander to the group as the primary value of political and cultural discourse and history. It should not be forgotten that every group is made up of individuals, who possess unique minds capable of abandoning the herd mentality regardless of the social costs that may befall independence of mind.

Nonetheless, despite the advantages that increased mutual dependency through trade and commerce can bestow, the benefits to be gained from a quick aggressive war remain immediately recognizable, whether they are material values such as land, or immaterial values such as honor and prestige. The longer term benefits are less certain, for ultimately aggression undermines the capacity for a people to produce the wherewithal needed for survival, never mind prosperity. Economics provides us with the ability to see the principles of human action beyond the short run and into the conditions of longer term economic growth, prosperity, and peace, and reason can elucidate the proximate conditions; but so often in man's history, the longer term benefits are given up in favor of the short run, and it does not assist matters for Keynes to have quipped, "in the long run, we're all dead"!

In effect, if the benefits from growing commercialism are to be had, reason alone is not sufficient — the market culture must be allowed to develop and to pursue its own ends as the active individuals producing, consuming, and trading see fit. The paradox is that this is a theoretical call employing reason, yet so often in history the appeal to reason has been made by those who can see through mankind's short comings and myopia but the appeal has gone unheard, for too much cultural momentum exists to sustain aggressive warfare. Perhaps at such junctions, peace should be externally imposed by forces who have the ability and resources to deploy: such is the vision of the United Nations peace keeping forces and can also be found in the musings of Michael Ignatieff.[5] On the other hand, often cultural barriers between peoples may be breached by voluntaristic, Hayekian spontaneous patterns of trade rather than by attempts to enforce a cultural or political hegemony on warring factions.[6] But to rely solely on a hope that people involved in intractable warfare will turn to trading with one another, also belies a naivety of the depth of human culture and motives. The theories of rational economic man who constantly seeks to maximize his utility cannot fathom why some would prefer to fight than to trade; unless that utility is broadened to encompass non-material aspects as well as material gains. In acting, we seek to substitute less favorable circumstances for more favorable circumstances, but what is deemed favorable does not have to entail material benefits — it can include the glory of one's name, the pride of one's regiment, the honor of one's principles, or the expected benefits of the after-life. We can admit that a person will not do anything unless it benefits them, but what can be included in the concept of benefit must not be constrained to material or economic benefits.[7]

The statesman's duty to see beyond the immediate is likewise not something that reason alone can teach. A person comes into the political realm (the original position if we were to take Rawls's conception of political discourse) with a host of cultural baggage. And this is before public choice theories are added to the complexity of public office and the principles of government. The veil between reason that seeks impartiality and universal justice is terribly thin and vulnerable to being sliced upon, often on the slightest of pretexts: parochialism is a much greater force than the desire to seek common understanding or cooperation, especially across warring peoples.

The final illustration of the tenacity of cultural and political momentum that channels men's energies into war is taken from the Second World War. In this case, however, the belligerent momentum is broken by the *post bellum* unification of the European States into a general free trade and political confederation overseen by French and American diplomats and the carrot of the Marshall Plan.[8] The recent revival of war in the European theater (e.g., Yugoslavia) involves nations that have yet to be brought within the generally liberal realm of the European Union.[9]

Europe in 1945 had been torn apart by yet another of its incessant wars. War was a perennial pastime for all the major communities, nations, polities, and warrior classes of the western flanks of the European continent. Viewed historically, the passages of peace surely seem like hiatuses before the next onset of bloodshed. Politically, the lands were vulnerable to any ignition to the latent discord that fulminated beneath the surface of treatises and alliances. But it is not true to conclude that these wars, so frequent, bloody and vast, were the sole policies of ruling élites, who exploited willing and obedient peasants until they were freed from their tutelage and permitted to judge political processes and hence refuse to fight as pawns in powerbrokers' games. That would be to imply the 18th century rationalist and democratic version of history is correct — the optimistic vision of humanity espoused in the Enlightenment that were it not for the misuse of power for political games and imperial aggrandizement, man would not wage war, for the common folk, those who pay for the wars and lose their lives in them, would not condone warfare. But things are much more complex. The so-called masses possess their own political and cultural momentum, which may both escape political control as well as frame it. The cultural momentum incorporates not just explicit philosophies, ideas, expectations, but tacit ones too: hence the fears and prejudices of long-ago eras are not easily controlled or abandoned. Political control — the optimism of dialogue and discussion to resolve disputes will not be sufficient, so long as there remains a tendency to hail the onset of violence.[10]

Accordingly, the cultural preferences as well as the political processes that emphasize war as means of conflict resolution need to alter. Reason alone cannot complete this task — too often in history, reason has been jettisoned by the more powerful forces that lie latent in man's nature, awaiting that spark from propaganda or demagoguery to set them aflame and let loose the dogs of war. In 1945, Europe heaved with a peace that in living memory had already seemed within the Continent's grasp — but the pacifist movements following the Great War of 1914-18 had been swept aside by political and cultural forces hell bent on war. Germany had not lost its bellicose momentum, which arguably was exacerbated by the reparation payments it was supposed to make following the previous war,[11] as well as a naïve optimism in Germany's attempt at social engineering and reclamation of its militaristic pride through Hitler's policies.

Certainly after the Second World War, the Allied powers acted to ensure that Europe could rebuild without recrimination and that its nations could be drawn together in a political union that would reduce the need for war. The American federal model of politics, so much on the tongues of European intellectuals both since the American Revolution and the influential tome of Immanuel Kant on *Perpetual Peace*, was imposed on Europe — this had not stopped the States themselves from waging a most brutal civil war, but by bringing the main powers peacefully into explicitly organized institutions of cooperation at least the *political momentum* for war could be curtailed. However, what was missing from the post Great War settlements were the important pacifying cultural channels that would have reduced the powerful forces that generated war. Trade was curtailed on the part of the major economies severely through inflationary policies, increased tariffs and economic isolationism. The drive to autarky — economic self-sufficiency — prompted the peoples of Europe to look inward once again and to view outsiders and neighboring nations with distrust, as indeed they might when their trading partners increased taxes on their exports. Intellectually, within one short decade of the First World War, Europe had cast off the gains from the post-Napoleonic peace and had returned to the siege mentality of the Middle Ages.

Accordingly, the post-bellum resolutions in 1945 acknowledged the failings of the Versailles Treaty (1919) and aimed to cultivate a grand free trade zone alongside increased international cooperation both within Europe and with exterior pan-global institutions such as the United Nations and the General Agreement on Tariffs and Trade as well as the International Monetary Fund and the World Bank. While the economic principles and policies behind the IMF and the World Bank cannot be accepted as good (they are based on the implicit and even explicit assumption that inflationist policies are useful mechanisms for increasing productivity), they certainly complemented the reduction of trade barriers and assisted the re-building of international trade.

Biologically of course, man does not radically change in a few, or even a few thousand generations. But culturally he can change quicker.

Reason may present a guide as to the direction that he should be heading in — to realms of increased mutual cooperation and trade — but cultural processes need to supplement that shift. Trade, which produces so many beneficial arrangements at the level of the individual, should be enhanced, as it was after 1945, and politics should resolve not to interfere with such arrangements that are voluntarily entered into between different nationalities. The key to Europe's successful maintenance of peace for over fifty years is not the product of politics alone, but of the expansion of the soft dissembling morality of commerce.

Whether it will be sustained though depends as much on that political framework as the expansion of commercial links across the borders. That is because free trade is not alone sufficient, especially when its nature and principles are not broadly understood either by the general public of the West or its intellectuals. For trade to flourish and for peace to be secured *the rule of law* is imperative. What the rule requires and implies cannot be elaborated on here, but suffice it to say that rules bring consistency and converge on a greater consistency between peoples: the ideal of an impartial and global body of laws is a useful guide for those interested in peace. Such laws may be exceedingly narrow in their application which would permit local divergences within the spirit of international law, yet the ancient stoical, cosmopolitan theory of an all encompassing theory and body of natural law, now resurfacing in human rights legislation, provides a useful benchmark in the dissembling of man's barbarity towards one another.

Throughout the work, I have attempted to dissemble reductionist theories of war, whether they claim war to be the product of man's genetic inheritance, of belligerent cultural structures, or of man's reason. Determinism — the theory that man does not choose his actions — is rejected, but in doing so the opposing thesis that man chooses war does not provide a thorough explanation either. Why he chooses war, as why he chooses anything, cannot be reduced to a simple explanation. We are thinking beings who deploy language to construct thoughts, we are social beings that live amidst cultural forces not of our making, and we accordingly we do not always act out of singular motives. In acting we choose, and our choices are predominantly a product of our ideas, but those ideas are not wholly of our construction, for they are part of the political and cultural environment; when a soldier declares, "for King and Country", does he *truly* understand what he says, or does he mimic what his contemporaries declare? And do they know what they utter, or are they mimicking what has always been said? Perhaps it is a little of both: the utterance requires an acceptance into the conscious mind that is formed by biological, social, and individual factors, but the acceptance can only take place by a *willing* creature.

War remains a perennial issue and shall do so for humanity as long as the supporting ideational structures are accepted. The difficulty is that it is not merely an alteration in explicit thinking that is required for man to embrace perpetual peace, but a change in the deeper cultural structures that provide the means for war's allure over generations. This is not likely to come about from pacifistic blue prints that demand a change in human nature or the abolition of war by decree, for such projects are inherently weak in terms of what they can alter in human motivation — in the complex matrix of rules and expectations that govern our every day actions as well as our conceptions of ourselves and others. Peace has a greater chance through the dissembling, pacifying tendencies of individualism and of the market place and its political corollaries of free trade, free movement, free speech and expression. Peace has a greater chance if governments reduce their power — and hence the temptation to use that power for wars and interventions; and peace certainly has a greater chance if the cost of war is imposed equally and immediately on the electorate, rather than deferring it through inflation or national debts.

But even then, the renouncing of war will remain historically shallow and vulnerable to challenge by martial rhetoric.

Notes

1. These may be entirely economic or nationalistic or spiritual.
2. The political relationship of companies and the state is complex, but suffice it to say, a political relationship with the state can only emerge where the state invites, attracts, or accepts lobbying and interest in protectionist measures.
3. E.g., in riots or in war-torn areas.
4. However, the expansion of prosperity also produces greater amounts of leisure time that economically permit standing armies to be supported — and wars, which are, for the most part, luxurious pursuits.
5. Cf. *The Warrior's Honor*.
6. E.g., the gradual ascent of peace across the England in the 16th century following centuries of conflict.
7. Cf. Mises, *Human Action*, Part One, Ch. 1.
8. The motivations for setting up the European Union are also complex and a sketch of the peace is all that is required here. Interestingly, France pushed the European Coal and Steel treatise to ensure that it had commercial access to the German Ruhrgebiet, i.e., that Germany could not intervene in the area and use its production for war purposes.
9. Before elaborating on the reasons why war could be put to rest in Europe, another highly pertinent example to illustrate the move to peace would be the American Civil War which brokered a peace following a turbulent beginning to the American nation in the Revolutionary War and the persistence of wars with Indians and Mexicans on various frontiers. Following the cessation of war in 1865, the American States relaxed into a peace built on republican principles and internal free trade and thereby pursued Kant's dream of perpetual peace. Of course, peace was not permitted for the Indian tribes who had to suffer several more decades of forced migrations and quasi-genocidal campaigns against them. But the reason for focusing on the European theatre of war rather than the peaceful settlement of the US Civil War, is that the United States was, for the most part, dealing with a civil war between countrymen — the wars against the Indians were also too one-sided in terms of technology to provide an intricate example of belaboring a peace between equals. Europe offers the historian and the philosopher the complexity of peoples of different tongues who had made war a second nature in terms of their political and cultural traditions. Yet a problem with choosing any example is that the historical conditions in which the peace was effected were unique, as any historical conditions are. The particular political conditions, the specific advancement in the division and specialization of labor, the state of technology, the cultural-political mindset, and so on, cannot be repeated. So the question arises as to the worth of presenting a specific example from which to draw philosophical conclusions. Principles may nonetheless be drawn from historical studies, even though the same conditions will never again apply. Generally, it can be asked if securing impartiality and the rule of law assists the brokering of peace or not, if a move to a more accountable government reduces the chances of arbitrary aggression, if a more stable economy with a sounder currency is more conducive to fostering peaceful cooperation than not, if free trade with other nations reduces culturally imbibed prejudices than not, if the formation of treatises of peace is useful for securing other methods of interna-

tional conflict resolution, and so on.

10. Witness the cheering crowds that ushered in the First World War — and that after a century of relative peace, of growing prosperity and the ascendancy of the free trade doctrine and the expansion of the franchise.

11. Although the actual reparations payments were not as onerous as the political capital that could be made from the perceived yoke.

Bibliography

Alexander, F. Matthias. *Man's Supreme Inheritance*. Mouritz: London, 1996.

Allen, Tim. "Perceiving Contemporary Wars. " In *The Media of Conflict*. Zed Books: London, 1999, pp. 11-42.

Almond, Brenda. *Ethics: A Traveller's Tale*. Blackwell: Oxford, 1998.

Augustine. *The City of God*. Trans. Marcus Dods. Hafner Publishing Company: New York, 1948. [426]

Ardrey, Robert. *The Territorial Imperative: A Personal Inquiry into the Animal Origins of Property and Nations*. Collins: London, 1967.

Aristotle. *Politics*. Trans. T. A. Sinclair and T. J. Saunders [Penguin, 1981]. Also in *A New Aristotle Reader*. Ed. J. L. Ackrill, Claredon Press: Oxford, 1992 [1987], pp. 507-539.

Aron, Raymond. *Peace and War*. Excerpts in Freedman, War. An Oxford Reader: Oxford, 1995

Barnes, Jonathan. *Early Greek Philosophy*. Penguin: Harmondsworth, 1987.

Barzun, Jacques. *From Dawn to Decadence 500 Years of Western Culture*. Harper Collins: New York, 2000.

Beitz, Charles. *Political Theory and International Relations*. Princeton University Press: Princeton, 1979.

Berkely, George. *Principles of Human Knowledge*. Collins Fontana: London, 1972.

Berlin, Isaiah. *The Power of Ideas*. Princeton University Press: Princeton, 2000.

Branden, Nathaniel. "Reflections on the ethics of selflessness. " In *The Art of Living Consciously*. Simon and Schuster: New York, 1997.

Brenner, William H. *Logic and Philosophy: An Intergrated Introduction*. University of Notre Dame Press: London, 1993.

Burckhardt, Jacob. *The Greeks and Greek Civilisation*. Trans. Sheila Stern. St Martin's Griffin: New York, 1999.

Butler, Joseph. *The Works of Bishop Butler: Volume 1*. Ed. J. H. Bernard. Macmillan and Co. : London, 1900.

Carrighar, Sally. "Aggression" In *Man and Aggression*. Ed. M. F. Ashley-Montagu. Oxford University Press: Oxford, 1968.

Carlton, Eric. *War and Ideology*. Routledge: London, 1990

Clausewitz, Carl von. *On War*. Trans. Col. J. J. Graham. Penguin Books: Harmondsworth, 1982 [tr. 1908, orig. 1832].

Coleridge, Samuel Taylor. *The Poems of Samuel Taylor Coleridge*. Edward Moxon: London, 1852.

Copleston, F. C. *A History of Philosophy: Volume II*. Image Books: London, 1985.

Copleston, F. C. *A History of Philosophy: Volume VII Fichte to Nietzsche*. Search Press: London, 1963.

Crane, Stephen. *The Red Badge of Courage*. Folio Society: London, 1964.

Creasy, Sir Edward. *The Fifteen Decisive Battles of the World*. MacMillan: London: 1905.

Darwin, Charles. *The Descent of Man*. (1871) http://www. infidels. org/library/ historical/charles_darwin/descent_of_man

Dawkins, Richard. *The Selfish Gene*. Oxford University Press: Oxford, 1989.

Dawson, Doyne. *The Origins of Western Warfare: Militarism and Morality in the Ancient World*. Westview Press: Colorado, 1996.

Davis, Norman. *The Isles*. Macmillan: London, 1999.

De Laclos, Choderlos. *Les Liaisons Dangeureuses*. Trans. Richard Aldington Folio Society: London, 1962.

De Rosa, Peter. *Rebels: The Irish Rising of 1916*. Poolbeg: Dublin, 2000.

De Tocqueville, Alexis. *Democracy in America*. Wordsworth Classics: Hare, 1998.

Dixon, Norman. *On the Psychology of Military Incompetence*, Pimlico, 1994.

Dobhzhansky, Theodosius. *Mankind Evolving: The Evolution of the Human Species*. Yale University Press: New Haven and London, 1962.

Doyle, Michael W. "Kant, Liberal Legacies, and Foreign Affairs, Parts 1 and 2. " In *Philosophy and Public Affairs*. Volume 12, Issue 3 and 4, 1983, pp. 205-235, pp. 323-353.

Dryden, John. "Song for St. Cecillia's Day", *Poetry, Prose, and Plays*. Ed. Douglas Grant. Hart-Davis: London, 1952).

Durant, Will and Ariel. *The Lessons of History*. Simon and Shuster: New York, 1968.

Dyer, Gwynne. *War*. The Bodley Head: London, 1986.

Ehrenreich, Barbara. *Blood Rites*. Metropolitan Books: New York, 1997.

Erasmus, Desideratus. "The Complaint of Peace. " In *The Essential Erasmus*. Trans John P. Dolan. New American Library, New York, 1964.

Fagan, Brian M. *People of the Earth: An Introduction to World Prehistory*. Seventh Edition. Harper Collins: New York, 1992.

Forde, Steven. "Classical Realism", in *Traditions in International Ethics*. Ed. Terry Nardin and David Mapel. Cambridge University Press: Cambridge, 1996. pp. 62-84.

Frazer, Sir James. *The Golden Bough*. Wordsworth: Ware, Hertfordshire, 1993.

Freedman, Lawrence. *War*. An Oxford Reader: Oxford, 1995.

Freud, Sigmund. "Why war?" In *War: Studies from Psychology, Sociology, Anthropology.* Eds. Leon Bramson and George W. Goethals. Basic Books: London, 1968. pp. 71-80.

Fromm, Erich. *The Anatomy of Human Destructiveness.* Penguin Books: Harmondsworth, 1977.

Frondizi, Risieri. "The Ideological Origins of the Third World War. " in *The Critique of War.* Ed. Robert Ginsberg. Henry Regnery Co. : Chicago, 1969. pp. 77-95.

Gallie, W. *Understanding War: Essays on the Nuclear Age.* Routledge: London, 1989.

Gibbon, Edward. *The History of the Decline and Fall of the Roman Empire.* Penguin Books: London, 2000.

Ginsberg, Robert. "Philosophy versus War. " In *Critique of War.* Ed. Robert Ginsberg. Henry Regnery Co. : Chicago, 1969, pp. ix-xxiv.

Glover, Jonathan. *Humanity: A Moral History of the Twentieth Century.* Jonathan Cape: London, 1999.

Graham, Gordon. *Ethics and International Relations.* Blackwells: Oxford, 1998.

Granatstein, J. L. *Yankee Go Home?* Harper Colllins: Toronto, 1998.

Gray, John Hables. *Postmodern War.* Routledge: London, 1997.

Hall, Willis. *The Long and the Short and the Tall.* Heinemann: London, 1975.

Harva, Urpo. "War and Human Nature. " In *Critique of War.* Ed. Robert Ginsberg. Henry Regnery Co. : Chicago, 1969. pp. 45-55.

Hastings, James. *Encyclopedia of Religion and Ethics: Volume XI.* T & T Clark: Edinburgh, 1934.

Havel, Václav. *Open Letters: Selected Prose 1965-1990.* Faber and Faber: London, 1992.

Hayek, Friedrich A. von. *Law, Legislation and Liberty: A New Statement of the liberal principles of justice and political economy. Volume I: Rules and Order.* Routledge & Kegan Paul: London, 1973.

Hayek, Friedrich von. *New Studies in Philosophy, Politics, Economics, and the History of Ideas.* Routledge and Kegan Paul: London, 1978.

Hayek, Friedrich von. *The Fatal Conceit: The Errors of Socialism.* The Collected Works of F. A. Hayek, Vol. I, Ed. W. W. Bartley III, Routledge: London, 1988.

Hayek, Friedrich von. "Dr Bernard Mandeville (1670-1733)", in *The Trend of Economic Thinking: Essays on Political Economists and Economic History, Collected Works of F. A. Hayek Volume III,* Gen. ed. W. W. Bartley III and Stephen Kresge, Routledge: London, 1991.

Hazlitt, Henry. *Economics in One Lesson.* Crown Publishing: New York, 1998.

Hegel, G. F. *The Philosophy of Right.* Trans T. M. Knox. Clarendon Press: Oxford, 1965.

Herodutus. *Histories.* Trans. Robin Waterfield. Oxford University Press: Oxford, 1998.

Hitler, Adolf. *Mein Kampf.* Trans. Ralph Mannheim. Hutchinson: London, 1972.

Hobbes, Thomas. *Leviathan.* Ed. C. B. Macpherson. Penguin Books: Harmondsworth, 1988.

Hoppe, Hans Hermann. *Democracy: The God That Failed.* Transaction Publishers, London 2001.

Howard, Michael. *The Causes of Wars*. Unwin Paperbacks: London, 1984.

Hume, David. *A Treatise of Human Nature*. Ed. L. A. Selby-Bigge, 2nd ed. Clarendon Press: Oxford, 1978.

Hume, David. *An Enquiry Concerning the Principles of Morals*. Ed. J. B. Schneewind. Hackett Publishing: Indianapolis, 1983.

Hume, David. "Of the Original Contract. " In *Essays Moral, Political, and Literary*. Liberty Classics: Indianapolis,1987 [1741], pp. 465-487.

Ignatieff, Michael. *The Warrior's Honor*. Owl Books: London, 1998

Ignatieff, Michael. *Virtual War*. Chatto and Windus: London, 2001.

Irwin, David. *Against the Tide: An Intellectual History of Free Trade*. Princeton University Press: Princeton, 1996.

James, William. *Talks to Teachers on Psychology: And to students on some of life's ideals*. Longmans, Green and Co. : London, 1911.

James, William. "The Moral Equivalent of War. " In *War and Morality*, ed. Richard Wasserstrom. Wadsworth Publishing Co. : Belmont, California, 1970, pp. 4-14.

Jaspers, Karl. *The Future of Mankind*. Chicago University Press: Chicago, 1951.

Jenkins, Karl. *The Armed Man*, Virgin Records, 2001.

Johnson, James Turner. "Sources of the Western Just War Tradition. " In *Just War and Jihad: Historical and Theoretical Perspectives on War and Peace in Western and Islamic Traditions*. Eds. John Kelsay and James Turner Johnson. Greenwood Press: London, 1991, pp. 3-30.

Johnson, Paul. *Intellectuals*. Phoenix Press: London, 2000.

Johnson, Paul. *The Offshore Islanders*. Weidenfeld and Nicolson: London, 1972.

Johnson, Paul. *A History of the Modern World: From 1917 to the 1980s*. Weidenfeld: London, 1983.

Kant, Immanuel. "Perpetual Peace. " In *Kant's Political Writings*. Trans. H. B. Nisbet. Ed. Hans Reiss. Cambridge University Press: Cambridge, 1970, pp. 93-130.

Kant, Immanuel. *Critique of Pure Reason*. Trans. Norman Kemp Smith. Macmillan: London, 1970

Kaufmann, Walter. *Existentialism from Dostoevsky to Sartre*. Meridian: New York, 1989.

Keegan, John, Richard Holmes, John Gau. *Soldiers*. Guild Publishing: London,1985.

Keegan, John. *A History of Warfare*. Hutchinson: London, 1993.

Leakey, Richard and Roger Lewin. *Origins* Reconsidered: In Search of What Makes Us Human. Abacus: London, 1992.

Lenin, V. I. "Socialism and War" In *A Handbook of Marxism*. Ed. Emile Burns. Victor Gollancz Ltd: London, 1935, pp. 678-687

Liddell, Basil Hart. *Thoughts on War*. Faber and Faber: London, 1944.

Locke, John. *Two Treatises of Government*. Ed. Peter Laslett, New American Library: Scarbourough, Ontario: 1963.

Longford, Elizabeth. *Wellington*. Weidenfeld and Nicolson: London, 1992.

Lorenz, Konrad. *On Aggression*. Trans. Marjorie Latzke. Methuen and Co: London, 1966.

Machiavelli, Nicolo. *The Art of War*. Trans. Ellis Farneworth. Da Capo: New York, 1965.

MacIntyre, Alasdair. *A Short History of Ethics*. Second Edition. Routledge: London, 1998.

Marx, Karl and Friedrich Engels. "The Communist Manifesto. " In *A Handbook of Marxism*. Ed. Emile Burns. Victor Gollancz Ltd: London, 1935, pp. 21-59.

McCrone, John. *The Myth of Irrationality: The Science of the Mind from Plato to Star Trek*. MacMillan: London, 1993.

McDougall, William. "The Instinct of Pugnacity". In *War: Studies from Psychology, Sociology, Anthropology*. Eds. Leon Bramson and George W. Goethals. Basic Books: London, 1968, pp. 33-43.

Mead, Margaret. "Warfare Is Only an Invention -Not a Biological Necessity. " *In War: Studies from Psychology, Sociology, Anthropology*. Eds. Leon Bramson and George W. Goethals. Basic Books: London. pp. 269-274.

Midgley, Mary. *Beast and Man: The Roots of Human Nature*. The Harvester Press: Hassocks, Sussex, 1979.

Midgley, Mary. *The Ethical Primate: Humans, freedom and morality*. Routledge: London, 1994.

Mill, John Stuart. "Civilization. " In John Stuart Mill *Collected Works: Volume XVIII*, Ed. John M. Robson. University of Toronto Press: Toronto, 1977 pp. 119-147.

Milton, John. *Areopagitica*. Dover: New York, 1981.

Mises, Ludwig von. *Socialism: An Economic and Sociological Analysis*. Trans. J. Kahane. Liberty Classics: Indianapolis, 1981.

Mises, Ludwig von. *Omnipotent Government: The Rise of the Total State and Total War*. Yale University Press: New Haven, 1945.

Mises, Ludwig von. *Human Action: A Treatise on Economics*. William Hodge and Company Limited: Edinburgh, 1949.

Mises, Ludwig von. *Theory and History*, Jonathan Cape: London, 1958.

Mises, Ludwig von. *Nation, State, and Economy: Contributions to the Politics and History of our Time*. Trans. Leland B. Yeager. New York University Press: New York. 1983.

Moseley, Alexander. "Is War a Spontaneous Hayekian Institution" *Peace and Change*. February 2002.

Moseley, Alexander. "Anti-Capitalist Children of Capitalism". *Ideas for Liberty*. March 2001.

Moseley, Alexander. "Political Realism. " *Internet Encyclopedia of Philosophy*, http://www. utm. edu/research/iep/p/polreal. htm 1998.

Nef, Stephen. "International Legal Aspects of Rescue" in *The Duty to Rescue*. Eds. Michael A. Menlowe and Alexander McCall Smith, Dartmouth Publishers: Aldershot, 1993. pp. 159-204.

Nicolai, Dr. G. F. *The Biology of War*. Trans. Constance A. Grande and Julian Grande. J. M. Dent & Sons Ltd. , London and Toronto: 1919.

Nietzsche, Friedrich. *The Will to Power*. Trans. Walter Kaufmann and R. J. Hollingdale. Weidenfeld and Nicolson: London, 1968.

O'Brien, Conor Cruise. *The Long Affair: Thomas Jefferson and the French Revolution: 1785-1800.* Pimlico: London, 1998.

O'Hear, Antony. *Karl Popper.* Routledge and Kegan Paul: London, 1980.

Pagel, Elaine. *Adam, Eve, and the Serpent.* Vintage Books: New York, 1989.

Paskins, Barrie and Michael Dockrill, *The Ethics of War*, Duckworth: London, 1979.

Peikoff, Leonard. "The Analytic-Synthetic Dichotomy", in Ayn Rand, *Introduction to Objectivist Epistemology*, New American Library: New York, 1967, pp. 119-164.

Peikoff, Leonard. *The Ominous Parallels: The End of Freedom in America.* Stein and Day: New York, 1982.

Peikoff, Leonard. *Objectivism: The Philosophy of Ayn Rand.* Meridian: New York, 1993.

Plato, "Phaedo. " In *The Last Days of Socrates.* Trans. Hugh Tredennick, Penguin Books: Harmondsworth, 1969 [1954], pp. 99-183.

Plato. "Laws. " In *The Dialogues of Plato: Volume IV.* Trans. B. Jowett. Clarendon Press: Oxford, 1953 [1871], pp. 189-544.

Plato. *The Republic.* Trans. Desmond Lee. Penguin: Harmondsworth, 1974.

Plato. *The Republic*, Trans. Alan Bloom. New York: Basic Books, 1968.

Popper, Karl R. *Objective Knowledge.* Clarendon Press: Oxford, 1979.

Popper, Karl R. *The Open Society and its Enemies: Volume I: The Spell of Plato.* Routledge and Kegan Paul, 1986.

Popper, Karl R. *The Open Society and its Enemies: Volume II: The High Tide of Prophecy: Hegel, Marx, and the Aftermath*, Routledge and Kegan Paul: London, 1974.

Popper, Karl, R. *The Poverty of Historicism.* Routledge and Kegan Paul, 1957.

Popper, Karl, R. *Conjectures and Refutations: The Growth of Scientific Knowledge.* Routledge and Kegan Paul: London, 1974.

Popper, Karl R. "Natural Selection and the Emergence of the Mind. " In *Evolutionary Epistemology, Rationality, and the Sociology of Knowledge.* Eds. Gerard Radnitzky and W. W. Bartley III. Open Court: La Salle, Illinois, 1987. pp. 139-153.

Porter, Bruce D. *War and the Rise of the Modern State: The Military Foundations of Modern Politics.* The Free Press: New York, 1994.

Priest, Stephen. *Theories of the Mind.* Houghton Mifflin Co. : London, 1991.

Rand, Ayn. *The Virtue of Selfishness.* New American Library: New York, 1964.

Rand, Ayn. *Philosophy: Who Needs It.* New American Library: New York, 1982.

Rand, Ayn. *Introduction to Objectivist Epistemology.* Meridian: New York, 1990.

Randall Jnr. , John Hermann, *The Making of the Modern Mind: A survey of the intellectual background of the present age.* George Allen & Unwin Ltd: London (no date).

Rapoport, Anatol. "Editor's Introduction. " In *On War*, by Carl von Clausewitz. Ed. Anatol Rapoport. Penguin Books: Harmondsworth, 1982.

Rauschning, Hermann. *The Voice of Destruction.* New York, 1940.

Ralws, John. *Law of the Peoples.* Harvard University Press: Harvard, 1999.

Regan, Geoffrey. *The Past Times Book of Military Blunders.* Guinness Publishing: London, 1999.

Reisman, George. *Capitalism: A Treatise on Economics.* Jameson Books: Ottawa, Illinois, 1998.

Robertson, Geoffrey. *Crimes Against Humanity: The Struggle for Global Justice.* Allen Lane Penguin Press, 1999.

Rousseau, Jean-Jacques. *The Social Contract and Discourses.* Trans. G. D. H. Cole. [First published 1913] Everyman: London, 1993.

Rousseau, Jean-Jacques. "*L'état de Guerre.*" Trans. Grace G. Roosevelt. In *Reading Rousseau in the Nuclear Age.* Temple Press: Philadelphia, 1990.

Russell, Bertrand. "Fear As the Ultimate Cause of War." In *Prophecy and Dissent, 1914-1916* (The Collected Papers of Bertrand Russell, Vol. 13), Unwin Hyman: London, 1988. pp. 30-31.

Russell, Bertrand, "Lord Northcliffe's Triumph." In *Prophecy and Dissent, 1914-1916* (The Collected Papers of Bertrand Russell, Vol. 13), Unwin Hyman: London, 1988.

Sakharov, Andrei. "Sakharov Speaks. " In *Continuity and Change: Cultural Traditions in the Modern World.* Second Edition. Ed. Philip C. Ensley. Simon and Schuster: Needham Heights, Massachusetts, 1996, pp. 168-172.

Santayana, George. *The Wisdom of George Santayana.* Ed. Ira Cardif. Peter Owen: London, 1964.

Sartre, Jean-Paul. *Existentialism and Humanism.* Trans. Philip Mairet. Methuen: London, 1990.

Sartre, Jean-Paul. "Existentialism is Humanism." Trans. Walter Kaufmann. In *Existentialism from Dostoyevsky to Sartre.* Meridian: New York, 1975, pp. 345-369.

Scruton, Roger. *Guide to Modern Culture.* Duckworth: London, 1998.

Scruton, Roger. *Modern Philosophy: A Survey.* Sinclair-Stevenson: London, 1994.

Seward, Desmond. *The Monks of War: The Military Orders.* The Folio Society: London, 2000.

Shakespeare, William. "Hamlet, Prince of Denmark." In *The Works of Shakespeare.* Odhams Press: London, 1947, pp. 441-531.

Shakespeare, William. "The First Part of King Henry." In *Shakespeare's Historical Plays, Poems, and Sonnets.* Everyman: London, 1910, pp. 130-199.

Shakespeare, William. "The Life of Henry V". In *Shakespeare's Historical Plays, Poems, and Sonnets.* Everyman: 1910. pp. 274-348.

Schoeck, Helmut. *Envy: A Theory of Social Behaviour.* Liberty Press: Indianapolis, 1997.

Singer, Peter. *The Expanding Circle: Ethics and Sociobiolgy.* Clarendon Press: Oxford, 1981.

Smith, Adam. *The Theory of Moral Sentiments.* Eds. D. D. Raphael and A. L. Mackie. Clarendon Press: Oxford, 1976.

Smith, Adam. *An Inquiry into the Nature and Causes of the Wealth of Nations.* Eds. R. H. Campbell and A. S. Skinner. Liberty Classics: Indianapolis, 1979.

Sokolovsky, Marshall V. D. "Soviet Strategy", in *War, Ed. Freedman. An Oxford Reader:* Oxford, 1995, pp. 235-238.

Sprigge, Timothy. *Theories of Existence.* Penguin Books: London, 1984.

Stevenson, Leslie. *Seven Theories of Human Nature.* 2nd Edition. Oxford University Press: Oxford, 1987.

Strachey, Alix. *The Unconscious Motives of War: A Psycho-Analytical Contribution.* George Allen & Unwin: London, 1957.

Thucydides, *History of the Pelopennesian War.* Trans. Richard Crawley. Everyman: London, 1998.

Tuchmann, Barbara. *The March of Folly: From Troy to Vietnam.* PaperMac: London, 1996.

Veale, F. J. P. The Mitre Press: *Advance to Barbarism: The development of Total Warfare from Serajevo to Hiroshima* London, 1968.

Vico, Giambattista. *New Science.* Trans. David Marsh. Penguin: London, 1999.

Vitoria, Francisco de. *Political Writings.* Eds. Anthony Pagden and Jeremy Lawrence. Cambridge University Press: Cambridge, 1991, [1528]. (On Dietary Laws, or Self-Restraint, On the American Indians, 'On Civil Power').

Wintle, Justin. *Dictionary of War Quotations.* Hodder & Stoughton: London, 1989.

Wolff, Christian. *Jus Gentium Methodo Scientifica Pertractatum,* Trans. Joseph Drake. Clarendon Press: Oxford, 1934.

Wright, Quincy. *A Study of War.* Second Edition. University of Chicago Press: London, 1971 [1965].

Zeldin, Theodore. *Conversation.* The Harvill Press: London, 1998.

Zeldin, Theodore. *An Intimate History of Humanity.* Vintage: London, 1998.

Index